ONE OF OUR
SUBMARINES

BY

EDWARD YOUNG
COMMANDER, D.S.O., D.S.C., R.N.V.(S.)R.

Is it not curious, that so vast a
being as the whale should see the
world through so small an eye?
Moby Dick

PEN & SWORD MILITARY CLASSICS

First published in Great Britain in 1952 by Rupert Hart-Davis
Published in this format in 2004 by
PEN & SWORD MILITARY CLASSICS
an imprint of
Pen & Sword Books Limited
47 Church Street
Barnsley
S. Yorkshire
S70 2AS

ISBN 1 84415 106 9

A CIP record for this book
is available from the British Library.

Printed and bound in Great Britain by
CPI UK

Pen & Sword Books Ltd incorporates the imprints of
Pen & Sword Aviation, Pen & Sword Maritime, Pen & Sword Military,
Wharncliffe Local History, Pen & Sword Select,
Pen & Sword Military Classics and Leo Cooper.

For a complete list of Pen & Sword titles please contact:
PEN & SWORD BOOKS LIMITED
47 Church Street, Barnsley, South Yorkshire, S70 2AS, England.
E-mail: enquiries@pen-and-sword.co.uk
Website: www.pen-and-sword.co.uk

ONE OF OUR
SUBMARINES

PEN & SWORD MILITARY CLASSICS

We hope you enjoy your Pen and Sword Military Classic. The series is designed to give readers quality military history at affordable prices. Pen and Sword Classics are available from all good bookshops. If you would like to keep in touch with further developments in the series, including information on the **Classics Club**, then please contact Pen and Sword at the address below.

Published Classics Titles

Series No.

1	The Bowmen of England	*Donald Featherstone*
2	The Life & Death of the Afrika Korps	*Ronald Lewin*
3	The Old Front Line	*John Masefield*
4	Wellington & Napoleon	*Robin Neillands*
5	Beggars in Red	*John Strawson*
6	The Luftwaffe: A History	*John Killen*
7	Siege: Malta 1940–1943	*Ernle Bradford*
8	Hitler as Military Commander	*John Strawson*
9	Nelson's Battles	*Oliver Warner*
10	The Western Front 1914–1918	*John Terraine*
11	The Killing Ground	*Tim Travers*
12	Vimy	*Pierre Berton*
13	Dictionary of the First World War	*Stephen Pope & Elizabeth-Anne Wheal*
14	1918: The Last Act	*Barrie Pitt*
15	Hitler's Last Offensive	*Peter Elstob*
16	Naval Battles of World War Two	*Geoffrey Bennett*
17	Omdurman	*Philip Ziegler*
18	Strike Hard, Strike Sure	*Ralph Barker*
19	The Black Angels	*Rupert Butler*
20	The Black Ship	*Dudley Pope*
21	The Argentine Fight for the Falklands	*Martin Middlebrook*
22	The Narrow Margin	*Derek Wood & Derek Dempster*
23	Warfare in the Age of Bonaparte	*Michael Glover*
24	With the German Guns	*Herbert Sulzbach*
25	Dictionary of the Second World War	*Stephen Pope & Elizabeth-Anne Wheal*
26	Not Ordinary Men	*John Colvin*
27	Plumer: The Soldier's General	*Geoffrey Powell*
28	Rommel as Military Commander	*Ronald Lewin*
29	Legions of Death	*Rupert Butler*
30	The Sword and the Scimitar	*Ernle Bradford*
31	By Sea and By Land	*Robin Neillands*
32	Cavalry: The History of Mounted Warfare	*John Ellis*
33	The March of the Twenty-Six	*R. F. Delderfield*
34	The Floating Republic	*G.E. Manwaring & Bonamy Dobree*
35	Tug of War: The Battle for Italy 1943–45	*Dominick Graham & Shelford Bidwell*
36	Churchill & The Generals	*Barrie Pitt*
37	The Secret War	*Brian Johnson*
38	Command on the Western Front	*Robin Prior & Trevor Wilson*
39	The Operators	*James Rennie*
40	Churchill and The Admirals	*Stephen Roskill*
41	The Battle for North Africa	*John Strawson*
42	One of Our Submarines	*Edward Young*

Forthcoming Titles

43	The Battle of Trafalgar	*Geoffrey Bennett*
44	Fire Power	*Shelford Bidwell & Dominick Graham*
45	Sieges of the Middle Ages	*Philip Warner*
46	Haig's Command	*Denis Winter*
47	Hitler's Death's Head Division	*Rupert Butler*

PEN AND SWORD BOOKS LTD

47 Church Street • Barnsley • South Yorkshire • S70 2AS

Tel: 01226 734555 • 734222

E-mail: enquiries@pen-and-sword.co.uk • **Website:** www.pen-and-sword.co.uk

FOREWORD

by Admiral Sir George Creasy, K.C.B., C.B.E., D.S.O., M.V.O.
Commander-in-Chief, Home Fleet

I HAD the honour and happiness to command the Submarine Branch of the Royal Navy from September, 1944, to October, 1946.

In pre-1939 days our Submarine Branch was regarded as very much the preserve of the regular Royal Naval officer and rating. It was my distinguished predecessor, the late Admiral Sir Max Horton, G.C.B., D.S.O., who, foreseeing the inevitable expansion that would be required of the Branch, insisted on opening the entry to officers of the Royal Naval Reserve and the Royal Naval Volunteer Reserve. This policy was pursued by his successor and my immediate predecessor, the late Admiral Sir Claud Barry, K.B.E., C.B., D.S.O.

Thus when I inherited the command I found that more than half the officers of our submarines were from the R.N.R. and the R.N.V.R., the latter in the majority owing to their larger numbers. And of these a considerable number had risen to the command of submarines.

This book gives some idea of what these officers had to face in transforming themselves from amateurs (and I am sure they will forgive me the term) into the equals and, at times, the superiors of the professionals. But I think the reader will have to use his or her imagination in reading between the lines to appreciate fully what this great achievement really entailed.

Of this gallant band of R.N.R. and R.N.V.R. submarine captains the author of this book had built up a fighting record which was second to none and he was, indeed, one of our greatest submarine captains.

I always enjoyed reading his Patrol Reports. Not only did they tell of good work and of well-earned success but they told their stories so clearly, so simply, that they always made good reading. I was not surprised when I was told that Commander Young was, by profession, a publisher. When he came to see me, on his final return from active service, I told him I hoped he would put his submarine experiences into book form. He was somewhat vague but implied that he hoped to do so "some day." Now he has done so, and this book tells in a simple and straightforward way the story of a very gallant and distinguished career in submarines. The story is told with the sincerity and modesty characteristic of the man. He has, however, included at the end of the book a list of the ship's company of H.M. Submarine *Storm* which gives the honours and awards won by himself, his officers and men. This list can well be left to tell its own story of skill, courage and efficiency in action.

I hope this book will be read by a wide public. I am sure that all its readers will share the admiration and affection of the officers and men of the Royal Navy for their brothers-in-arms of the Royal Naval Reserve and the Royal Naval Volunteer Reserve.

GEORGE CREASY
Admiral

H.M.S. *Vanguard*,
   at Portland,
      22nd May 1952.

CONTENTS

PAGE

INTRODUCTION 12

Part One
APPRENTICESHIP

CHAPTER

I MY FIRST DIVE 17

II MY FIRST PATROL 30

III DISASTER 46

IV "THE BAY" AND NORTH RUSSIA 60

V FIRST LIEUTENANT 79

VI MEDITERRANEAN 88

VII RECALLED HOME 109

VIII "PERISHER" 115

IX MY FIRST COMMAND 127

Part Two
H.M. SUBMARINE "STORM"

X BUILDING 139

XI TRIALS AND WORKING-UP 152

XII INSIDE THE ARCTIC CIRCLE 165

XIII PASSAGE TO CEYLON 187

XIV IN THE NARROWS : MALACCA STRAITS 201

XV BETWEEN PATROLS : CEYLON 225

XVI ANDAMAN ISLANDS 230

XVII CLOAK AND DAGGER 242

9

CONTENTS

		PAGE
XVIII	DESTINATION PENANG	262
XIX	MERGUI ARCHIPELAGO	274
XX	GUN ATTACK ON CONVOY	292
XXI	THROUGH THE LOMBOK STRAIT	302
	EPILOGUE	317
	THE SHIP'S COMPANY	318

LIST OF PLATES

1 S-class submarine leaving harbour
2 "The sea rolling along the bulging curve of our saddle-tanks"
3 Control-room of a T-class submarine, from a painting by Barnett Freedman
4 Captain at the periscope
5 Hydroplane operators
6 U-class submarine
7 In the conning-tower
8 Motor-room and engine-room
9 Target sinking, taken through the periscope
10 Destroyer hunting a submarine, taken through the periscope
11 (a) Ben Bryant (b) George Colvin
12 Torpedo-stowage compartment, or "Fore Ends"
13, 14, 15 Diving and surfacing
16 Underwater photograph of *Auriga*'s bridge
17 Underwater photograph of torpedo being fired
18 Fuelling alongside the depot ship
19 *Saracen* in Malta
20 "The maze of pipes"
21 The galley
22 *Storm* on her first run in the River Mersey

LIST OF PLATES

23 Down the hatch
24 H.M.S. *Forth*, submarine depot ship
25 Unloading kit after a patrol
26 Loading a torpedo into its tube
27 Returning from the North Cape patrol, November 1943
28, 29, 30, 31 *Storm*'s officers
32 *Storm* nearing Trincomalee after a patrol
33 *Storm*'s bridge
34 Picking our Japanese prisoner out of the sea
35 The Oerlikon
36 Three stalwarts : Taylor, Evans and Greenway
37 Dicky Fisher and boarding party in action
38 *Storm* entering Haslar Creek on return from Far East
39 Home again !

COPYRIGHT ACKNOWLEDGMENTS

LIST OF MAPS

	PAGE
NORTH SEA, NORWAY AND MURMANSK	66
MEDITERRANEAN	98
INDIAN OCEAN, CEYLON TO MALACCA STRAITS	200
MALACCA STRAITS, IN THE NARROWS	206
ANDAMAN ISLANDS, PORT BLAIR	231
PULO WEH AND SABANG	243
MERGUI ARCHIPELAGO, NORTHERN HALF	275
LOMBOK STRAIT	311
WESTERN AUSTRALIA AND DUTCH EAST INDIES (inset)	311

(The maps were prepared by K. C. Jordan)

INTRODUCTION

THE average man's almost superstitious horror of submarines is surely due to ignorance of how they work and of what the life is like. One of my reasons for writing this book was to try to remove that ignorance and to show what a fascinating life it is. Some people genuinely suffer from claustrophobia; others imagine they would do so inside a submarine, yet cheerfully travel in aeroplanes and underground trains. It is, I suppose, a matter of temperament. In spite of its uncomfortable moments I found wartime life in a submarine preferable to being shelled in a trench knee-deep in mud, or being shut up in the belly of a tank in the heat of a desert battle, or bombing Germany night after night, or working down in the engine-room of any large surface ship.

I once heard a junior submarine officer, in the presence of his commanding officer, refer to submarine pay as "danger money." "DANGER?" roared the C.O. "Danger! What you get extra pay for, my boy, is skill and responsibility. What the hell do you mean, *danger?*"

In times of peace submarines rarely hit the newspaper headlines unless something goes wrong and one of them is sunk; and then every man who has never been to sea is ready with suggestions for raising her off the bottom and getting the men out. Unfortunately this aspect of the submarine service has acquired a grossly exaggerated importance in the public eye, and every time there is a disaster we hear on all sides well-meaning people demanding more safety devices and better methods of escape. These demands never come from submariners themselves. A submarine is a war machine, and though reasonable safety devices are essential, and indeed are continually being improved, they must take second place to fighting efficiency. Fatal railway accidents could be abolished if all trains were limited to a speed of five miles an hour, and the safest submarine in peacetime (but not in wartime!) would be one that could not dive at all. The submarine service prefers to concentrate rather on making its ships and its men so efficient that the chances of an accident are reduced to the minimum. And though submarines travel thousands of miles every year, surfaced and submerged, fatal accidents are in fact remarkably rare. My own story does happen to include one of the rare disasters, but I hope the perspective of the whole book will reveal the incident in its proper light and even help to underline the point I am trying to make.

I wish to thank my old shipmate Mike Willoughby, not only for putting me right on several technical and historical points, but also for making the black-and-white drawings which are scattered through the book. The diagrams on the end-papers and on page 16 are his too. I find I have nowhere mentioned that in addition to his other attainments he is also an inventor. During the war Mike invented an entirely new method of firing torpedoes from a submarine, illustrating his proposals with some first-class engineering drawings which received serious consideration at the Admiralty. He also designed an improved submarine camouflage, which was first tried out on *Sealion* and later adapted by some of us for use in the Far East.

I wish also to thank my friend Barnett Freedman (together with the Trustees of the Tate Gallery) for allowing me to reproduce a photograph of his painting of a submarine control-room. I was first introduced to Barnett when he was working on this picture as a War Artist at Fort Blockhouse, Gosport. "Not *the* Barnett Freedman?" I exclaimed amidst the Philistines, and made a friend for life. He was not content, as many artists would have been, to fudge the complexity of his subject by a cowardly impressionism; instead he spent several weeks, months even, going to sea and diving in the submarine until he knew the exact function of every lever, pipe and valve. The result is not only a fine picture but the most detailed and technically accurate drawing of a control-room that has ever been made.

For their valuable help in checking the typescript and the

proofs, and for many suggestions gratefully adopted, I am indebted to David Garnett, Rupert Hart-Davis, Ruari McLean, and Commander M. R. G. Wingfield, D.S.O., D.S.C., R.N.

I wish to thank Commodore B. Bryant, D.S.O., D.S.C., R.N., for lending me several photographs, particularly those taken through his periscope and here reproduced opposite page 64; my First Lieutenant in *Storm*, Brian Mills, D.S.C., R.N., for the photographs numbered 27, 30, 34, 35 and 37; Mr N. F. Carrington, formerly Lieutenant R.N.V.R., for sending me many years ago the photograph of *Saracen* in Malta which faces page 97; also Captain B. W. Taylor, D.S.C., R.N. (Chief of Staff to Flag Officer Submarines) and Mr E. G. A. Thompson in the Department of the Chief of Naval Information, Admiralty, for their helpful co-operation.

Finally I thank my wife, not only for typing the final draft of the book, but for her forbearance during my spare-time labours over two-and-a-half years.

E. Y.

July 1952

PART ONE
APPRENTICESHIP

So ignorant are most landsmen of some
of the plainest and most palpable wonders
of the world, that without some hints
touching the plain facts, historical and
otherwise, of the fishery, they might scout
at Moby Dick as a monstrous fable, or
still worse and more detestable, a hideous
and intolerable allegory.

Moby Dick

HOW A SUBMARINE DIVES

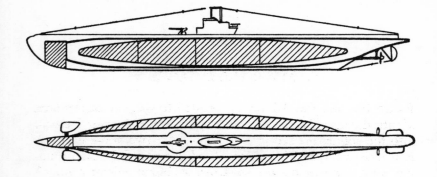

A submarine dives by allowing her main ballast tanks to fill with water. In the above diagrams (side view and bird's-eye view) the main ballast tanks are indicated by shading. These tanks are outside the pressure-hull. On the surface they are full of air; when the air is allowed to escape, through vents at the top of the tanks, the sea comes in through holes at the bottom, and the submarine loses its buoyancy and dives. Under water the ship is controlled by internal trimming tanks and hydroplanes. The hydroplanes, which can be seen in the lower of the two diagrams above, are external fins which can be tilted from the control-room, one pair for'ard and one pair aft; they are really horizontal rudders.

The diagram below shows the centre cross-section of a submarine diving: (1) on the surface, ballast tanks full of air; (2) starting to dive, main vents open, air escaping and sea entering the tanks; (3) fully submerged, tanks full of water, main vents now shut ready for surfacing when necessary. To surface, compressed air is released into the tanks, forcing the water out through the bottom holes.

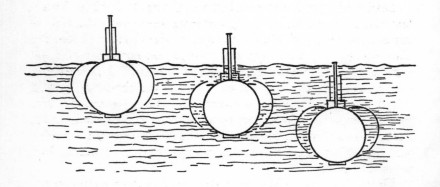

I

MY FIRST DIVE

Early in 1940 the Admiralty decided to risk the experiment of introducing officers from the Royal Naval Volunteer Reserve into the submarine service. A request for two volunteers was sent in April to H.M.S. *King Alfred*, the new R.N.V.R. training establishment on the sea-front at Hove, where a search through the files discovered an officer under training who had had experience as an amateur diver. This officer immediately accepted the astonishing opportunity and, warned to secrecy, was asked to find the other volunteer. He approached a close friend of mine who had joined up at the same time as myself, and the same night, in the digs we shared, Harold confided to me his decision to volunteer. I told him he was crazy; submarines were generally considered dangerous and unpleasant, and neither of us had ever seen even the outside of one. At the same time, I was very envious, for the two volunteers were to be promoted into the special higher navigation class due to start in a few days' time, and I would miss it. One thing I had hoped to get out of the war was a knowledge of celestial navigation.

During the break between lectures the next morning, I way-laid the Commander in charge of instruction and told him of my earnest desire to join the navigation class. He said that the class was already made up; moreover, I had not completed the regulation three weeks of elementary training. I pressed my case more urgently. At last he regarded me thoughtfully and asked my age. I told him, twenty-six. Was I married? No. Sea experience? Only week-end yachting. He then said, "Come to my office," and I followed him down the corridor with a beating heart and the conviction that my temerity had done the trick.

Up to this point it had not entered my head to volunteer for

B

service in submarines. It was therefore with something of a shock that, after being told to shut the door and sit down, I heard the Instructor Commander asking me whether I would consider doing that very thing. The Admiralty had only asked for two volunteers, he said, but he was prepared to put me forward as a third if I was really keen.

"You needn't make up your mind immediately. Think it over and let me know tomorrow."

"If I agree, does that mean I can do the navigation course?"

"It does."

"In that case, sir, I will give you my answer now. It is Yes."

I emerged from the interview with an uneasy stirring in my bowels. I tried to convince myself that I was doing the right, the heroic thing. But in my imagination I saw submarines as dark, cold, damp, oily and cramped, full of intricate machinery. Chances of survival at that time seemed small; death when it came would come coldly, unpleasantly; and the recent loss of the *Thetis* on trials in Liverpool Bay was still fresh in everyone's memory. But it was too late now: I should never have the courage to retract.

At the end of our course at *King Alfred* the three of us were posted to different Hunt-class destroyers based on Scapa Flow, so that we should get a couple of months' above-water naval experience as a background to our submarine training. But before we left for the north, at the end of May, an outing in a submarine on a day exercise was arranged for us. Through losing our way we arrived five minutes late at H.M.S. *Dolphin*, the submarine base in Fort Blockhouse, Gosport, and when we hurried across the narrow plank on to the saddle-tanks of the submarine *Otway* the Captain was leaning over the bridge, far from pleased at being kept waiting by three sub-lieutenants —and R.N.V.R. at that.

I was rather disappointed at the fragile and rattly appearance of this submarine. It was so different from the sleek, stream-lined craft of my imagination. I was unaware that most of what I could see was a sort of outer shell which filled with water when the submarine dived. The whole of the long, narrow deck, and most of the bridge structure, were in fact pierced by innumerable holes, so as to allow this outer casing to flood when diving and drain away when surfacing. The pressure hull itself was barely visible above the surface of the water. As we were led for'ard and told to climb down through a round hatch into the innards of this monster, I don't think any of us felt very happy about it.

We had gathered a few details about submarines when we were at *King Alfred*. We knew, for instance, that the pressure hull was roughly the shape of a long cigar, circular in section and tapering slightly towards each end. We knew that the lower half of it was occupied by trimming tanks, fuel tanks, huge electric batteries and so on. We knew that a submarine had diesel engines for driving her along on the surface and for charging her batteries, and that she changed over to her electric motors when submerged. But we were not prepared for the myriad impressions that bewildered us as we were led aft along the passage-way, past the various compartments to the wardroom. First of all, I was astonished at the size of the boat. In most places you could stand up to your full height. You had to duck your head to avoid various overhead obstructions, or when you passed through the water-tight doors, but in general you could walk about quite easily. The hull was wider than a London tube train. Another thing that surprised me, strangely enough, was the brightness of the lighting everywhere. And in the messes there were wooden bunks, and wooden cupboards, and curtains, and pin-up girls, and tables with green baize cloths. I had not expected to find so much comfort and cosiness. But alas! what a confusion and complexity of pipes, valves, electric wiring, switches, pressure-gauges, junction-boxes, above our heads and on every side of us! How could anyone so unmechanical as myself ever hope to master it all?

In the wardroom, a snug compartment about the size of the saloon of a twelve-ton yacht and with every inch of space as cunningly used, we were handed over to a tall, good-looking sub-lieutenant who introduced himself as Jewell. He suggested we might like to go up on the bridge while we were leaving harbour. We followed him into the control-room, where our eyes boggled at the appalling concentration of levers, valves, wheels, depth-gauges and other mysterious gadgets, and then found ourselves climbing a vertical brass ladder which led up from the centre of the control-room through a hatch into the conning-tower. Here another vertical ladder took us through the upper hatch and on to the bridge. We clustered at the after end behind the periscope standards and tried to take in what was happening.

We were already going astern on the motors, emerging from Haslar Creek into the main fairway of Portsmouth's harbour-mouth. Below us, on the casing fore and aft, the seamen, in white jerseys and bell bottoms, were stowing away the wires and ropes which had secured us to the jetty. Soon we were pointing. out to seaward and beginning to move ahead. The Captain, who seemed to be in a bad temper, perhaps because we had kept him waiting, was issuing a bewildering succession of orders. A throbbing and spluttering towards the stern told us that the diesels had started up. To starboard the walls of Fort Block-house slipped past us like a sliding door, opening up the familiar vista of the Solent, where I had sailed so often before the war. It was now an impressive scene of activity, full of ships of every kind. Soon we were kicking up a creamy wake that shone like snow in the morning sun.

Looking down over the bridge, we watched the sea rolling along the bulging curve of our saddle-tanks. Jewell explained that it was the air in these saddle-tanks, or main ballast tanks, that kept us on the surface; indeed, we were actually riding on air, for the holes at the bottoms of the tanks were permanently open, the sea being kept out merely by the pressure of the air; when we wanted to dive, the air would be let out of the vents which we could see along the tops of the tanks.

At the end of the channel we swung to starboard and pointed our nose westward towards the Needles. The Isle of Wight looked green and peaceful. An aircraft came over, flying south. "Is everybody blind?" roared the Captain. "Why has no one reported that aircraft?" This was addressed to the look-outs, but we felt personally guilty, and it was a relief when Jewell proposed that we should go below and see the after end of the submarine.

We climbed down the conning-tower, a veritable wind-tunnel now that the diesels were thundering away and sucking in air with every stroke of their sixteen cylinders, and followed him through the control-room again and into the engine-room. I am not an engineer—at this time in my life I could not even drive a car—and all I took in was a pandemonium of noise. These diesels were no noisier, I suppose, than diesel engines usually are, but in that confined space (although it was the largest compartment in the submarine) the racket was terrific. It was a madhouse of brass and steel and frantically moving pieces of machinery. We passed on farther aft, through the motor-room, flanked by panels of switches, ammeters and volt-meters, and into the stokers' mess-deck, a nightmare of dis-comfort surrounded by machinery. At last Jewell led us back, past those pounding diesels again, until, with our brains reeling from the noise and the multiplicity of new impressions, we regained the comparative quiet of the control-room.

The submarine was rolling a bit now, and we guessed we must be clear of the Solent and meeting the swell from the Channel. "We'll be diving soon," said Jewell.

He had hardly spoken when the order "Diving stations" came down the voice-pipe and was shouted from compartment to compartment fore and aft along the submarine. Now we were for it. And as the sailors came hurrying into the control-room to their stations it seemed suddenly incredible that this thundering mass of metal and machinery was about to be deliberately submerged. What would it feel like? Would it be like going down in a lift? Or would we dive like an aircraft, nose down? And I imagined there would be a sensation of being under pressure as we went deeper. It was all rather alarming.

Trying to keep out of everybody's way, I found myself standing under the conning-tower. Looking up, I saw the blue sky framed by the upper hatch, and a cloud rolling from side to side. A pair of legs suddenly swung through the hatch and began climbing down the ladder. The raucous explosion of a klaxon hooter close to my ears set my heart thumping wildly, and I caught sight of Jewell grinning at our startled faces. So much happened during the next few seconds that it was difficult for us to sort it all out. Wheels were turned, levers pulled, valves shut off, orders passed, reports made. The look-outs tumbled down the ladder, followed by the officer-of-the-watch. I began to feel a little sick. There was a muffled thud somewhere overhead; the Captain was shutting the upper hatch. His voice came sepulchrally from the tower: "One clip on. . . . Both clips on." He then descended calmly to the control-room, removed the binoculars from around his neck, handed them to the signalman, said "Shut the lower hatch," and then, to the First Lieutenant: "Thirty-two feet, Number One."

I looked across at the two large depth-gauges on the port side and saw that the needles, which before had pointed steadily to zero, were now alive and moving. Already they had passed the figure 10 and were moving on to 15 . . . 17 . . . 20 . . . and I realised that up to this moment I had not appreciated the fact that we were actually diving. For there was an unexpected absence of sensation. Everything had become very peaceful. I supposed that the diesels must have stopped when the hooter went and that we were now being driven by the electric motors, though I could not hear them. We had a slightly bow-down angle: perhaps five degrees, no more. There was no feeling of pressure—and, after all, if the hull was pressure-tight why should there be? We had stopped rolling: even at this shallow depth the swell seemed to have lost its effect. The change from the noisy, turbulent surface world to this sub-marine peace amazed and delighted me. My stomach began to recover.

The Captain stood watching the depth, and when the needle reached 30 feet he ordered "Up periscope." A bronze column which led up through the hull overhead slid quietly upwards from a deep well in the deck. As the foot of it emerged from the well, he bent down, snapped open the two handles and put his eyes to the eyepiece while the periscope was still rising. In its fully raised position it allowed him to stand comfortably

at his full height, with his arms crooked over the handles. First he turned the periscope rapidly through a complete circle, his body moving round with it and his feet just outside the edge of the well. Finally he came to rest on one bearing, examining something on the horizon. I wondered if there would be a chance of having a look for ourselves, but dared not ask. Standing close by him, I could see the pupil of his eye pierced by a point of light; all the rays from the outside world miraculously drawn together through the many lenses of the periscope into this tiny orb of illumination, and re-distributed by his optical nerves into a corresponding picture somewhere inside his brain.

"Now then," he said, "where are these wavy-navies from Hove? Want to have a look?"

At first I had difficulty in seeing anything, until I found exactly the right angle for my eyes. Then I saw, far more clearly than I had expected, a flurry of tumbling grey-green sea. It looked rougher than it really was, because I was seeing it from so close to the surface. Occasionally a wave sprang towards me and engulfed me in a smother of bubbling foam, and then the top lens broke through again, momentarily blurred, like a windscreen in heavy rain, until the water drained off and left it suddenly clear again. It was surprising how wide the field of vision was. I pushed the periscope round and saw land, the Isle of Wight, and immediately identified the Needles.

"Now I'm going to show you something," said the Captain. "Keep on looking and watch carefully. Can you see the Needles? You're in low power at the moment. Now watch." And he put his hand over my right hand, gave the handle a sharp half-turn towards me, and the Needles suddenly appeared astonishingly near. The field of vision had narrowed, but I could see every detail of those rocks as though they were less than a mile away. "You're now in high power," said the Captain, "normal vision magnified four times. Try it again yourself." I swivelled the handle again, and the Needles clicked back to their normal distance. "Now try moving the other handle," he said, "and see what happens." I did so, and found I could move sea, land and sky up or down; I could look at the sea quite close to me, or I could look above the land at the clouds. In fact I could swivel the top lens until I was looking at the sky right overhead. "That's so that we can keep a look-out for aircraft," said the Captain. "Now it's about time one of the others had a go."

I took my eyes away with the greatest reluctance, for I was fascinated by this remarkable toy and could have gone on looking through it all day. I had never realised that a submerged submarine could see so much of the outside world, or see it in such brilliant clarity and detail. I was curious to know what it would be like when the periscope was under water, and how far you could see into the surrounding depths, and whether you could see fish, or perhaps the submarine itself. For the periscope was the only means of looking beyond the steel walls which enclosed us. Because they would have been a weakness in the hull structure, there were no portholes through which I had imagined we might catch glimpses of the jade-green sea and its inhabitants.

I had no further opportunity that day for periscope explorations. The Captain was only staying down for an hour, and the time passed far too quickly. I could not get over the feeling of excitement at being so comfortably below the surface, the great length of the ship now invisible to the outer world, with her weight so finely adjusted between positive and negative buoyancy that she rode in her liquid element as delicately and majestically as an airship in the air. I was impressed by the quiet way in which orders were given, the informal yet firm discipline, the warm lighting everywhere, the unexpected lack of any discomfort in breathing or standing or moving about, the murmurs from the other compartments as the sailors cracked jokes for all the world as though they were safe on dry land.

All too soon the Captain ordered "Stand by to surface." At the order "Shut main vents" from the First Lieutenant, the rating at the control panel on the starboard side moved a group of small levers. A series of muffled thuds indicated the shutting of the vents, but the First Lieutenant waited for confirmation from the various compartments before he in turn reported to the Captain, "All main vents shut, sir." By this time the signalman had opened the hatch into the conning-tower. The Captain had one final sweep round with the periscope, snapped the handles shut, said "Down periscope," and then, as he began climbing the ladder, gave the order "Surface."

"Blow all main ballast!" Valves on the control panel were opened one after the other, and there came a roar of air under high pressure expanding into the ballast tanks. The hydroplane operators turned their wheels to put the planes to "rise." The ship took on a slight bow-up angle as we began moving towards the surface. Number One stood at the foot of the ladder calling up the changing depths to the Captain, who was now releasing the clips on the upper hatch: "Twenty-five feet, sir. . . . Twenty feet, sir. . . . Fifteen feet, sir . . ." and then the Captain thrust his arm up and swung the hatch open. A few drops of water came down the tower, the signalman and the look-outs clambered up, and as the Channel swell took charge of us again I had to hang on to one of the periscope wires to steady myself. "Stop blowing," shouted Number One above the din of roaring air. Orders came down the voice-pipe from the Captain, and soon the diesels were thundering and the ship began to gather speed. I stood under the conning-tower and felt the cool draught on my face as the air came whistling down to feed the engines. Then we climbed up on to the bridge and stood in the wind and sun once more, while the submarine swung round on to a course for home.

Comparing notes with the others, I found that neither of them quite shared my feeling of excitement. Harold confessed to having experienced a strong sense of claustrophobia, but thought that perhaps in time he might get over it. For myself, I was filled with exultation. I had been to sea in a submarine; I had dived; I had looked through the periscope. Not many of my contemporaries could say as much. I began to like the idea of serving in these extraordinary ships.

But first we had to serve our two months in destroyers, above water. So a few days later I left London by the night train to look for H.M.S. *Atherstone* at Scapa Flow. After a wearisome train journey from Edinburgh to Scrabster in the north of Scotland, and a boat trip across the boiling Pentland Firth to Orkney which made me thoroughly seasick, I arrived at Scapa only to find that *Atherstone* had sailed for Rosyth two days ago. Without pause for rest I had to turn about and suffer the boredom of the whole journey all over again. When I reached Rosyth I was told that *Atherstone* had been in, but had left the previous day; she was, however, expected to return shortly. Two days later she duly turned up, and at last I reported on board. Within the hour we were off to sea again: destroyers were given little peace in those days.

So began my first sea appointment. *Atherstone* (Commander Browning, D.S.O., R.N.), the first of the new Hunt-class destroyers (she was really little larger than a sloop), was based on Scapa and spent her days in escorting convoys or in fruitless searches for U-boats reported by aircraft in doubtful positions. We were too far north to be of any use at Dunkirk during the eventful early days of June; we fretted with impotent rage as the full story of the evacuation came through. Sometimes we escorted large units of the Home Fleet, and once, just under a year before her tragic end at the hands of the *Bismarck*, we were part of the screen for H.M.S. *Hood* sailing westward into a moderate Atlantic gale; even though I was being extremely seasick at the time, I had to admit that she made a majestic picture as she thrust her beautiful lines through the breaking seas with the spray lifting right over her bridge.

For watch-keeping I understudied the First Lieutenant, Mike Tufnell, and at action stations I was supposedly in charge of "B" gun, the after four-inch. It was fortunate that we never had to shoot in earnest, for I had not the slightest understanding of the drill, or of how the gun worked. But my most important job was being Correspondence Officer, the job that is always given to the youngest and greenest sub-lieutenant in the ship. That is all very well when the officer is regular R.N., for at least he has been a midshipman and knows something of naval routine and the hierarchy of rank and rating and how to address superior officers. But I had gathered little of these matters during my six weeks at *King Alfred*, three of which had been devoted solely to navigation. As Correspondence Officer of H.M.S. *Atherstone* I was plunged immediately into a morass of paper work which might have been in code for all I could make of it. How could I know that an A.F.O. was an Admiralty Fleet Order, or that L.T.O. stood for Leading Torpedo Operator but actually meant a rating trained for electrical duties? And when a sailor came to me and claimed that his pay was in arrears, what was I supposed to do about it? For I was responsible for paying the ship's company, and this part of the job alone presented innumerable problems. At first I began to believe that all the jokes about service red tape were only a pale reflection of the truth. Later on, when it all became clear to me, I developed a great respect for the way the general business of the Royal Navy was run; considering the complexity of the organisation, the amount of paper work was extremely small.

In addition to my other duties I had to look ahead to the day when, as I hoped, I would get my appointment to a submarine training class. And here I was lucky, in that both the Captain and the First Lieutenant had been submariners in their time and were able to give me much help. Mike Tufnell, in particular, lent me his old submarine notebooks and answered my endless questions. The result was that I went to my training class with a sound basis of elementary knowledge about submarines that I should not otherwise have had.

At last, about the end of July, the signal came appointing me to H.M.S. *Dolphin*. But I arrived at Fort Blockhouse without my two R.N.V.R. friends from *King Alfred*, for in the meantime Harold had, quite rightly, not felt justified in going further with submarines in view of his proneness to claustrophobia, and the third member of our trio had been reported as "temperamentally unsuitable for submarines" by his destroyer C.O., himself an ex-submariner. And so it was that, by pure chance, I became the first officer of the Royal Naval Volunteer Reserve to enter the submarine service.

The training class which I joined in August 1940 lasted the usual wartime six weeks. During this time the Battle of Britain was at its height, and our instruction and sleep were continually interrupted by visits to the air-raid shelters. Somehow, by skilful concealment of my ignorance of some of the most elementary facts about electrics and the internal-combustion engine, I managed to scrape through the course. That I did so was due to the preliminary coaching I had received in *Atherstone*, and to the fact that the expansion of the submarine construction programme was producing a desperate shortage of officers.

At the end of the course we were posted to various submarines. Three of us—Dearden, Tait and myself—were appointed to the pair of H-boats based on Harwich and operating against German coastal shipping along the Dutch coast. Dearden joined *H.49* at Harwich and went straight off on patrol; Jock Tait and I travelled to Sheerness, where *H.28* was just completing a refit before resuming her North Sea patrols.

I am glad I did not know as much then as I did later about submarines and operational conditions. *H.28* was the oldest and one of the smallest submarines in the Royal Navy: she was built in 1918. Needless to say, Jock and I had been instructed

in the later types of submarine, and although the basic prin-
ciples were the same, we found we had to forget much of what
we had learnt and start afresh. Our Captain, Lieutenant
M. R. G. Wingfield, who looked older and sterner than he was,
had only recently completed his C.O.'s course, and *H.28*'s next
patrol was to be his first in command. Challis, the First Lieutenant, had several war patrols to his credit, but about half the
crew were fresh from training class and some of them had never
before been to sea. Such was the country's desperate lack of
trained men, after a full year of war.

Jock and I, the greenhorns in the wardroom, stuck together
for mutual support. Jock was R.N.R. and a Scot, with a snub
nose and an aggressive chin. He had the merchant seaman's
intolerance of the punctilious discipline of the Royal Navy; and
this, coupled with an innate tendency to be "agin" authority,
was to lead at times to an almost mutinous attitude towards the
Captain when criticised; then Jock's small dark eyes would half
shut with suppressed anger. But these moods never lasted, and
he and Wingfield got on very well. For Jock was desperately
keen on the job, and really very humble in spirit.

A week or so after we had joined the boat the refit was complete and we moved round to Harwich. The submarine base
here was built on Parkeston Quay and formed part of the railway station. As we busied ourselves in preparation for our first
patrol, ordering stores, learning how to decode signals, and
bringing our charts up to date with the latest minefields, we
were surrounded by posters urging us to visit the Continent.

A few days before we were due to sail, our sister ship *H.49*
returned from her patrol. We stood on the quayside watching
her approach. The weather had been rough, and the men on
the bridge looked wet and weather-beaten. We waved to Dearden, but it was a tired smile that responded. In the mess that
evening Jock and I pumped him for all we were worth to tell us
what it had been like; but though we had been in the same
training class there was a gulf fixed between us: he had completed a war patrol and we had not.

II

MY FIRST PATROL

It was a grey October morning when we waved good-bye to
our friends from the base who had gathered on Parkeston Quay
to wish us well. We pushed off down the river to the open sea
and took station astern of the Admiralty trawler that was to
escort us out.* The visibility was poor, and a chilly east wind
was knocking up the usual North Sea chop. All day we zig-
zagged up the coast until, in the late afternoon, we reached the
beginning of the secret route through the East Coast mine barrier. Here our trawler parted company, flashing us a final
"Good hunting" as he turned away in the falling dusk. Now
we were really alone. We pointed our nose eastward and shaped
a course towards the enemy across the no-man's-land of the
North Sea.

When, after an uneventful passage, we reached our area, we
had some difficulty at first in fixing our position. We dived
shortly before dawn a little way out from the Dutch coast and
crept in towards it during the day. The sea was calm, the sky

---

* His job was to protect us, not so much from the enemy as from friendly ships
and aircraft. In our own shipping lanes an unescorted submarine was assumed to
be hostile and therefore fair game. Although Coastal Command was always informed of our own submarines' movements, the sight of a lone submarine on the
surface, even when air protection was supposedly in force for its benefit, was sometimes too much for the aggressive spirit of our pilots. It was usually advisable to
get down out of their way. One of the earliest signals of the war came from one
of our submarines which was being harassed by the R.A.F. in the North Sea on
her return from patrol: "Estimated time of arrival 1100, friendly forces permitting."

grey, and the visibility indifferent. By noon we had sighted the low-lying land, and the Captain and Jock spent the afternoon taking bearings through the periscope and trying to make a lighthouse and various white buildings on an otherwise featureless coast agree with the landmarks shown on the chart. At last they were satisfied that they knew where we were, and we turned to patrol up and down a five-mile line parallel with the shore, waiting for something to come along. But it was not until the third day that anything happened to disturb the monotonous routine of "watch diving."

This was the routine that was to grow so familiar during the next four years. At "diving stations" every one of the forty-odd men in the ship had a job to do, either when diving and surfacing or when carrying out an attack. But during the long hours of waiting for something to happen, we were at "watch diving," the crew divided into three watches (red, white and blue), two hours on and four off. The watch consisted of just enough men to maintain the required depth and work the periscope: the two planesmen, sitting on the port side facing the large dials of the depth-gauges and giving occasional turns to the control wheels; the helmsman in the port for'ard corner, steering by gyro compass; an E.R.A.* responsible for operating the vent-and-blow panel on the starboard side and the lever which raised and lowered the periscopes. Besides these men in the control-room, there was an L.T.O. in the motor-room aft who obeyed the speed-telegraphs † operated from the control-room; a seaman for'ard who listened, through headphones connected to an external revolving disc called a hydrophone, for the sound of approaching ships; and finally, in a tiny compartment under the control-room, a stoker who, by operating the ballast-pump motor and opening various valves, could flood or pump on any of the trimming tanks throughout the submarine in obedience to the orders of the First Lieutenant or the officer-

* Engine-Room Artificer.
† Exactly similar to those in all surface ships: hand-operated dials with pointers to the speed required—slow, half or full, and ahead or astern—with repeaters in the engine-room and motor-room.

of-the-watch. The rest of the crew would be sleeping, reading, eating—but mostly sleeping.

I now had to learn the arduous art of keeping watch through the periscope. It was with a disturbing mixture of apprehension, pride and curiosity that I went into the control-room to take over my watch from Number One for the first time. He took me first to the chart-table, an uncomfortably small space in the passage-way leading for'ard, pointed out our position on the chart and the landmarks on which I must take a fix every half-hour, and then showed me those landmarks through the periscope to make sure I could identify them. Finally, with a cheery "She's all yours, chum," he retired to the wardroom and left *me* in charge of the ship.

"Up periscope," I said, trying to make it sound like an order I had been giving for a long time. First, following the standard periscope drill, I had a quick look all round in low power. Satisfied that no ships or aircraft were close to us, I followed this by a slow, careful search in high power of one quarter of the horizon. As I turned the periscope, my panoramic eye, seemingly pivoted a few inches above the gently heaving water, sometimes obscured as a wave lapped over the top lens, moved slowly across the empty edge of the grey horizon, looking for the masthead or the breath of smoke that might announce the approach of a target. Then another all-round sweep in low power to make sure that nothing had crept up behind me. Then "down periscope." Then again "up periscope," a quick all-round sweep, and a thorough examination of the next ninety degrees of horizon. Training carefully along the misty coastline, I could not help thinking it was rather amusing, almost impudent, that we two-score Englishmen should be living, sleeping and eating here, so close, and so invisible, to the enemy.

At least we hoped we were invisible. All the time, when you were keeping periscope watch, you had to take care that you were not showing more than a few inches of periscope. If the planesmen did not keep to the exact periscope depth of thirty feet, whether from lack of skill or attention, or because the boat was not properly trimmed, you might find the periscope stick-

ing up several feet out of the water, with the danger of being
sighted through some shore-watcher's telescope. You could
correct this by having the periscope lowered a little and bend-
ing down to keep your eyes still on the eyepiece, but the constant arching and straightening of the back was tiring. Much
better see to your trim.

As officer-of-the-watch, therefore, besides watching for the
enemy and taking a periodic navigational fix, you had to keep
a severe eye on the depth-keeping. Primarily, the First Lieutenant was responsible for "putting on the trim," or adjusting
the amount of water in the various trimming tanks so that the
ship rode level and in neutral buoyancy (neither light nor heavy).
But owing to the movement of men about the ship and changes
in the density of the surrounding water, occasional corrections
to the trim were necessary throughout the day. It was up to the
officer-of-the-watch to make these corrections and maintain a
good trim. It was not always easy, if you were as inexperienced
as I was, to estimate from the way the boat was behaving
whether she was, for instance, heavy for'ard, or light aft, or
just bodily heavy or light. Should the trim be so lost that the
planes could no longer keep the depth, you could recover control by speeding up and so giving more effect to the planes. But
if the ship got badly out of trim, you might be unable to hold
her despite your speeding up; you would then exhibit the morti-
fying and unforgivable spectacle of a submarine wallowing and
churning about on the surface in sight of the enemy coast. You
would soon have an angry Captain in the control-room. Or you
might be too heavy, and go sinking below periscope depth, ren-
dering the submarine blind until you had regained control. All
this speeding up would, moreover, be a drain on the precious
amps in the battery. So from all points of view it was essential
to keep a good trim.

Two hours of periscope watch were enough. It was more of
a strain than it sounds, particularly at first, when the muscles
of the eyes were not used to such meticulous, thoughtful searching. Efficient periscope work demands a constant and deliberate exercise of the imagination. All the time you have to say

c

to yourself: "At this very moment an enemy vessel may be approaching just beyond the horizon; every second that it is in sight without my spotting it will mean so much less time for the Captain to get into an attacking position if it is a target, or to get out of the way if it is hunting for us." After a long period of seeing nothing it is easy to submit to a softening of the will-power. You cease to believe in the imminence of danger or of a target. And so one morning, sweeping dreamily round an over-familiar seascape that has been empty for days, you fail to notice the needle-point of a mast emerging from the horizon's rim, and when you get round to that bearing again—heavens alive! here's a ship coming at you, and much too close—mast, funnel and upperworks all clearly visible.

It fell to Jock to make our first sighting. I was dozing in my bunk in the wardroom, after lunch on the third day, when I was woken by a cry of "Captain in the control-room!" Wingfield was out of his bunk and at the periscope in a flash. Number One and I strained our ears to listen to what was going on. We heard the Captain's "What is it, pilot?" and Jock's reply: "A mast, I think, sir." A pause, and then the Captain again: "Ah, there he is. Well done, pilot. Hullo, here's another one. Right. . . . Diving stations!" As the order was repeated for'ard and aft, the submarine sprang to life with a rush of men hurrying to their stations. Number One took over the depth-keeping, standing behind the planesmen, watching the depth-gauges and the hydroplane tell-tales, passing a few quiet flooding and pumping orders to restore the trim, which had been upset by the sudden movement of the crew.

As "Third Hand" I had nothing to do at diving stations unless we were attacking, when my duty was to work a calculating instrument known as the "fruit machine." * So far, however, the Captain had not started to attack, so I could concen-

---

* This is a calculating machine connected electrically to the ship's gyro compass. When the information from the Captain is fed into it, it gives a running diagrammatic picture of the attack in progress and, providing the Captain's estimations are sufficiently accurate, tells him when to fire.

trate on watching him at the periscope. I was shivering with excitement. It was maddening not being able to see what was going on up top. We had to be content with what we could guess from the expression on the Captain's face. For a long time he said nothing at all. He seemed to be trying to decide what sort of ships they were. The pin-point of daylight glittered on his eyeball.

At last he snapped the handles shut, ordered "Down periscope, starboard fifteen, steer two-eight-five," then turned to the First Lieutenant and said, "Two minesweepers, I think, Number One. Shows we're on the coastal shipping route all right. There's no point in attacking—we'd only spoil our chance of a better target later on. We'll just keep out of the way and watch."

The tension in the control-room deflated like a punctured tyre. The news that it was "only a couple of minesweepers" rippled through to the ends of the boat, and we settled down to wait until the trawlers had passed. We crept slowly away at a right angle to their track, the Captain making frequent observations of them and taking ranges and bearings so that Jock could plot their course and speed on the chart. When they were out of sight we reverted to "watch diving" and returned to our patrol line.

Nothing more happened for the rest of the day, but our first contact with the enemy had made us feel that something might happen at any time, and there was a sense of increased alertness through the ship when we were due to come up at nightfall.

The most dangerous time for a submarine on war patrol is this moment of surfacing at night. We must wait for complete darkness, and for the last half-hour or so the light has been too bad for the periscope to be of any use, so we have gone deep to avoid accidental collision. For half an hour, therefore, we have been blind, relying on our hydrophone amplifier to give audible warning of approaching vessels. The air in the boat has become pretty foul: in the long days of summer we dive, perhaps, at four in the morning and come up at nine in the evening, and even at the end of the briefer winter day the air is getting short of oxygen and causing a certain amount of discomfort in breathing. Night vision is affected by physical condition, and when we surface our eyes will not reach their full efficiency in the dark until blood and lungs have got used once more to the fresh sea air.

About twenty minutes before surfacing, the order is passed to "Darken ship." The lights in the control-room and every compartment for'ard of it are switched out and replaced by the dimmest of bulbs, so that the Captain, the officer-of-the-watch and the look-outs can get their eyes used to the dark. The eyes use an entirely different set of muscles for seeing in the dark, and it takes at least fifteen minutes for them to dilate to full efficiency. Ordinary lighting has the same effect on these muscles as a touch on the end of a snail's horn.

As we go to our diving stations preparatory to surfacing, the scene in the semi-darkness is dramatic. The men are aware that this is a dangerous moment. Up top it is night: perhaps we have, unknowingly, been detected during the day and a destroyer is up there waiting quietly for us to surface under his nose. The Coxswain and the Second Coxswain watch the hydroplanes with more than their usual concentration; the helmsman is dead on his course; the officer-of-the-watch and the look-outs are ready in their duffel coats and balaclavas, binoculars slung round their necks. The Captain comes quietly into the control-room, severe and alert with the responsibility of forethought and decision. He passes an order to the hydrophone operator to make a final careful listening sweep. As we wait in silence for the answer, we come gently up to periscope depth, and the Captain has a slow look all round. He does not expect to see anything but utter blackness, because of the loss of light through the lenses of the periscope, but he might just be able to make out the shape of anything that happened to be very close. And it would be foolish to surface straight into the beams of a searchlight. However, he sees nothing. The report comes back from the hydrophone operator: "No H.E.,* sir."

"Stand by to surface," says the Captain, and the signalman

---

* Hydrophone effect, or propeller noise.

reaches up and opens the lower hatch of the conning-tower. Number One, who has been ready to surface for the last five minutes, reports, "All ready to surface, sir."

The Captain says, "Down periscope. . . . Surface," and climbs up into the tower, followed by the signalman; the two look-outs wait at the foot of the ladder. Amid the roar of compressed air bursting into the ballast tanks, we rise to the surface. The Captain flings open the hatch; the air pressure inside the boat, which has built up during the day from minute leaks in the system of compressed-air pipes, releases itself into the night atmosphere with a gush which raises a small hurricane in the conning-tower, drawing with it a sickening stench of dirty oil from the bilges and cabbage-water from the galley, where the cook has already started preparing the evening meal. The look-outs clatter up the tower after the Captain, we stop blowing, and then wait in suspense for the first order down the voice-pipe. We roll gently; it is fairly calm; I look up through the tower and observe that the sky has cleared, for I can see a star swinging back and forth across the hatch. We are still going slowly ahead on the electric motors. Up there on the bridge the Captain and the look-outs are searching the blackness; we cannot start the diesels until they are sure there is nothing close enough to hear us.

"Control-room!" The Captain's garbled words crackle in the voice-pipe. The helmsman answers, "Control-room," and we all listen for the order. "Start main engines." And we know it is all right up top. The telegraphs clang as the orders go to the engine-room, and presently the engines roar to life and begin sucking down into the submarine a delicious stream of cool fresh air which blows away the cobwebs from our sleepy brains. The order is passed for "Patrol routine," cigarettes are lit and the surface watch-keeping rota begins. I go to the wardroom to get a hot supper before I have to go up on the bridge.

We saw those same minesweepers almost every other day after that. In bad visibility they served as a useful check on our navigation. And on about the ninth day they came escorting a large laden barge. It was not a very promising target, but as nothing else had come our way, the Captain felt we must do something "to maintain the offensive" and decided to fire two torpedoes set to a running depth of four feet.

His order to "Start the attack" set my heart pounding, but I turned to my "fruit machine" and stood by to manipulate the dials as I had been trained to do. The game was on.

"Up periscope. The bearing is . . . that! Range . . . that! Down periscope. I am ten degrees on his starboard bow. Port thirty. Give me a course for a sixty track."

The enemy bearing and range were read off the periscope by a Petty Officer standing behind the Captain. My job was to feed these data into the instrument and produce from it the answers that would assist the Captain to get into an attacking position and fire his torpedoes at the precise moment. Some of my answers were passed on to Jock for his plot of the attack, the main purpose of which was to estimate the enemy's speed.

The attack developed slowly. The Captain's ranges from his frequent periscope observations showed the enemy's speed to be somewhere between six and eight knots. From my settings on the "fruit machine" I could tell that the moment for firing was drawing near; now all my efforts must be concentrated on producing for the Captain what was known as the D.A., or Director Angle, or in plainer English the "aim-off" to allow for the target's speed and the time the torpedoes would take to reach his track. Fortunately this was a simple attack, and when the Captain asked, "What's the D.A.?" I was able to read off the answer, "D.A. five red, sir," with fair confidence.*

"Stand by One and Two tubes. Up periscope. Down periscope. Up periscope. Put me on red five. Stand by . . . FIRE ONE! . . . FIRE TWO! Down periscope."

As each torpedo was fired in the tube-space for'ard I felt a sudden increase of pressure on my eardrums and a slight backward lurch, as though the boat had momentarily bumped into

* Bearings and firing angles are expressed as so many degrees off one's own bow—"red" for port, "green" for starboard.

something large and soft. And then we waited for the bangs, in an almost unbearable tension, imagining the torpedoes racing at forty knots towards the target. Meanwhile we turned to starboard, and the Captain had two or three quick looks at his intended victim. The seconds dragged by interminably.

But alas, there were no bangs. "Sorry, boys, I'm afraid we've missed," said the Captain at last, puzzled and angry with himself. It was bitterly disappointing. And now what was the enemy's reaction going to be? At his next look, the Captain saw that both the minesweepers had turned in our direction; they had obviously sighted the tracks of the torpedoes, and they were angry. "Take her down to a hundred feet, Number One, shut off for depth-charging, absolute silence through the boat." The depth-gauge needles moved round as we dropped down from periscope depth . . . 40 feet . . . 50 feet . . . 70 . . . 90 . . . and then slowed up as the planesmen corrected the dive and brought her gently on to 100 feet. Once more we waited for a bang, but this time with somewhat different feelings.

A message came through from the hydrophone operator for'ard that he could hear propeller noises astern. Almost at the same moment a sharp crack, as of a giant hammer, struck the pressure hull, followed by a frightful reverberating roar which seemed to echo through all the subterranean ocean caves of the world. To my astonishment the lights stayed on. "Not very close," said the Captain. Not close! As he spoke there was a second mighty crack, and again that thundering, rumbling aftermath. And still we suffered no damage. And again we waited. "Faint H.E. on red 160," came another report from for'ard, followed by "Asdic transmissions on the bearing." A little while later the Captain, listening intently, said, "I think I can hear his asdic," and presently I too heard a faint, slow, regular knocking, as though someone was tapping gently on the outside of the hull. I thought of Pew's stick tapping along the road in *Treasure Island*. It was like being shut up in a dark room, with a blind maniac reaching out sinister fingers to find you. Perhaps the enemy had already detected our echo from his transmissions and was even now closing in for the kill.

However, to our surprise, there were no more depth-charges. I was after all to be let off with an easy baptism. At last, after an hour of tedious suspense, we could no longer hear the transmissions, the propeller noises grew fainter astern, and the Captain decided to return to periscope depth and see what was going on. With tremendous relief we heard him report that they were well astern of us and appeared to be making for home.

And for the rest of that patrol we saw nothing more of them. Three days later we received our recall signal. It warned us that we might meet *H.49* during the night, on her way out to relieve us, but we did not sight her. We had one more moment of excitement, however. Approaching the Suffolk coast on the surface soon after daybreak in poor visibility, I was officer-of-the-watch when a German fighter suddenly appeared out of the mist, very low and close. As I gave the order to dive, and the look-outs scrambled down the hatch, the German saw us and began circling to come at us. By the time I was in the hatch myself, we were started on our way down, but he had made his turn and was coming straight for us. I could hear his engines roaring. As I reached my arm up to pull the hatch down over my head he opened up with his machine-guns. I banged the lid down, put the clips on, and tumbled down the ladder to the control-room so fast that there was a roar of laughter when I reached the bottom, badly bruised, with the sound of bullets clattering round the bridge structure overhead. There was no damage to the pressure hull, however, and after staying deep for half an hour we surfaced and proceeded on our way.

In the bad visibility we took some time to find our escort at the rendezvous, but we did so at last, and came finally into Harwich to revel in hot baths, fresh food and the good feeling that, although it had proved abortive, at least we had survived our first war patrol and gained valuable experience. Half of us were given leave; I was one of the lucky ones. I went off to London for four days, and then returned to Harwich to make preparations for our next patrol.

Our departure was fixed for the day after *H.49*'s return. On the morning of the day she was due to arrive I was in the Staff

Office collecting the tables of recognition signals for our patrol period. The only other person in the room was the Staff Officer. He seemed to be unusually preoccupied. Gradually I sensed an atmosphere of strain, and the more casual our desultory conversation became the more I grew convinced that something serious had happened. He looked as though he had been up all night. As innocently as possible I asked what time he was expecting *H.49* to arrive. He took a long time to reply. "I may as well tell you," he said finally. "*H.49* hasn't turned up at the rendezvous with her escort, and she hasn't replied to any of our signals. She may of course be damaged and her W/T may be out of action. But it doesn't look very good. Only for heaven's sake keep it under your hat for the moment."

By the following evening the continued silence from our sister ship turned fear into certainty. The word was passed for "Clear lower deck" at 1800, and all officers and men from the base and from *H.28* mustered in one of the quayside sheds to be addressed by Captain Submarines.* Captain Phillips, D.S.O., R.N., had distinguished himself in December 1939, while in command of the submarine *Ursula*, by sinking a Köln-class cruiser through a screen of six destroyers in shallow water off the Elbe estuary. What he had to say to us came better, perhaps, from a man who had made his reputation in action so recently and in much the same waters. He said quite simply that he was sorry to have to tell us that *H.49* was overdue and must be presumed lost. He asked us not to mention it outside the base. He was himself going immediately to break the news to any of the wives who were living in Harwich or the neighbourhood. He then went on, to our surprise, to say that in the meantime the sailing of *H.28* had been postponed indefinitely, and that he was waiting for further Admiralty orders concerning our future. Finally he thanked us, and we were dismissed. I felt very sorry for him. He was now faced with a painful and difficult duty; and the Commanding Officer of *H.49* had been a friend of his.

Jock and I went off for a long walk. I felt very cold and dead

* Usually abbreviated to "Captain S/M."

inside, and we hardly spoke. We thought of Dearden, who had been in our training class. He seemed now impossibly remote; I fancied him smiling again that same tired smile with which he had greeted us on his last return to harbour. Once more he had crossed a gulf ahead of us. Later Jock was to cross it too, and in less than a year I was to come very close to doing so myself.*

We lived the next few days in an atmosphere of anticlimax until orders came through that H-class submarines were to cease operational patrols forthwith and join the Seventh Submarine Flotilla, which consisted only of training submarines and was based at Rothesay in the Clyde estuary. Harwich was to be abandoned as a submarine base. We packed our gear and sailed up the East Coast, round the north of Scotland to the Clyde, spending a week or two at Dundee on the way. It must have been about the beginning of December when we arrived off Rothesay and secured alongside H.M.S. *Cyclops*.

In normal times Rothesay is a popular summer resort. Now the lovely bay, with its long prospect of Loch Striven and the blue hills of Argyll, was dominated by the dirty coal-burning merchant-ship that had been converted into an inadequate and uncomfortable submarine depot ship. Only the wartime shortage of shipping had saved old *Cyclops* from the scrap-heap. Throughout the submarine service she was known, almost affectionately, as the "Cycle-box." Once a year she was taken to sea on exercise, to disprove (some said unkindly) the rumour that she was aground on a self-made reef of empty tins. But between these annual jaunts she rode peacefully at anchor, with her submarines berthed on either side of her, a mother hen with her chicks, disturbed only by the frequent gales and squalls which came sweeping down the hills and churned the bay into an angry ferment, so that the submarines began bumping badly and had to lie off.

* Our submarine flotillas took some hard knocks in 1940, both in the North Sea and the Mediterranean. By the middle of the year we had lost *Seahorse*, *Starfish*, *Undine*, *Thistle*, *Sterlet*, *Tarpon* and *Seal*; in July, *Shark* and *Salmon*; in August, *Oswald*, *Odin*, *Orpheus* and *Spearfish*; in September, *Narwhal* and *Thames*; in November, *H.49*, *Swordfish* and *Rainbow*.

The purpose of the Seventh Submarine Flotilla was twofold: to give sea-training to new submarine officers and ratings, and at the same time to provide live practice targets for destroyers and other escort craft. Many of the boats in this flotilla were therefore dispersed at the various bases where anti-submarine forces carried out their training. So we spent the next few winter months up and down the rugged and beautiful coastline of Western Scotland, dividing our time between Rothesay, Campbeltown, Ardrishaig and Tobermory, acting as "clockwork mouse" to the crews of destroyers and corvettes who were being trained in the use of asdic. Each morning we proceeded to the exercise area, followed by the surface ships, and then dived to 80 feet for perhaps two hours at a time, usually on a pre-arranged course, while the asdic instructors initiated officers and ratings into the art of "pinging" on us, picking up an echo from our hull, plotting our movements, and making dummy attacks.

This was inordinately dull work for us. When off watch we spent most of the day sleeping. But gradually we grew so accustomed to submarine life (away from the depot ship we lived entirely in the boat for weeks on end) that diving and surfacing became second nature. And sometimes we managed to get in a practice attack on the surface ships at the end of the day.

There were continual changes in the crew, as is inevitable in a training flotilla, and by February I was the only officer left in *H.28* out of the four that had taken her on her last patrol. Jock Tait left to join an operational boat: our paths thereafter crossed only briefly once or twice; and in the end I heard that he had been lost on patrol. I took over the duties of navigator. We also had a change of First Lieutenant, and shortly afterwards Wingfield went off to take command of a new U-class submarine called *Umpire* and was relieved by Lieut. L. W. A. Bennington.

Bennington, who already wore a D.S.C., had been Number One of the submarine *Triumph* just over a year earlier when she struck a mine in the Skagerrak. They were on the surface on a very dark night, charging batteries as usual, and Bennington was officer-of-the-watch on the bridge. He saw the horned mine poised on the crest of a wave ahead of him, too late to do anything but shield his face. There was a tremendous explosion: it seemed certain they were done for. But to his amazement the boat remained on the surface. Inspection of the damage revealed that eighteen feet of the bow had been blown off, but the for'ard bulkhead, split and leaking badly, was by some miracle still holding. The torpedoes had not detonated (in a T-boat there were eight of them ready for firing in the bow tubes), but one had been blasted clean out of its tube, another had nothing left but its tail, and the T.N.T. warhead of a third had been utterly crushed. Amidships there was a ten-foot vertical crack in the pressure hull. And after all this they discovered a seaman still snoring in his hammock only ten yards from the point of the explosion. They were in a sorry state. They could not dive, and it was all the pumps could do to cope with the flooding from the leaks. The Captain, Lieut.-Commander J. W. McCoy, wirelessed for help, and they set off for home across the North Sea. They were sighted by German aircraft next morning, but as the enemy began to attack they were met by air escort and destroyers, and struggled into the Firth of Forth late the following night.

Bennington was short and stocky, with fair hair, a ruddy complexion and a dark chuckle. He talked endlessly in his deep voice about submarines and the submarine service, which for him was a kind of religion: the Royal Navy was immeasurably superior to the other services, and within the Navy the submarine branch was the most efficient and potentially the most powerful as a striking force. He never spoke of "subs" or "tubes" or "boats"; submarines were "submarines" and no nonsense. He was a quiet but strict disciplinarian, and had an unobtrusive way of showing his appreciation of good work. He professed to have no interest in women, and liked nothing better, when ashore, than to sit drinking beer and talking submarines by the hour. He was a terrible man to wake in the morning; when we were living in the boat he would lie in his bunk smoking cigarettes and drinking cup after cup of tea until two minutes before harbour stations, when he would miraculously appear on the dot of time and give orders with his accustomed precision. He never to my knowledge ate breakfast.

He was a wonderful teacher; from him I learnt much which stood me in good stead when I eventually had a command of my own. We got on well together. But in April, almost exactly six months after I had joined *H.28*, a signal came ordering me to report to Chatham. Wingfield had asked for me as his Third Hand in *Umpire*.

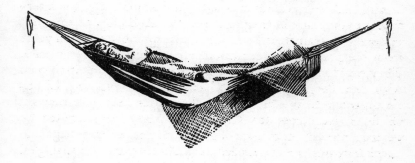

III

DISASTER

Umpire's dockyard trials had been successfully completed, including the usual static basin dive to prove that the hull was water-tight. The last welding leads had been removed, the bunks, cupboards and other wooden fittings were a bright mahogany gleam, new curtains hung in the messes, and the whole boat was resplendent with fresh-smelling paintwork, white inside and battleship grey outside.

Mervyn Wingfield was plainly delighted with his new command, though he tried to conceal his pleasure behind a demeanour of severity and icy reserve. The First Lieutenant, Peter Bannister, I had not met before; he was tall, energetic and humorous, easy to get on with. Tony Godden, the navigator, had been in the same training class with me at Fort Blockhouse; I was delighted now to find we were in the same boat, for he was a most amusing and endearing shipmate, and we had many good evenings ashore together during our stay in Chatham.

Umpire moved out at last into the River Medway on a day towards the end of July, spick and span, a brand-new white ensign flying, bound north-about for the Clyde, where we were to carry out sea trials and training with the Third Flotilla based at Dunoon, before setting forth on a "working-up" operational patrol in the North Sea. After that, the Mediterranean.

We stopped overnight at Sheerness to wait for a convoy of merchant-ships leaving the Thames the next day. In the morning we got under way early and found the convoy congregating off Southend under an escort of motor launches and Admiralty trawlers. We took up our station astern, and by the time we turned the corner at Shoeburyness the convoy had more or less sorted itself out.

All day we moved up the East Coast, passing Burnham,

Clacton, Walton-on-the-Naze, Harwich, Felixstowe, Orford-ness, and when we were somewhere off Aldeburgh a German bomber came in low from seaward and began attacking the leading ships of the convoy. I was officer-of-the-watch at the time, and in accordance with our convoy instructions gave the order to dive.

Now, we had never dived before at sea and under way. Nor-mally a brand-new submarine carries out numerous dives in slow motion, with the crew already at diving stations, before it is committed to a full-speed dive. We had to make our first dive on the klaxon, and it is to the great credit of all concerned —the Chatham men who built her; Wingfield, who as Captain had thought ahead and trained his officers and men to his satis-faction; Bannister, who as Number One had organised the crew in their duties and had also worked out the first trim; and the crew, who went calmly to diving stations and performed their jobs correctly—it is to the credit of all these that *Umpire's* first dive was a complete success. Within two minutes Bannister had caught a trim and the Captain was able to concentrate on the periscope. We did not want to stay down longer than we need, because the convoy was drawing ahead of us. Five min-utes later the Heinkel seemed to have vanished, so we surfaced and pressed on to regain our station in the convoy, which had sustained no damage from the attack.

We felt very pleased with ourselves, and boyishly proud of our boat that had behaved so well. Then, about nightfall, one of the diesels developed trouble and had to be stopped. At first this did not affect our speed, our propulsion being diesel-electric, and we continued to maintain our station. But as the evening wore on, the engine-room staff were unsuccessful in their attempts to get the defective engine going. The other one produced insufficient power by itself to balance the batteries' output when driving two propellers, and we were obliged at last to reduce our speed. The Captain flashed a signal to the Com-modore of the convoy, reporting the situation. An M.L. was detailed to drop back and act as our escort, and we were to catch up as soon as possible.

We knew from the latest W/T situation report that, some twenty miles to the north of us, a southbound convoy was approaching down the same buoyed channel. The two convoys were due to meet somewhere about midnight.

The international rule at sea is that in a channel-way ships must keep to the starboard side. Ships meeting in a channel should therefore pass *port to port*. It was revealed afterwards that when the two convoys met, some miles ahead of us, they passed on the *wrong* side, starboard to starboard. So when Tony Godden, the officer-of-the-watch, presently sent down a message that the southbound convoy was approaching, Wingfield was surprised to find on reaching the bridge that the oncoming convoy was not on our port bow, as he expected, but right ahead, with part of it actually extending across our starboard bow. It was a calm night, very dark, but with reasonably good visibility; lights could have been seen at a fair distance. But the German E-boats were raiding the East Coast convoys nearly every night, and no one was showing any lights. Our escorting M.L. had lost touch with us some time earlier. We were quite alone and almost invisible to other ships even at close range.

The normal action would have been to alter course to starboard, but this would have taken us across the bows of the approaching merchant-ships and we might not have had room to get clear. Wingfield altered a few degrees to port, and the first six ships of the convoy passed safely down our starboard side about two hundred yards away. Although we did not know it, our own convoy, now several miles ahead, had taken the same action.

Suddenly a dark shape appeared ahead of us, detached from the nearest column of the convoy. Examining it through his binoculars, Wingfield saw that it was a trawler, presumably part of the convoy's escort, and that we were directly in its path. In the next second he realised that it was alarmingly near to us and apparently unaware of our presence. He had to decide quickly what to do. The trawler was fine on his starboard bow and seemed certain to pass dangerously close. By the rule of the road it was the trawler's right of way and our duty to keep clear. According to the rules Wingfield should have altered course to starboard, but only two hundred yards to starboard was the endless line of southbound merchant-ships forming an impenetrable barrier. With every ship fully darkened, this was a predicament not visualised by the authors of the Regulations for Preventing Collision at Sea. Wingfield ordered "Hard-a-port." But, even as we began to turn, the trawler seemed to see us, low and dark in the water, and turned instinctively to starboard. This made collision inevitable. Wingfield yelled his last order down the voice-pipe, "Full astern together!"—but before the order could be carried out, the bows of the trawler struck *Umpire* with a sickening metallic crash, some twenty or thirty feet abaft the starboard bow. The submarine lurched to port, and for a few seconds the two vessels stayed locked together, held by the impetus of the trawler's headway. During these seconds Wingfield clutched the trawler's side as it swung in towards him, and shouted furiously, "You bloody bastard, you've sunk a British submarine!" Then the trawler fell away, and Wingfield found his boat sinking under him by the head. In less than thirty seconds she plunged under, leaving Wingfield, Godden and the two look-outs in the water. In the darkness there was shouting and confusion, but the four kept together at first. But presently one and then the other of the look-outs dropped out of the small circle. Tony Godden, who was wearing long fur-lined seaboots, gasped out that he could not kick them free and that he was sinking. For a while Wingfield helped to support him, but Tony finally let go and sank out of sight. It seemed a long time before the trawler's boat appeared, and Wingfield was unconscious when he was hauled on board. When he came to and realised that he, the Captain, was apparently the sole survivor, his feelings can be imagined.

When the Captain left the wardroom to go up on the bridge in response to Tony's message about the approaching convoy, Peter Bannister and I were sitting at the wardroom table,

D

decoding a routine wireless signal that had been passed to us by the telegraphist on watch.

The wardroom was divided from the control-room only by a thin steel partition, and by curtains from the passage-way; at sea these curtains were drawn back, and Peter and I could hear the helmsman repeat the orders which came to him down the voice-pipe from the bridge.

When we heard him repeat the Captain's emergency order, "Hard-a-port," we pushed back our chairs and stood up, our eyes meeting in question and alarm. We stumbled out into the passage-way, and Peter at once gave the order to "Shut water-tight doors!" Almost immediately we heard another urgent yell down the voice-pipe, but before this last order from the bridge could be repeated by the helmsman there was a violent crash for'ard in the torpedo-stowage compartment, followed by the blue-white flare and muffled thump of an electrical explosion. The boat rocked to port, stayed there a few seconds, and then slid drunkenly forward and over to starboard as she began her plunge to the bottom. If the water were deep here, its weight would crush us like an egg-shell. Most of the lights had gone out. Then men were running past us from the next compartment, Peter was yelling "Shut that door!" and I had my hand on it, letting the men run through, disobeying Peter because I hadn't the courage to deny any of them a chance so long as the water was not yet actually at their heels. Somehow the further door to the damaged compartment had shut, whether blown to by the explosion or deliberately shut from the inside by a last nameless act of self-sacrifice as the sea came flooding in, we shall never know. "Shut that bloody door!" repeated Peter in a fury, but by now all the men from the intervening compartment were through. With some difficulty, because of the angle of the boat, I pulled the door up towards me and clamped it shut.

I turned, and struggled up the tilting deck into the control-room. The boat was listing to starboard and sloping forward at an angle of about ten degrees. Water was pouring in from what seemed to be a hundred places. Peter was struggling with the

outboard battery-ventilation-valve overhead, desperately seeking an explanation for this inrush of water, and acutely aware
of the fatal danger of chlorine gas if the sea-water should find
its way into the battery cells under the deck. I reached up to
help him, glad in my numbed state of something positive to do.
But the valve was already shut, as we knew it should have been,
and we must look elsewhere for the breach in our defences. To
my paralysed brain it seemed that the shock of the collision had
cracked the hull and started rivets along the whole length of
the ship. Surprisingly enough, no water was coming down the
conning-tower; presumably the upper hatch had fallen shut
when the boat took on a list immediately before she went
under.

Peter was now calling for more light, and one or two of the
men searched about for the emergency hand-lamps. I remembered that I had a torch in my drawer in the wardroom, so I
retraced my steps, moving with difficulty down the wet and
sloping deck. In the passage-way the water was already knee-
deep. I sloshed through it and pulled myself up into the wardroom. Streams of ice-green water were cascading from somewhere overhead, drenching the beautiful new curtains and
bunks in a universal deluge. If I had brought a conscious intelligence to bear on the source of this waterfall I should have
hit on something that ought to have been obvious to all of us.
But not until the whole thing was over did I realise that all this
water must have been coming from the *ventilation shaft*, now
open to sea pressure through the damaged torpedo-stowage
compartment. By reaching up my hand over the Captain's
bunk I could have shut the valve on the bulkhead quite easily,
and the flow of water would have stopped. But my brain, as
though stunned by the catastrophe, had become incapable of
constructive thought.

I found the torch and splashed my way back to the control-
room. As I did so, it occurred to me to wonder what depth we
were at. I shone the torch on the depth-gauges and found, to
my surprise, that they were both reading only a little over 60
feet. This meant we were in very shallow water, with the bow

presumably resting on the bottom at something like 80 feet. I
asked Peter whether it was possible to *blow* her up. It seemed
unlikely, since we had been at full buoyancy at the time of the
collision, and a vast quantity of water must have entered for'ard
to have overcome that buoyancy so suddenly. It was obvious
that a large gash had been torn at the top of the pressure hull in
the torpedo-stowage compartment, and that the compartment
had filled up in a matter of seconds. We should never get her
up with all that weight of water in her. However, Peter
thought it would do no harm to try, so one by one he opened up
the valves of the high-pressure air-panel until all five ballast
tanks and the two main internal tanks were blowing. But it
was no use: the depth-gauges did not even flicker.

The sea continued to pour in on us, with a terrible and re-
lentless noise, and the water in the compartment grew deeper
every minute. As the level crept up the starboard side, live
electrical contacts began spitting venomously, with little lightning flashes. Vaguely I wondered if we were all going to be
electrocuted.

In the half-darkness the men had become anonymous
groping figures, desperately coming and going. There was no
panic, but most of us, I think, were suffering from a sort of
mental concussion. I discovered one man trying to force open
the water-tight door that I had shut earlier. "My pal's in
there," he was moaning, "my pal's in there." "It's no good,"
I told him; "she's filled right up for'ard and there's no one left
alive on the other side of that door." He turned away, sobbing
a little.

For some reason we decided it would be useful if we could
find more torches. I knew there must be one or two others
somewhere in the wardroom, so I made yet another expedition
down the slope, wading through the pool that was now waist-
deep and already covering the lowest tiers of drawers under our
bunks. I spent some time in the wardroom, shivering with fear
and cold, ransacking every drawer and cupboard, pushing aside
the forsaken paraphernalia of personal belongings—under-
clothes, razors, pipes, photographs of wives and girl-friends.

But I could find only one torch that was still dry and working. Holding it clear of the water, I returned to the control-room.

It was deserted.

The door into the engine-room was shut. Had I spent longer in the wardroom than I thought? Perhaps they had all escaped from the engine-room escape hatch, without realising that I had been left behind. Even if they had not yet left the submarine, they might already have started flooding the compartment in preparation for an escape, and if the flooding had gone beyond a certain point it would be impossible to get that door open again. I listened, but could hear nothing beyond the monotonous, pitiless sound of pouring water. In this terrible moment I must have come very near to panic.

I could at least try hammering on the engine-room door. Looking round for a heavy instrument, I found a valve spanner and began moving aft towards the door. As I did so I heard a voice quite close to me say, "Christ, who's that?" I looked up and found I was standing under the conning-tower. In it, to my infinite relief, I saw Peter with an able seaman and one of the E.R.A.s. "Where the hell have you come from?" said Peter. "Where the hell's everybody gone?" I retorted. "Any room for me up there?" "We ought to be able to squeeze you in. The others are going to escape from the engine-room."

I climbed up through the lower hatch, grateful as never before for the company of my fellow-creatures. Four of us in the tiny space made a tight squeeze, Peter at the top of the ladder with his head jammed up against the upper hatch, the A.B. half-way up the ladder with his bottom wedged against the side of the tower, leaving just room for me and the E.R.A. standing at the foot of the tower, with our feet on the edge of the lower hatch-opening. The E.R.A. was in a bad way, vomiting continuously and hardly able to stand.

In the centre of the upper hatch was a small port, or round window, made of glass thick enough to withstand tremendous pressure. Number One said that he could see a glimmer of light through it, and supposed it to be caused by a searchlight from some vessel waiting overhead. This encouraged him to think we ought to be able to swim to the surface and be picked up without much difficulty. We knew the control-room depth-gauges were reading just over 60 feet; the upper hatch was something like 15 feet higher than the normal surface water-line (the point of reference for the depth-gauges) and was there-fore probably only about 45 feet from the surface, say the height of eight men standing on top of each other. It ought to be easy.

"Shut the lower lid," said Peter, "and let's just think this out." I bent down, shut the hatch and pulled the clip over. We then discussed exactly what we were going to do. We agreed that to wear Davis escape gear would be an unnecessary com-plication in the confined space. One of the dangers was that on our way up we might crack our skulls on the cross-bar between the periscope standards, but we decided there was little chance of this owing to the starboard list. We hoped (vainly, as it turned out) that we might be assisted in our rise to the surface by the bubble of air which would be released from the conning-tower as the hatch opened. The drill was simple. Peter would open the hatch, and as the water came in each man would fill his lungs with air and climb out as fast as he could. Except for the poor E.R.A., who was sick beyond comfort or encouragement, we were by now quite calm, even cheerful.

How long we considered the situation I cannot remember; but at last Peter said, "Well, the next thing is to see if we can open this hatch against the sea pressure." Bracing himself against the side of the tower, he pushed upwards with all his strength. The hatch remained firmly shut. Somehow we must raise the pressure inside the tower.

It occurred to me that while we had been talking the pressure had still been building up in the control-room below us, owing to the continuing inrush of water. I eased off the clip of the hatch under my feet, and sure enough there came the sharp hiss of air forcing its way into the tower. I allowed the air to come in until, after a minute or two, I became aware of a peculiar, faint smell. Perhaps it was merely the odour of fear, but my first thought was that the sea-water had at last found its way into the batteries. "Hullo," I said; "I think I can smell chlorine gas." "All right," said Peter; "shut the lid again and I'll have another shot at opening this one." This time he managed without much effort to lift the hatch slightly off its seat, allowing a trickle of water to come through.

"O.K.," said Peter. "Well, boys, take your time. There's no hurry. You say when you feel you're ready."

I said I was for having a go at once, before we weakened ourselves any further by breathing foul air, and the others agreed. We stripped down to vest, pants and socks.

"Ready?" asked Peter.

"Ready," we all replied, though I think the E.R.A. had reached the point in his sickness where he wanted to die more than anything else.

"Right. Stand by," said Peter cheerfully. "Here we go for fourteen days' survivor's leave. We're off!"—and he pushed up the lid with all his strength.

I took as deep a breath as I could, and then the sea crashed in on us. There was a roaring in my ears, a blackness everywhere, and there was nothing for it but to fight for life with all one's primitive instincts of survival. Hauling myself up by the rungs of the ladder, I found my head obstructed by the A.B.'s bottom. With the strength of a desperate man I pushed up at him, his heel struck me in the face, I pushed again, and then we were through the hatch and clear of the submarine. I swam upwards with quick, jerky breast-strokes. It seemed a terrible distance. Time stretched out of its normal span until I thought my lungs must surely crack before I reached the surface. And then suddenly I was there, coughing, spluttering, gasping in great draughts of the sweet night air and drinking in the blessed sight of the stars shining in the immensity of space.

The sea was fairly calm, with no more than a gentle popple. Seeing two heads in the water not far away, I called out and found they were Peter and the A.B., both in good heart. Of the E.R.A. there was no sign. We could make out the dark shapes of several ships around us, so we began shouting to attract attention. Some of them were throwing searchlights on the water, and one of these seemed to me nearer than the rest. "Come on," I said, "let's swim to that nearest one," and began swimming towards it with my rather feeble side-stroke. I pressed on for a few minutes, imagining the other two were following me, but after a while I turned and could see no sign of them, although I heard them shouting at intervals not far off. The vessel I was making for was farther away than I had thought. I am not a strong swimmer, so I turned over on to my back and relaxed into an easy backward leg-stroke, calling "Help!" at the top of my voice from time to time. Sometimes a wave lopped over my head and I swallowed a little more water. I seemed to be swimming for a long time. Whenever I looked round, the ship seemed to be as far away as ever. Surely, after all this, I was not going to drown in sight of safety? I began to feel rather exhausted. Suddenly I heard voices shouting, the churning of propellers going astern, and I turned to find a searchlight blazing in my eyes and below it the shape of an M.L. quite close, with a scrambling-net down over the side and men running along the deck. A heaving-line shot out, I grabbed it and was hauled in. A sailor clambered down the net and helped me on to the deck, where I fell into the arms of two R.N.V.R. officers. Exhausted and groaning for breath, with my lungs half full of sea-water, I must have appeared in a worse state than I was, but while they wrapped me in blankets and hustled me below I managed to tell them that there were some more of us out there in the water and many others still down in the submarine trying to escape from the engine-room.

In a cabin below they rubbed me down, gave me dry clothes, and put me into a bunk, where I lay shivering from delayed shock. About half an hour later they came and told me our men were starting to come up from the bottom. I couldn't bear to stay in my bunk while this was happening, so I wrapped myself in a blanket and tottered along to find out what the situation was. They were coming up at fairly frequent intervals, strange Martian creatures with their D.S.E.A.* goggles and oxygen

* Davis Submerged Escape Apparatus.

bags, and rendered almost unrecognisable by black oil which had floated up from the bilges when they flooded the engine-room for the escape. But they were in extraordinarily good spirits, half intoxicated with their unexpected return to life. Every one of them was full of praise for the way in which the Chief E.R.A. and the Torpedo Gunner's Mate had organised the escaping party and carried out the escape drill. When finally these two reached the surface, the Chief E.R.A. last of all, they reported there was no one left in the engine-room. There had been enough D.S.E.A. sets for all but two of the party. Two men had volunteered to go up without them, each holding on to the legs of one of the others; one of these was never seen again. A final roll-call showed that the only other casualty of the engine-room party of twenty was a civilian technician from Chatham dockyard, who had joined *Umpire* as passenger for the trip north: the Chief E.R.A. and the T.G.M. had fitted him with a D.S.E.A. set and patiently explained its simple operation to him several times, but the man was so unnerved by the catastrophe that, although he succeeded in getting out through the hatch, he failed to reach the surface. But altogether the engine-room escape was a remarkable justification of the submarine escape drill.

It was only afterwards I discovered that, half-way through the escape, the Chief E.R.A. thought it would be advisable to make sure none of the escapers was getting caught up in any obstruction outside the hatch. He therefore clipped on the oxygen mouthpiece of his D.S.E.A. set, made his way up through the hatch, walked about on the outside casing of the submarine in the vicinity of the hatch, and then, although he could easily and without shame have made his ascent to safety, he climbed down through the hatch into the engine-room once more and carried on with the business of supervising the escape of the remaining men. Not until every other man had left the compartment did he make his own get-away.

For his part in the escape Chief E.R.A. Killen was later awarded the British Empire Medal.

It was not until the M.L. landed us at Yarmouth that I heard Peter Bannister was missing. I had been told that another vessel had rescued some survivors from the water, and I had assumed these were Peter and the A.B. who had been with us. In fact only the A.B. had been picked up. When I saw him later at Yarmouth, he said that he and Peter had swum together for some time and that when they were rescued he had thought Peter was immediately behind. A long search failed to find him. I was staggered by this news, for Peter was a strong swimmer and had seemed in excellent fettle when we spoke together on the surface. To have got so far and be lost at the last moment was an appalling tragedy.

It was daylight when we reached Yarmouth and were met by Lieut.-Commander J. F. B. Brown, who had flown up from submarine headquarters in London to get the facts at first hand. During the day, in the intervals of answering questions, we enjoyed the generous hospitality of the Naval Base.

That evening I strolled alone after dinner in a small grassy courtyard. A gentle drizzle of rain was falling, and it was what one would call a miserable evening, but to me the sound of the soft rain falling like a benediction on the living grass seemed inexpressibly sad and sweet, and life itself so desirable that I could not imagine myself ever again being dissatisfied with it. For the first time I knew the delirious joy of not being dead.

At the same time I felt that in the emergency I had failed to act in the manner expected of a submarine officer. Running over again and again the sequence of events following the moment of collision, I was tortured by two nagging thoughts. First, why had I not had the sense to realise that all the water coming into the control-room had been pouring in through the ship's ventilation system? Secondly—and this has haunted me ever since—I knew that I should have been in the engine-room with the men.

There was also the problem of the future. At first I was sure I never wanted to see the inside of a submarine again. But the conviction grew in me that to ask to leave the submarine service would be such an admission of defeat that I should never recover my self-respect. For the purely egoistic reason of patching up my pride, I therefore decided to remain in submarines—if I was allowed to. On the principle of immediately remounting the horse that has thrown you, I resolved to ask to be sent on an operational patrol as soon as possible.

With thoughts like these crowding my brain, I was still awake when Wingfield walked into my cabin about midnight. He had just landed, having stayed on the scene of the collision until nightfall. He was looking ten years older, grey and haggard from worry and lack of sleep. He told me how Tony Godden had been drowned, and asked about Peter Bannister. I told him the story up to the point where we had separated after reaching the surface. He said the final casualty total was two officers and twenty men, almost half the ship's complement.

The next day, after further interrogation, they sent us off on fourteen days' leave. In the middle of it we were recalled to attend the official Board of Inquiry at Chatham, a dreary and gruelling experience.* At the end of my leave I reported to H.M.S. *Dolphin* at Gosport, and in answer to my request for an early return to sea I was appointed to relieve Freddie Sherwood† as Torpedo Officer of the submarine *Sealion*, then based on Fort Blockhouse and operating off the French coast under the command of the famous bearded Ben Bryant.

* The Admiralty apparently did not attach too much blame to Wingfield, for he was given another command soon afterwards and remained in command of operational submarines until the end of 1944, winning a D.S.O. and two D.S.C.s.

† Lieut. F. C. Sherwood, the first Canadian V.R. officer to join submarines.

IV

"THE BAY" AND NORTH RUSSIA

SEALION had been almost continuously in the fighting line since the beginning of the war. During the German invasion of Norway the S-boats had suffered heavy losses in desperate battles in the constricted, shallow and heavily-mined waters of the Skagerrak.

One of the most remarkable characters in *Sealion* was the Chief E.R.A., "Skips" Marriott, a tall, saturnine submarine E.R.A. of the old school, with a highly developed sardonic humour. At sea he wore a peculiar headgear of his own invention, a long oblong of cardboard twisted into strange shapes and stuffed into a dirty old navy-blue balaclava, and when he walked through the control-room on his way to the engine-room, with his loping gait and eyes twinkling in a dead-pan face, he might have been a crafty old monk straight out of the pages of Boccaccio. Sometimes in harbour when it was my turn to be duty officer in the boat, I would join the E.R.A.s in their mess so that I could listen to some of old Skips's yarns. I have brought him in here because many months later, glancing through his rough Engine-Room Register, I came across several verses scrawled on the oil-smudged pages in his firm bold hand, and among them the following lines, which tell the tragic story of the S-boats in the early months of the war better than I can:

Twelve little S-boats "go to it" like Bevin,
Starfish goes a bit too far—then there were eleven.

Eleven watchful S-boats doing fine and then
Seahorse fails to answer—so there are ten.

Ten stocky S-boats in a ragged line,
Sterlet drops and stops out—leaving us nine.

Nine plucky S-boats all pursuing Fate,
Shark is overtaken—now we are eight.

Eight sturdy S-boats—men from Hants and Devon,
Salmon now is overdue—and so the number's seven.

Seven gallant S-boats trying all their tricks,
Spearfish tries a newer one—down we come to six.

Six tireless S-boats fighting to survive,
No reply from *Swordfish*—so we tally five.

Five scrubby S-boats patrolling close inshore,
Snapper takes a short cut—now we are four.

Four fearless S-boats too far out to sea,
Sunfish bombed and scrap-heaped—we are only three

Three threadbare S-boats patrolling o'er the blue,
. . . .

Two ice-bound S-boats . . . .
. . . .

One lonely S-boat . . . .
. . . .

His completion of the list, leaving the blanks to be filled in later (I am glad to say it was not necessary: *Sealion*, *Seawolf* and *Sturgeon* survived to the end of the war), is an example of the buoyant sense of humour, fatalistic but far from defeatist, which inspired most of *Sealion*'s crew. Contact with men who had soldiered on through hard fighting and seen their "chummy boats" go down one after another was the best possible antidote to my state of nerves.

The officers were all strangers to me: McVie, the First
Lieutenant, usually diffident, with his quiet Scots voice, but
aggressive enough when occasion demanded; Stroud, the
R.N.R. navigator, commonly known as "Vasco," a boisterous,
noisy fellow with a heart of gold but little tact; and "Chiefy"
Francis, Engineer Officer, short, tubby and full of chuckles, a
first-rate technician. By accepting me at once on equal terms,
despite their many patrols in *Sealion*, they helped to put my
personal problem in the right perspective. And to complete my
cure I could not have had a better commanding officer than
Lieut.-Commander B. Bryant.

Ben Bryant was one of those men who are big enough to give
you confidence in yourself by assuming you can do your job
without appearing to check up on you. He believed in taking
the game of war seriously; nevertheless it somehow always
seemed a game. He strove continuously to make himself and
his men as efficient as possible, and was out to hit the enemy
with all he knew, but he did so with such an air of gay bravado
that half the time you had an odd feeling that you were playing
at pirates. With his erect height, his sea-dog beard and arro-
gant eye, he was the typical submarine captain of the public
imagination. He had a fine command of the English language,
which he used to good effect in recounting yarns in the wardroom, inventing ballads, or expressing his opinion of some in-
eptitude on the part of one of his officers or men. He had the
rare gift of being able to switch without loss of dignity from
commanding officer to entertaining messmate.

On the evening of September 12th we sailed from Portsmouth for fourteen days' patrol in the Bay of Biscay. A mine-
sweeper escorted us past the Nab Tower to the end of the swept
channel, where we dived to catch a trim and wait for darkness.
I disliked that first dive very much, but it was worse after we
had surfaced and were pressing on down the Channel through
a pitch-black night. Sitting in the wardroom or lying in my
bunk, I expected every moment to hear the telegraphs ring
down for full astern together as a prelude to the crash of a collision. I was like a nerve that has been jabbed and is afraid of

being jabbed again. During my first watch on the bridge that night I spent the two hours in a state of near-panic. It was so dark that I could barely distinguish the horizon through my binoculars, and wherever I looked I imagined I saw ships suddenly close and about to hit us. I began to think it was no use, that I was going to be no good. Luckily, in my second watch towards morning the visibility improved and I calmed down a little. But it was a great relief when the sky showed signs of growing lighter and the Captain decided to dive. I felt safer under water; it was the thought of another surface collision at night that worried me.

We reached our billet* off Lorient just before dawn on the second day. One of the objects of this patrol was to make a night rendezvous with a French fishing-boat and pick up some important secret documents that were being smuggled out of occupied France. The fishing-boat was to identify itself from time to time during daylight by allowing its sails to flap unsheeted and by sending a man up the mast. On the appointed day, as luck would have it, the wind fell light, and we found ourselves in the middle of a small fleet of fishing-boats, all lying becalmed on an oily swell with their sails slatting lazily from side to side. The Captain nearly went crazy. Using the periscope in that glassy calm without allowing it to be seen was in itself an exacting job, without the added difficulty of weaving our way in and out of all these boats and trying to identify our fisherman. It was not until the late afternoon that we spotted a man climbing up a mast. There might be several reasons for any of them to have a man up the mast, but we had to take a chance, and as dusk was falling we closed him submerged.

As soon after nightfall as we dared, we surfaced within hailing distance. We had brought with us a young Frenchman, who had made several trips in and out of France since the occupation; we sent him over in a collapsible canoe to identify his friends and make sure there was no monkey business. In case of trouble we had the gun's crew closed up, with the barrel

* Term commonly used in the Submarine Service when referring to one's patrol area or patrol position.

trained on the fisherman. The canoe went alongside, there was some rapid conversation, and then our Frenchman called out to us, "O.K., *Commandant*!" The fisherman sent over a boat. Two suitcases full of papers were handed up to us, followed by a bottle of wine as a *"cadeau pour le Capitaine,"* and in return we passed down a bottle of Scotch. While this was going on the look-outs observed another fishing-vessel, without lights, drifting suspiciously close to us. We cut short our genial conversation, hurriedly re-embarked our French passenger and the canoe, and retired discreetly into the night.

Apart from this and a couple of false alarms, we had an uneventful patrol. By the end of it I felt confident that my nerve was almost restored, though I never afterwards quite got over my feeling of uneasiness on the surface at night, particularly in home coastal waters, and I always felt happier under water.

On the 25th we were back in Fort Blockhouse, enjoying our drinks in *Dolphin*'s wardroom before dinner, and sitting long over our port in the gracious dining-hall, with its minstrels' gallery and polished mahogany tables. We had plenty to talk about, for two surprising pieces of news had greeted us on our return. Ben Bryant was leaving *Sealion* to take over *Safari*, the first of the new improved S-class submarines nearing completion at Cammell Laird's; he was to be relieved by George Colvin, whom none of us knew. And *Sealion* was to winter in the Arctic Circle, based on a Russian port near Murmansk.

Lieutenant George Colvin, our new Captain, had been in command of *Sunfish* until a German bomb had damaged her in dry dock beyond repair. More recently he had brought back from Iceland the first German U-boat to be captured in the war.* He had a pale skin, and at this time sported a small square-trimmed bright red beard. When he smiled, tight wrinkles ran

---

* It was also the first, and only, instance of a U-boat captured by an aircraft. *U-570*, on her maiden voyage, was caught on the surface by a Hudson bomber, which dropped four depth-charges with such accuracy that the crew came on deck and showed the white flag. The Hudson flew round the U-boat until surface forces were able to reach the spot and tow the surrendered vessel into Iceland. Later it was repaired and put into operational service as H.M.S. *Graph*.

along the bridge of his pink nose. I grew to like him more than any other submariner I ever met.

Autumn was already well advanced when we sailed, and every mile would take us nearer to the polar regions. We stopped at Dunoon in the Clyde to take in special stores and arctic clothing, and called in at Scapa Flow for a final refuelling. The night we left Scapa, with fifteen hundred landless miles ahead of us, it was blowing a full gale from the north. As we battled our way into it, the wind and sea increased to a fury that I had never imagined possible. It was a fitting start to a voyage that seems in retrospect to have been a succession of mountainous seas and nights of misery. From now on I had to get accustomed to a routine that was typical of the winter drudgery experienced by all submarines operating in northern waters. Night after night of roaring wind, hurtling seas, scratch meals and dampness everywhere: water pouring down the conning-tower and sluicing over the control-room deck to find its way into the bilges, and no chance of ever drying your clothes. Worst of all was the torture of being woken up when it was your turn to go on watch at night.

"Ten to two, sir, your watch and the First Lieutenant says to tell you it's still very wet up top, sir." Someone is shaking you by the shoulder, but you can't believe it, and return protesting to the warm cocoon of your dream of fair women, until the brute shakes you again more roughly. "Five minutes to go, sir." With a great effort of moral courage, you force yourself on to one elbow and survey the hideous scene in the half-darkness, envying the others who can still go on snoring behind their curtains, and trying to make yourself believe that the motion of the ship is not quite so bad as it was when you turned in four hours ago. But the hanging lamp over the table is still swinging violently and you can feel the boat under you rolling and crashing as wildly as ever. Groaning, you tumble out on to the heaving, shuddering deck, and you are not sure if you are going to be sick. You struggle into your wet Ursula suit * and

* A special form of clothing for wet weather, designed by Captain Phillips when he was in command of the submarine *Ursula* at the beginning of the war.

E

sea-boots, and stagger along the passage. As you climb the tower another sea fills the bridge and cascades down over you and into the control-room. With a curse you pull yourself through the hatch and on to the bridge. The night is black as the devil, the screaming wind full of vicious spray; another thundering mass of water tumbles on board, and you hang on to save yourself from being swept away. You step up to the front of the bridge. You are three minutes late, and Number One is not pleased. He waits until you think you can see efficiently, and then hands over the watch and scrambles thankfully below. How you envy him. You settle down to endure your two hours of timeless misery, peering out into the storm, ducking as the water leaps over the gun platform and springs up at you with seemingly deliberate malice. Binoculars are useless in this weather. Water is in your boots, down your neck, up your sleeves, and your fingers are frozen in your sodden gloves. You watch the sea for some sign of an abatement of its violence, but ahead of you in the darkness the long shape of the submarine's fore-casing goes on lifting, plunging, staggering, like a tormented whale, now rearing to heaven, now hurtling down into the valley, now vanishing altogether in a cauldron of boiling fury. You grit your teeth and force yourself to resist the siren sleep. When the end of your watch draws near, the minutes drag on interminably. If your relief is late you begin to hate him with a passion you would never have believed yourself capable of. When at last he arrives, full of apologies and absurd excuses, you can hardly trust yourself to speak to him. But soon you are on your way below and climbing into your bunk for another four hours of blissful oblivion.

Vasco was a terror for being late on watch. Number One refused to be relieved by him, so it fell to my lot to suffer the agonies of having an extra ten or fifteen minutes added to my watch. Later Number One and I conceived the brilliant idea of starting all the watch-keeping periods at ten minutes past the hour, without letting on to Vasco, who thereafter never ceased to complain bitterly of Number One's tardiness in relieving *him*. Vasco and I got into the habit of speaking comic German when handing over the watch, solemnly acting the parts of two humourless, pompous U-boat officers and always ending with *"Gott strafe England!"* and the ridiculous Nazi salute. In high winds this was transformed into Wagnerian opera. The lookouts thought we were quite mad.

While the rough weather continued, we had little peace even when submerged by day. The waves were often so deep that at periscope depth we rocked like a crazy pendulum and had the greatest difficulty in keeping the required depth. Through the periscope we saw a desolation of tossing water, the horizon (when we could see it at all) swinging wildly up and down, and every other wave drowning the periscope in a tumbling welter of green water and aerated foam. Sometimes it was so bad, and so expensive on the battery because of our constant speeding up to keep the depth, that we were forced to drop down to the blindness and comparative peace of deep water, though after many days of high seas the wave motion was still perceptible as far down as eighty feet.

Surfacing in really rough weather was a frightening business. There was a tricky moment before we reached full buoyancy, and before the water had drained out of the bridge casing, when the boat was extremely unstable, and if we surfaced with our beam to the waves there was a serious danger of being rolled right over. These early S-boats were particularly tender in this respect, and one of them is believed to have been lost through turning turtle. We had to be careful to come up with our bows heading almost directly into the sea. When diving, on the other hand, we had to turn beam on to the waves; otherwise their lifting tendency would prevent us from forcing the bows under.

As we drew nearer to the Arctic Circle the winds began to moderate a little, the sky cleared, and we were able to check our position by observations. At night the flaming curtains of the Aurora Borealis ran among the stars in green and purple undulations, and every day at noon the sun was perceptibly lower in the southern sky. Gradually we recovered from the effects of the stormy weather, dried our clothes, ate proper meals, caught up on lost sleep, and settled down to the numerous amusements that pass the time of submariners at sea.

We played many games. Pontoon, backgammon, chess and cribbage were fairly common. My favourite game was the peculiar version of poker dice known as "Liars," which grew subtler the more you played with the same people. But most popular of all was "Uckers," a special form of ludo which was played with great enthusiasm every night; Uckers competitions between the various messes, wardroom included, were a regular feature of our daily life.

One day the Captain, with a little embarrassment, produced from his drawer several skeins of coloured wool, a needle and canvas, and began working on a half-finished cushion-cover in *gros-point*, a hobby which he said he found creative, absorbing and soothing to the nerves. He would design his own patterns, and many and fierce were the arguments over choice of colours when he was ready to start a new one. Some of us began whittling away at wooden scale models of *Sealion*; the E.R.A.s, with all the resources of the engine-room at their disposal, were a superior lot and made their models in brass. Our Torpedo Gunner's Mate was forever making violins, working happily by himself in the tube-space; he did, I believe, occasionally finish one, but more often he would be dissatisfied with the elegant curves on which he had lavished weeks of care and break the thing up. He was the oldest T.G.M. in the submarine service, and his only ambition in life was to kill Germans; when the alarm went, he sat at his torpedo tubes with his fingers itching on the triggers, and bitter was his frustration if the alarm turned out to be false. He also played the accordion with skill, and sometimes of an evening he would settle down with his squeeze-box among the sailors in the overcrowded torpedo-stowage compartment and play tune after tune until for an hour or two their present dangers and discomforts were forgotten.

So the time passed as we climbed the world's shoulder and crossed into the Arctic Circle, with the days growing steadily shorter and colder. We took a wide sweep round the northern tip of Norway, passed mid-way between North Cape and Bear Island, and began to converge on the coastline towards the Kola Inlet, where a Soviet destroyer was due to meet us and escort us in. Expecting to sight the Russian coastline during the night before the rendezvous, we were puzzled by seeing only what appeared to be long dark banks of cloud above an empty horizon, and began to doubt the accuracy of our navigation. But when we dived shortly before dawn Vasco felt sure we were in the correct position, and as it grew light we saw that the land was in fact quite close. The high cliffs were white with snow, standing out from the higher ground behind them, and it was the moonlight shining on these which had given us our illusion of sky and cloud.

Fifteen minutes before the appointed hour, Number One at the periscope reported a destroyer coming out towards us. The Captain watched until she was only a few cables off, and then surfaced on her quarter on the exact second of the rendezvous time. After an exchange of recognition signals, we took station astern and followed her in towards the wide entrance to the Kola Inlet, eagerly scanning the snowbound shores of the strange new land as it opened up ahead of us. Soon, turning a bend, we had our first view of Polyarnoe, the small naval port which was to be our base. Murmansk, the terminus of the British convoys which were then beginning to come through, is several miles further up the river.

All Russians wear beards, we had said to ourselves when we left England, and thought the long sea trip an excellent opportunity of making a start with our own stubbly growths. As it turned out, every Russian in Polyarnoe was clean-shaven, and the only beards we saw were our own. The Senior British Naval Officer was horrified at the hirsute appearance of the latest representatives of the Royal Navy. Indeed, everything about Polyarnoe horrified the Admiral. He was unable to disguise from our Russian allies his disapproval of the whole Soviet *régime* and his suspicion of all their motives. His disapproval was not mitigated by his being restricted to certain routes for his daily constitutional; on one occasion he was actually arrested when he inadvertently strayed from the pre-scribed path. The Russians on their side were equally suspi-cious of us; their sentries were belligerent in manner, held their rifles very much at the ready whenever they examined our passes, and always gave us a most uncomfortable feeling in the small of our backs as we walked away. Their jumpiness was perhaps hardly surprising, since we were only about thirty miles from the frontiers of Finland and German-occupied Norway. Sometimes at night we saw ghost figures dressed in white assembling softly in the snow, and knew them for Russian sol-diers moving up to the front, the most northerly front of the whole world war.

It was an important front because Murmansk was the only northern Russian port that remained ice-free throughout the winter, and the supplies brought in by our convoys passed to the heart of Russia down the slender thread of one vulnerable railway line. The R.A.F. had already sent a squadron of Spit-fires to operate here and provide local air superiority. The pur-pose of our visit was to assist the Russian submarines in their attacks on the sea route up the Norwegian coast to the ports of Kirkenes and Petsamo, through which the Germans were try-ing to supply and reinforce their army on this front. These attacks would also help to divert attention from the passage of our convoys. *Sealion* was the third British submarine to reach Polyarnoe. *Tigris*, with "Boggy" Bone in command, had been the first and had already, after many successful patrols, returned to England with a live reindeer as passenger. Sladen was still operating here with *Trident*. Before their arrival the Russian submarines had been rather ineffectual, but the example of these two aggressive and experienced submariners had spurred them to improve their tactics and increase their rate of sinkings.

At first we found the strangeness of it all tremendously stimulating. Our breath fell like smoke on the frozen air. In the sharp clarity of the atmosphere, sea and sky took on subtler shades of grey and blue against the contrasting whiteness of the landscape. We found a childish pleasure in stumping through the crisp snow and seeing skis and horse-drawn sledges used as normal methods of getting about. The tall red-brick buildings looked impressive at a distance, in their skyscraper style of architecture. Closer to, they were cheap and shoddy, but at least their central-heating was efficient and the food was good. When we were in harbour resting between patrols we lived in one of these block-houses. We had a Russian cook, and two Russian girls to wait on us at meals. They served up superb greasy soups full of vegetables, and always on the table were bowls of caviare and thick chunks of smoked salmon to which we freely helped ourselves between courses. From the wardroom we had a splendid view over the bay, and on the wall hung a huge map of Europe with the usual flags, and one lonely Union Jack stuck into Polyarnoe near the ceiling. The Submarine Staff Office was in the same building. Senior Officer Submarines was Commander Davies, and his Staff Officer a black-bearded R.N.V.R. officer called Bray. Bray had multifarious duties and was often missing when required by S.O.S/M; then an angry "BRA-A-A-Y" would echo down the corridors and staircase. Attached to us for liaison and interpreting was a rather tiresome Russian woman called Gellina, without humour or feminine grace that I could discover. She was for ever arguing politics, and produced all the old outworn clichés of Communist propaganda with a persistent fervour. In self-defence we would pull her leg about the wonderful life in Soviet Russia until she swept off with a red face and the conviction that we were a hopeless lot of diehard capitalists and imperialists.

Considering that we were supposed to be allies, we saw very little of our Russian brothers-in-arms. This was partly due to the language difficulty, but also, I am sure, to the absence of mutual trust and confidence at higher levels. The British have always had a short memory for their minor wars, but the Russians had still not forgotten that we had fought against the Bolshevik armies in the early days of the revolution. Equally, many of the British officers still remembered the bloodiness of the revolution and could not help regarding their opposite numbers as a gang of murderers.

It happened that the occasion on which we saw most of our allies was the evening of the day we first arrived. We were invited to a Fleet Concert, and took our places with numerous Russian officers and commissars at the back of a large and sumptuously fitted hall. We were the object of much curiosity on the part of the packed audience. Dead tired from our arduous journey, we hoped the concert would not be long. To our dismay, it was preceded by a political meeting which lasted an hour. The long and excitable speeches meant nothing to us until from time to time the speakers mentioned the name of Stalin. Every time this happened, and it happened at least fifteen times in the hour, the orchestra played the whole of one verse of the *Internationale* and the audience responded with a round of automatic clapping. At last the concert began. It consisted of numerous turns, all given by sailors from the ships in harbour. I doubt whether the whole of the British Navy could have produced such brilliant talent. The dancing turns were vigorous and stirring, but best of all was the singing of the Red Sailors' Choir. They sang marching and traditional songs in the manner of the Cossack singers until the blood tingled. Next, to our astonishment, the curtain rose on the solitary figure of *Sealion*'s T.G.M. How he managed to get himself into the programme we never discovered, but he now proceeded to treat the audience to the whole of his accordion repertoire, concluding with *Black Eyes* amid demonstrations of enthusiasm. The concert ended with another singing of the *Internationale*, and we stumbled out at last into the snow.

One evening we invited the officers of one of the Russian submarines lying alongside *Sealion* to come aboard for drinks. It had been arranged that an interpreter would accompany them, but at the last minute he was unable to come. This promised a rather sticky party, with no common language. However, they arrived, shook hands formally all round and sat round the wardroom table. We opened up the wine locker and produced gin, whisky, brandy, rum and sherry, inviting them by signs to take their choice. They chose whisky, which they drank neat and straight down in one. Next they thought they would sample the sherry. We were taken aback, but said nothing, and for ourselves stuck to whisky. Meanwhile I discovered that one of them had a smattering of German, and casting back into what I remembered from school I managed to establish a bridge of communication in the language of our common enemy. But alcohol was the better interpreter. By the time they got round to trying our gin (which they pronounced inferior to vodka) the party was going like a bush fire and conversation was animated. We produced an atlas and compared home towns. They told us, wistfully, that they would never have the chance to see other countries: foreign travel was not encouraged by the rulers of Soviet Russia. When at last the party broke up, every one of our guests needed assistance across the gang-plank. Unfortunately this successful example of allied intercourse was not repeated.

Before we left England we had imagined that at sea we should have icebergs and pack-ice to contend with. But on this fringe of the Arctic Ocean the water is kept from freezing by the Gulf Stream, here making its last effective sweep before surrendering to the rigours of the Barents Sea. In our patrols between the Kola Inlet and North Cape we encountered no floating ice, but during the brief daylight visibility was hampered by the spray which froze on the periscope and by frequent snowstorms which blotted out the land for hours on end. And on the surface in the long hours of darkness we faced the beastliness of spray which turned to ice even before it struck our faces. It froze on the gun, on the periscope standards, in the voice-pipe, and all over the bridge. Icicles hung from the jumping wire from one end of the submarine to the other, and sometimes formed so much top-weight that the Captain became concerned about our stability. Another anxiety was lest the main vents should freeze solid and prevent us from diving; we had to test them frequently during the night. The spray also formed a film of ice round the edge of the conning-tower hatch, so that it was necessary to wipe round it every fifteen minutes. One particularly bitter morning when I was officer-of-the-watch and last off the bridge as we made our routine dive, I found I could not quite shut the hatch because of the coating of ice. We were already on our way down, and in a moment the sea would be over the bridge. I called down the tower to Colvin: "I can't shut the hatch, sir!" His ginger-bearded face appeared below me. "Well, just hang on to it," he said; "I daresay it will shut presently." So as the sea spilled through the open crack I hung on to the clips, angry with the Captain for taking so calmly what appeared to me rather a dangerous situation. Half the Arctic Ocean was pouring over my head and down my neck. My mind flashed back to the last time I had been inside a conning-tower with the sea coming in, and this no doubt exaggerated my alarm. But gradually, as Colvin knew it would, the solid water melted the ice, the pressure of the sea on the hatch increased, and by the time we reached periscope depth the flow of water stopped and I was able to force the clips home. Speechless with cold and anger, I climbed below and made my way to the wardroom to change my sodden clothes. It was half an hour before I was able to see the funny side of the incident.

We encountered little excitement on these Arctic patrols. Targets had become rarer, partly owing to the successes of *Tigris* and *Trident* in this area, partly because of the deterioration of the weather. Two incidents have stuck in my memory.

Somewhere not far from North Cape one morning we intercepted a small ship of not much more than a thousand tons, and Colvin decided to come up and gun her. We fired a round across her bow as a warning, but she took no notice. After our second round had landed in her engine-room, however, she turned broadside on to us and stopped. We ceased firing and waited while the crew lowered a boat and rowed over to us. We now discovered that our victim was a Norwegian. It was unfortunate, but the Norwegians were carrying German cargoes, under duress, and the traffic had to be stopped. I was sent down on to the fore-casing to assist the men aboard over the port side. Meanwhile Colvin continued to sink the ship by gunfire, with the three-inch gun trained only about five degrees off our starboard bow. The crack of a three-inch is bad enough when you are behind it, but when the shells are whistling past your head no more than two yards away the noise is appalling. As the first shell went off I turned in alarm, gesturing a protest towards the bridge, but Colvin only grinned through his beard and carried on. While the shooting was still proceeding we suddenly saw a German aircraft flying slowly along the coastline less than four miles away. It was an awkward moment, as we still had the Norwegians, one of them badly wounded, on the casing. Fortunately the German never saw us, and flew steadily away into the distance. At last we had put enough holes along the target's water-line to sink her, and with our prisoners safely below we were able to return to the peace of periscope depth. Although his Chief Engineer had been badly wounded in the back by the shell which burst in the engine-room, the Norwegian Captain was charming and friendly, and we came to like him very much.

Eventually the Norwegians were all sent to England. A month later Colvin's mother found herself faced with a situation not covered by any book of etiquette. Ought one to express regret or pleasure, she wrote, when a complete stranger knocks at one's door and announces himself as the Captain of a ship which has been sunk by one's son? However, she had asked him in and found him a delightful guest, entirely without resentment at the loss of his ship.

Colvin, being more sensitive than most naval officers, never managed to acquire the crust of emotional indifference towards his targets which would have been natural in one whose business was war. It was not that he was blind to the necessity of inflicting destruction and loss of life in the merciless struggle in which we were all engaged, but I believe that when one of his torpedoes scored a hit on a target he could not help picturing vividly in his imagination the twisted steel, the torn flesh, the inrush of water, the choking lungs. I remember an occasion on another patrol when we attacked a merchant-ship making for Kirkenes. Colvin fired three torpedoes. Watching through the periscope for the result, he suddenly looked quite sick and said, in tones of great distress, "God, how I hate doing this." There was a loud bang as one of the torpedoes blew a hole in the ship's side just under the bridge, and it was as much as Colvin could do to keep his eyes at the periscope. There were no escorts to worry about, so several of us were presently able to take a look. It was the first time I had seen a ship sinking. She was going down slowly by the head. Men were running back and forth along the sloping deck, and presently, to Colvin's relief, we saw they were lowering a boat. They got well clear before their ship finally stood on her head and plunged vertically to the bottom. Between the dips of the sea's swell we could see the men in the boat rowing strongly towards the nearby land. There was no point in revealing ourselves, so we turned slowly away to resume our patrol. But Colvin was not elated by his success.

We were glad when, shortly before Christmas, orders came for us to return to England. *Trident* had already gone home, her place being taken by our sister-ship *Seawolf*. The novelty of our spartan environment had soon been obscured by a growing homesickness for more temperate climes and the warmth of human intercourse. Our spirits were oppressed by the gloom of the long arctic night and protracted twilight, the brevity and the lukewarmness of the sunlight, the bleakness of a landscape of eternal snow without trees or grass, and the unfriendliness and suspicion of the allies we had come so many miles to assist.

Our excitement at leaving for home was slightly dashed when we received orders to interrupt our fifteen-hundred-mile voyage for a few days' patrol among the Lofoten Islands. On Christmas Day we were still on our billet, with nothing in sight but the snow-capped mountains of Norway. But we arrived at last in Lerwick in the Shetlands, very weary and getting low in fuel. The next day we pressed on southward through the Minches and the Irish Sea and so back to Portsmouth, where we tied up once more alongside the jetty at Fort Blockhouse.

On our return from leave important changes were afoot.

McVie and Vasco were leaving *Sealion* to take up other appointments. To my great pride and pleasure, Colvin (now Lieut.-Commander: he had put up his half stripe in Polyarnoe) asked to have me promoted to First Lieutenant. My place as Torpedo Officer was taken by Sub-Lieut. Iwan Raikes, R.N., and Vasco's place as Navigator by Lieut. Mike Willoughby, R.N.R.

V

FIRST LIEUTENANT

THE First Lieutenant (called "Number One" by his fellow officers, and known as "Jimmy" amongst the men) is responsible to his Captain for seeing that the ship *works*. He organises the watch-keeping, allots the men their duties, trains them, looks after their health and welfare, and in general keeps his finger on all the details that are vital to the smooth running and efficient operation of the ship. In submarines the First Lieutenant has an additional responsibility that is literally a matter of life or death—the Trim.

All submarine watch-keeping officers have to adjust the trim as necessary during their watches, but it remains the duty of the First Lieutenant to work out the original trim. At the beginning of a patrol many changes have taken place in the submarine's weight since the last dive, owing to the intake of torpedoes, ammunition, stores, fuel, fresh water, and sometimes extra passengers—and he must compensate for these changes by altering the amounts of water in his various trimming tanks. He has to know not only the total weight of the changes, but also how the weight is distributed through the boat. All this calls for careful and elaborate calculation. A serious error might send the submarine plunging headlong to the bottom at her first dive. We had all been taught how to work out a trim in our submarine training class, but my mathematics are so poor that when I became First Lieutenant, and was faced with having to do these sums frequently, I determined to find some simpler method. All the calculations were in terms of "moment"—weight × distance from the centre of the ship—and I soon discovered they could be worked out very easily on an ordinary slide-rule. I had one made with the various tanks marked at their correct positions, and I was then able to work out my trims in a few minutes and with less chance of error.

It was not long before I had to put on my first trim. A few days after our return from leave, we were ordered to make hasty preparations for an emergency patrol in the Bay of Biscay. The rumour was that the German battle cruisers *Scharnhorst* and *Gneisenau*, which had been in Brest for nearly a year, were expected to make a dash for a German port at any moment, and we were to form part of an arc of submarines patrolling off Brest. Our submarines had in fact been maintaining a constant vigil ever since the enemy ships had first been spotted in Brest by air reconnaissance in March of the previous year. This had become known as the Iron Ring, but it would have required a large number of submarines to form an impassable cordon. Submarine commitments had increased with Italy's entry into the war and the defeat of France, and most of our submarines had to be sent to the Mediterranean. Our losses in the Norwegian campaign had not yet been made good. But every submarine that could be spared during the last ten months had been kept patrolling in the Bay of Biscay, with no reward except the occasional chance at a U-boat or a blockade-runner. And now, although she badly needed a rest for repairs and general overhaul, and was already overdue for a complete refit, *Sealion* was sent out to reinforce this iron ring. We had no idea whether the German battle cruisers would choose to run the gauntlet of the English Channel or would try a dash out into the Atlantic, and make their way well to the north of Scotland to a Norwegian port.

On the night of February 6th we reached our appointed patrol position a few miles west of Ushant. Nothing happened for the next forty-eight hours, but on the 8th we decoded a wireless signal which threw us into a fever of excitement:

Sealion from Capt. S/M 5.

It is anticipated that the German main units will carry out sea trials before sailing. Proceed at once to position 48° 05′ N, 5° 11′ W and endeavour to enter Iroise Bay tide and currents permitting to carry out reconnaissance and attack if opportunity offers.

This was big stuff indeed, although the more we looked at the chart the more we realised what a tough proposition we were in for. Apart from the certainty of anti-submarine patrols and the possibility of minefields, the strong currents running among the rocks and reefs of the Chaussée de Sein would present difficult navigational problems to a submerged submarine. But as we began moving in towards the French coast that night, charging our batteries at the same time, discussion in the wardroom raged over another and most unusual problem.

At this period of the war the submarine service was faced with a serious shortage of torpedoes. Expenditure had risen greatly since the flaring up of the Mediterranean war, and mass production of the new Mark VIII torpedo had not yet got into its stride. *Sealion* carried twelve torpedoes: six in the tubes ready for firing, and six in the torpedo-stowage compartment standing by for a reload. When we were storing up at Fort Blockhouse for this patrol, there were no more than six of the Mark VIII torpedoes available, and we had to make up the other six with torpedoes which had the Mark VIII body but a Mark IV warhead. This was slightly longer and heavier than the one designed for the Mark VIII. Unfortunately there was no reliable information as to how these bastard torpedoes would run, and no S-boat had carried out trials to see what would happen when they were fired. Because the composite torpedoes were just too long to fit into the stowage racks, there was no alternative but to make them the first salvo in the tubes, keeping the proper Mark VIIIs for the reload.

Doubts about what would happen on firing were an acceptable risk in the emergency so long as our billet was in deep water with room to manœuvre. But now, Colvin felt, the situation was rather different. We might have to make our attack in constricted and probably calm water, and almost certainly through a protective screen of destroyers; any misbehaviour on the part of torpedo or submarine would at once give away our firing position and lead to our probable destruction. Moreover, we had a new First Lieutenant (myself) who had had no experience of controlling the submarine at the moment of firing a full salvo, even of normal torpedoes; we had a new Torpedo Officer and a new Torpedo Gunner's Mate. Altogether Colvin thought the situation singularly inauspicious, and he was damned if he was going in specifically to attack two of the major targets of the war with doubtful torpedoes. How long would it take to withdraw them from the tubes and substitute the Mark VIIIs? Because of the extra length of the Mark IV warheads they would have to be detached before the bodies could be stowed in the racks. Even to withdraw a normal torpedo from a tube when the racks are full of reloads is not an easy operation, and now there was the additional problem of where to stow the Mark IV heads. However, it might have been possible. After a careful estimate, we thought the whole operation could be completed in about eighteen hours, working at full stretch. But reloading at sea can only be done when the submarine is submerged; on the surface there is too much motion, and the torpedoes would take charge and cause fatal havoc in the confined space of the fore-ends. We should therefore need two days dived to finish the job. But we might have to attack tomorrow.

It was Colvin who finally put into words the unprecedented decision that was staring us in the face.

"All right," he said, "we'll fire the bloody things into the Atlantic."

Chiefy Francis took a long pull at his cigarette and exhaled slowly towards the shaded lamp swaying over our heads. We sat in silence, watching how the wreathing smoke shuddered almost imperceptibly in the diesel-vibrated air.

"After all," continued Colvin, laughing rather bitterly, "they only cost three thousand smackers apiece." He stood up, pulled on the hood of his Ursula suit, and went off to have a look at the weather up top.

The decision taken, no more time was wasted in argument. And when we dived shortly before dawn we carried out a full-scale mock attack and fired the torpedoes in the general direction of America. It was too dark to see how they ran, but *Sealion* herself just broke surface on firing. It was a valuable, if expensive, exercise; from it I learnt enough to be reasonably certain of preventing the boat from breaking surface on future occasions.

The job of loading the spare torpedoes, the Mark VIIIs, into the now empty tubes was comparatively simple, and soon after daylight we were once more ready to fire a full salvo at a moment's notice.

This was the morning of February 9th. During the afternoon we sighted the whistle buoy which marks the seaward end of the Chaussée de Sein, a dangerous tongue of rocks and shoals extending over fifteen miles into the Atlantic from the Pointe du Raz on the mainland. This line of rocks forms the southern arm of the stretch of water known as the Iroise, the wide bay in which the German battle cruisers were expected to carry out their sea trials. Our orders were to penetrate this bay as far as possible during daylight. To avoid being swept on to the southern rocks we had to go in with the first of the north-going tide and withdraw before the ebb reached its full strength. We could not enter until the following morning, and meanwhile there was the problem of where to patrol while we were charging batteries during the night. The enemy would break out either round the north-west corner of the bay, which seemed the obvious route if they were going up Channel, or round the south-west corner where we were now patrolling.

"As the Irishman said," murmured Colvin, puzzling over the chart, "not being a bird I cannot be in two places at once."

He supposed that by putting him in this south-west position the Admiralty had reason to expect a break-out into the Atlantic, so he decided to make his night patrols in the vicinity of the whistle buoy. "Night dark, sea calm, poor horizon," he wrote in his patrol report. "Observed air and patrol activity to the north. Various lights seen to the north of the whistle buoy indicated at least two patrol vessels."

The morning was fine and clear, and we entered the Iroise for the first time, spending several hours in the glassy calm water, with a good view across to the entrance to Brest Roads and Douarnenez Bay. There was no sign of the enemy. "Had any ships been in the Iroise," wrote Colvin, "I must have seen them. No ships of any description having been seen, and the tide now running to the south, I set course to withdraw along the same route."

That night, except for a Dornier aircraft which, without seeing us, flew close over our heads with all its cabin lights showing, we were undisturbed, and the following day, February 11th, we made a second periscope examination of the Iroise, again without result. We surfaced after dark in our usual position, and soon after midnight, when I was officer-of-the-watch, an aircraft glided noiselessly in and dropped a flare so close that we could see its fuse spluttering before it lit up the bridge in a blinding light. As he opened up his throttle we scrambled down the hatch and dived, expecting him to plaster us with depth-charges. But nothing more happened, and half an hour later we came up and spent the rest of the dark hours in peace. We did not know that the *Scharnhorst* and *Gneisenau* were already on their way north through the narrow channels inside Ushant. The expected sea trials did not take place.

The aircraft had seen us all right, for at dawn four anti-submarine trawlers and an aircraft came out to hunt for us. They proved so troublesome that Colvin had to abandon his attempt at a third inspection of the bay and withdraw to the northward. After surfacing that evening we received a signal telling us the galling news that the battle cruisers had escaped up the Channel and ordering us to leave patrol forthwith.

We were back at Fort Blockhouse on the morning of the 15th. Colvin immediately went off with Captain S/M (Admiral Darke) to give the full story of the patrol and confess to the wasted salvo of torpedoes. Two hours later I met him in the wardroom looking extremely worried. "Well, Number One, it looks as if I've had it," he said. "Captain S/M is *very, very* angry. He's been on the blower to Northways * and is now wearing out his carpet waiting for the answer." As we were drinking our coffee after lunch, Colvin was sent for. He was away for over an hour, and we feared the worst. Then he returned with a broad grin all over his face. It seemed that Flag Officer Submarines in London, after considerable thought, had replied that although Lieutenant-Commander Colvin's action was not to be regarded as a precedent, it was, in the very special circumstances, entirely justified.

Sealion was now very much in need of a refit: minor defects were becoming more and more frequent. But we had to carry out one more patrol, this time off the coast of Norway. On the 26th we were on our way up the Irish Sea, in weather so warm it seemed like summer, and Mike Willoughby and I talked for hours on the bridge. Mike, who has one of those nice-ugly faces, had had a kaleidoscopic life. After an unhappy childhood he went to sea at the age of fifteen as a boy apprentice in the Blue Star Line; he left it four years later and spent the 1930s in a breathless variety of jobs: quartermaster, yacht skipper, shipyard hand, vacuum-cleaner salesman (but he never sold one), silk-stocking salesman, second mate of a sailing ship, clerk to a shady business-man who ended up at the Old Bailey, studio artist, chauffeur to a wealthy judge, and advertising manager to a concrete firm, a steam instrument firm and finally a motor-boat firm. In the summer of 1939 he skippered the yacht *Windward* across the Atlantic with an extremely amateur crew of ex-International-Brigade refugees from the Spanish civil war. Since September 1939 he had been second mate of a tanker on the North Atlantic run, sub-lieutenant in charge of a yacht at the Dunkirk evacuation, and then navigator at the original Combined Operations base at Hamble. He had passed his submarine training course in November 1941, and *Sealion* was his second submarine.

Early the following morning we arrived in Holy Loch off Dunoon and berthed alongside H.M.S. *Forth*, the depot ship

* Submarine wartime headquarters in London.

of the Third Submarine Flotilla. Here we spent a few days preparing for our patrol, and then set off.

It was a dismal patrol. I can remember only one amusing thing about it. Colvin had adopted the practice (which I followed later in *Storm*) of making the morning dive without the klaxon, taking it slowly and using only the men already on watch. This made it unnecessary to disturb the entire crew, and it was very pleasant in rough weather to turn in after a miserable watch on the bridge and wake up to find the submarine peacefully under water. It was also good practice for the junior officers to learn to put on the day's first trim. On diving one morning, however, Iwan Raikes inadvertently got such a bow-down angle on the boat that Mike, who was sleeping soundly in the athwartships bunk at the after side of the wardroom, was shot out and landed heavily on the deck. The following day it was Mike's turn to dive the boat, and determined on revenge he too put on a steep angle—not realising that on this particular occasion it was I who had the athwartships bunk. Not to be outdone the next morning, I put on an even steeper angle, and this time it was Iwan who found himself on the deck. His retribution was not yet complete, for the planesmen, over-correcting the angle, brought the bow up so sharply that a pile of books and navigational instruments slid off the wardroom table and landed on Iwan's head as he was struggling to his feet. After this Colvin called a halt to the sport.

Not a single target came our way, which was perhaps lucky, because we were full of troubles. I have preserved some notes written at the time:

15.3.42. This is one of those patrols when things go wrong the whole time. The muffler-trunking outboard has flooded. On the first day we had a continuous leak thence through the Group Exhaust into the port engine and so into the bilges. This meant continual pumping to prevent the flooding from reaching the motors. Even so, on surfacing that night a heavy roll to port splashed the port armatures enough to put a full earth on the for'ard armature and on both fields. This is so far uncured. Thus the port motor is out of action. Then on diving two days ago someone left A vent open inadvertently and we got 400 gallons heavy for'ard and sank to 270 feet before we pulled her up; after we had corrected this the Skipper (who used to help us out by doing one dived watch each day as Officer-of-the-watch) forgot to shut A suction before opening W, so that the water rushed back and forth from A to W and the bubble became uncontrollable. And yesterday also we were terribly heavy for'ard, and we found some waste jammed under A.I.V. suction valve, so that the tank had flooded. Other troubles: a fish leaking in the tube and the air bubbling out through the bow cap; full earth again on the navigation lights; leaking telemotor system; W/T trouble in getting a signal through; the usual bad leak in the for'ard periscope gland; but so far no trouble with the cell in No. 1 Battery which caused such a panic before sailing.

16.3.42. Still another disaster last night. Starboard main motor bearing ran hot and "wiped" during the charge. With the port motor already out of action, this is really serious. Spent the day under strictest amp economy. Vied with the Captain in seeing who could keep the longest stopped trim, and just beat him!

17.3.42. The bearing was repaired just in time to dive at dawn, but no charge was possible. When we surface tonight we shall have gone over thirty-six hours without a charge.

We were in no state to remain on patrol. We asked permission to return home, and finally limped back to Holy Loch to face a Board of Inquiry into the reasons why we had been so careless as to allow the port motor to be flooded. As First Lieutenant I came in for a large share of Their Lordships' displeasure. But at last we took *Sealion* round to Blyth for her long-overdue refit, and here Colvin left us, to take over command of *Tigris*. A few days later a signal arrived appointing me as First Lieutenant to a new S-boat, *Saracen*, then building in Cammell Laird's yards at Birkenhead.

Poor old *Sealion* was a sad sight when I left her, propped up in dry dock out of sight of her natural element, stripped of her motors, her batteries, her furniture, her crew and her glory. I felt a brute for deserting her so. But I was to meet her again.

I am sorry to have to record that a year later dear George Colvin was lost in *Tigris* after a devastating depth-charge attack while on patrol in the Mediterranean. He had just been awarded the D.S.O. for a previous operation.

VI

MEDITERRANEAN

WHEN I left Blyth to make my way to Birkenhead I did not know who my new C.O. was to be, and it was not until I walked into the submarine office in Cammell Laird's shipyard that I discovered it was Lieut. M. G. R. Lumby, whom I had already met a few months before and taken a liking to when he was doing his C.O.'s course at Fort Blockhouse. Mike Lumby was tall, wiry, a man of iron, a skilled squash player and cricketer, and one who was clearly cut out for great things. I was a little apprehensive at finding myself his First Lieutenant.

I now plunged into the life of the great shipyard, surrounded every day by the hammering of the riveters resounding among the metal hulls like a thousand woodpeckers in a forest of steel, by the groaning and rumbling of the giant travelling cranes, the sputtering and sparking of the electric welders, and the pervading smell compounded of scorched metal, new-sawn wood, varnish and paint. I familiarised myself with the various workshops, overseers, managers and foremen concerned in the building of our submarine. The hull had been launched some weeks before; it was now a matter of filling her up with machines, engines, compressed-air pipes, water-pipes, electric wiring, periscopes, lighting, heating, ventilation, bunks, cupboards, drawers, curtains and all the rest of it.

Warrant Engineer M. N. Stevenson had arrived before any of us, and had been working on the boat for some months. He was responsible for the mechanical efficiency of the engines and all the working parts of the boat, and for the organisation of the E.R.A.s and stokers in the engine-room department. It was my job to know how everything worked, to supervise the fighting efficiency of the ship, and, as the rest of the crew began to arrive, to get to know them all and start kneading them into a cohesive team.

Building a new submarine in wartime involved a friendly but none the less persistent battle between the officers and the ship-yard authorities. Every submarine C.O. worth his salt has his own ideas about the multifarious details that go towards making an efficient fighting machine and a reasonably comfortable ship to live in. The precise positions of the bridge voice-pipes, the telephones in each compartment, the pumping and flooding in-dicators, the torpedo firing tell-tales, the lighting, the electric radiators, the fans, the arrangement of bunks and cupboards, the layout of the galley, the design of the chart-table—all these details were thrashed out between Lumby and myself. To us it seemed that they were extremely important and that it was only right that we, who after all were going to live in the boat and attack the enemy with it, should have our way. The ship-yard, though sympathetic to our point of view and willing to humour us as far as possible, also had to consider the need to standardise fittings so as not to interrupt the flow of new sub-marines through the yard. It therefore behoved me as First Lieutenant to be tactful but determined, to discover the most diplomatic method of gaining each point, whether by a quiet word with the man who was actually doing the job, by a friendly chat with the departmental foreman, by a frontal attack on the ship manager, or, when an important problem proved too diffi-cult, by persuading the Captain to pay a visit to the Admiralty Overseer. There were also many ingenious gadgets of our own invention which could usefully be made in the dockyard work-shops. Lumby, for instance, had designed his own slide-rule for working out torpedo firing intervals and "spreads," while I wanted an improved version of my trimming slide-rule. Cam-mell Laird's were very good about all this, and pandered to most of our vagaries with resigned humour.

Gradually the submarine became ship-shape, the crew began to settle down into some sort of unity, and the programme of dockyard trials ran its course. The last two officers arrived: one of these, the Torpedo and Gunnery Officer, I already knew because he was young Iwan Raikes from *Sealion*; and the Navigator was an R.N.V.R. officer called Tony Johnson, a tall, good-looking, madcap Irishman who had been an agricultural student and always took a selection of fascinating microscope slides of bacteria to sea with him. And finally the day came when we were ready for sea, the last wild rush of storing ship was over, and we cast off the dockyard wires and set off under escort for Dunoon to join the Third Flotilla and carry out trials and exercises. Our eventual destination, we knew, was the Mediterranean.

At the end of two months' exacting work, during which we rehearsed every imaginable situation likely to be encountered in the face of the enemy and practised emergency drills to cope with all foreseeable damage and breakdown, we were sent on what was known as a "working-up" patrol, to get the crew used to patrol conditions and to give the Captain experience of reaching his patrol billet and finding his way home again. For this patrol we were sent to a quiet area where we were unlikely to encounter any enemy anti-submarine opposition. It was also unlikely that any targets would come our way.

Lumby, however, distinguished himself on his working-up patrol by sinking a U-boat and bringing back a German prisoner.

We were somewhere in the middle of the North Sea, with nothing to look at day after day but a grey, undulating horizon. Tony Johnson, on watch at the periscope as dusk was falling on a day towards the end of the patrol, could hardly believe his eyes when he saw the box-like shape of a U-boat's conning-tower emerge from the empty sea less than a mile away, the water streaming off it in a foaming cataract. His astonished cry of "Captain in the control-room. . . . Sound the alarm. . . . U-boat surfacing, sir!" sent us rushing to our attack stations. Lumby started cracking out bearings and ranges almost before Raikes and Johnson were ready at the "fruit machine" and the plot. This was to be a snap attack all right. The light was bad, and the U-boat's speed would be altering as he got under way after surfacing. At my post behind the hydroplane operators, with the pumping and flooding order-instrument under my hand, I had to cope with the change of trim caused by the men rushing aft to the control-room. Water must be put in for'ard and pumped out amidships. An eye must be kept on the Coxswain and Second Coxswain at the hydroplanes to see they were taking the necessary action in time. At all costs the Captain must not be blinded by our sinking below periscope depth, and we must not give our presence away by breaking surface. The trim and the depth-keeping must be as near perfect as possible, to enable the Captain to concentrate on the enemy. Within two minutes of starting the attack came the order, "Stand by all six tubes," and then . . . "Fire one. . . . Fire two. . . . Fire three . . .", but I hardly heard the last three because I was now concentrating on putting water in for'ard and speeding up to prevent our breaking surface. As calmly as though it were just another practice attack, Crosby, the asdic operator, reported, "All torpedoes running, sir," and soon we heard the crack and reverberation of a tremendous explosion. We had got him.

After a prolonged search all round the horizon, Lumby gave the order to surface. As soon as we had reached full buoyancy and the engines were running, I asked permission to go up on the bridge. As I climbed out of the conning-tower, taking a deep breath of fresh air, I could see a few faint stars pricking the evening sky, the very stars which had, I supposed, tempted the German to surface early for a sight. The Captain was now making towards the scene of the explosion. Already we could see in the falling light one or two objects bobbing in the water, and soon we were in amongst broken pieces of wood and other flotsam. The smell of oil-fuel spilt and spreading over the sea stank in our nostrils. And in the middle of all this debris were three men. One of them was treading water, but when we turned towards him to pick him up he deliberately put his arms straight over his head and sank out of sight. The next body was floating bottom up and was quite clearly dead. The third man, however, looked as though he might be still alive, and we manœuvred towards him until two of our seamen could reach down and pull him up on to the casing. Groaning dementedly and vomiting sea-water and oil, he was carried to the bridge. Here he became conscious for a brief moment, long enough to open his eyes and look straight at me with an appalling expression of despair and hatred, before our men somehow lowered him down the conning-tower to be looked after below.

We now dived to reload the torpedo tubes, surfacing again later than usual that night.

Keeping a prisoner in a submarine is a tricky business. There is nowhere he can be locked up, and a really determined man with a knowledge of submarines can fairly easily cause fatal damage, providing he is prepared to sacrifice his own life in the process. He must be kept under a constant armed guard, which means detailing out of each watch a man who can ill be spared from his normal duties. Even in the lavatory there are valves within easy reach which might prove a temptation, so that we were obliged to inflict on our captive the indignity of being kept under observation whenever he wished to relieve himself. We put him to work on cleaning duties, which he performed willingly and well. He was altogether a model prisoner. By what little interrogation we were able to carry out, we discovered he was the U-boat's signalman and had been on the bridge with the Captain and the Navigator when our torpedo hit them. He remembered nothing after that, but said that immediately before the explosion another of our torpedoes had hit them abaft the bridge and penetrated the engine-room without exploding.

So it was that when we returned to Dunoon and tied up alongside H.M.S. *Forth* we felt like a Cup Final team that has scored a goal in the first five minutes of play. But soon we were busy with preparations for our departure to the Mediterranean. Each watch was given four days' leave. And one morning towards the end of August we cast off from the depot ship and pointed our bow south towards Gibraltar.

It was just as Browning described it. There Gibraltar surprisingly was, grand and gray in the dimmest north-east distance. I had expected the lion to be facing south, but with the

seaward approaches secure in the hands of the Navy it is perhaps only appropriate that he should keep guard towards the
mainland. To me, arriving here for the first time, the landfall
was fantastically exciting. For the last two nights we had been
smelling the scented land-breezes of Portugal, the previous
afternoon we had had Cape St Vincent in view through the
periscope (for we travelled dived by day), and all night Cadiz
Bay had been invisible but somehow palpable on our port hand.
Now at daybreak, making our appointed rendezvous with the
M.L. which had come out from Gibraltar to escort us through
the narrow Straits (only half the width of the English Channel
at Dover), we had Cape Trafalgar and the Spanish coast in sight
to the north of us, and to starboard the mountains of Africa
thrusting away southward behind Cape Spartel. All these
names were an incantation to raise the immortal past, and the
spirit of Nelson moved about the ruffled face of the water.

Soon our six-inch Aldis * was clacking away, making our
identification to the Port War Signal Station on Europa Point.
Close under the shadowed slopes of the Rock we began to distinguish the upperworks of several warships in their Mediterranean suit of pearly grey, berthed on the inside of the Mole
with awnings spread; most prominent among them, to our
eager eyes, being the high, liner-like hull of H.M.S. *Maidstone*,
depot ship of the Eighth Submarine Flotilla. Over the whole
prospect shimmered the certainty of yet another perfect summer day. Lumby now appeared on the bridge for the first time
in tropical uniform—white cap-cover, white open-necked shirt
with gold-lace epaulettes, white shorts, white socks and white
shoes. As he stood there and examined the Rock through his
binoculars, I could not help envying him this moment, entering
the Mediterranean in command of his own ship with a U-boat
already to his credit.

When we were less than a mile off, our escort left us and a
sunburnt young Lieutenant came out in a launch to board us
and show us the way in. The boom-nets being drawn aside for

* Standard naval trigger-operated signalling lamp; four-inch diameter for
short-range, six-inch for long-range.

us, we nosed our way in, turned to starboard along the South Mole past the battleship *Malaya*, and berthed on *Maidstone*. Three other submarines were alongside, painted dark blue to make them less conspicuous when submerged in the clear Mediterranean water. Waiting to greet us at the foot of the gangway was Bertie Pizey, last seen by us in England as a two-and-a-half-striper and now, as Commander Submarines of the Eighth Flotilla, looking improbably resplendent and ferocious in his gold-peaked cap. It was exciting to look up from our bridge at the great bulk of *Maidstone* towering above us and spot familiar faces among the many grinning at us from the shelter-deck rail. The early heat of the morning, now that we were no longer under way, came at us like the opening of an oven door. High above the crowded harbour, and dominating the closely-packed town huddled at its feet, the famous Rock leaned massively against the burning sky, seeming scarcely more than a ship's length away until the sight of the villas, barracks and gun emplacements perching like gannets on the upper slopes rolled it back into perspective and startled the eye into an awareness of its overpowering size and solidity.

It was my first Mediterranean port, and I was tremendously moved.

Gibraltar, for all its limitations of space, was a good spot to be in. Almost every form of sport awaited our pleasure: tennis, squash, football, hockey, sailing. Best of all, perhaps, was to walk through the fabulous tunnel and go swimming in Catalan Bay below the precipitous cliffs and great water-catchments of the eastern face of the rock. The town of Gibraltar itself had a pseudo-Oriental fascination of its own. Besides the absurdly expensive curios to lure the innocent traveller, the shops were full of English goods which were rationed or "under the counter" at home. The narrow streets were full of noise; forbidden by law to use their horns, drivers forced their cars and trucks through the congestion with the aid of much slamming of the hand on the outside of the door; traffic blocks were frequent and the din appalling. In our daytime tropical rig of shorts and open shirt, I could not get over the delightful feeling of being on perpetual holiday. At night the pleasantest feature to recent arrivals from England was the absence of blackout. With the lights of Algeciras blazing away on the Spanish mainland in full view across the bay, the inconvenience of a blackout would have served no useful purpose, though I believe arrangements for one were in force. So at night the dark mass of the Rock was spangled with lights, and windows and scuttles could be left open to the warm night air. In the town there were plenty of good places for eating and drinking. All officers were honorary members of the Yacht Club; there were good cocktails at the bar of the Bristol, with its Moorish archways; excellent Spanish cooking at the Victoria, especially its ham omelettes; and across the road the Capitol provided a background of hot dance-music to one's drink and food. It was here that Tony Johnson, our Navigator, an unrestrainable maniac when in his cups, leapt on to a table with a wild cry one night and danced an Irish jig, to the great joy of the band, who thereafter, whenever Tony appeared in the place, stopped whatever they were playing and broke into *Phil the Fluter's Ball*. One night we went to the theatre to see a Spanish ballerina of exquisite grace and astonishing skill with the castanets. And there happened to be in Gibraltar at this time a particularly charming collection of Wrens.

During these enchanted days I first made the acquaintance of another R.N.V.R. submarine First Lieutenant, Stephen Spring-Rice. Spring-Rice, known to everyone as "Sprice," was one of those whom the gods love and was to lose his life early in the following year, when *P.45*, the U-class submarine in which he was serving, was lost with all hands, just before he was due to return to England for his C.O.'s course. But at this time, in September 1942, the future spread invitingly before us, and we were beginning to wonder whether, as R.N.V.R. officers, we were to be allowed to do our "perisher" (as the C.O.'s course was called) and get a chance of having our own commands. In age and length of time in the submarine service I was senior to Sprice, and it was obvious that if submarine time were any criterion it could not be long before I was "in the zone" for a C.O.'s course. The possibility of one day having my own command had naturally been in my mind for some while, but I began to realise that with any luck I might have my chance before many months were out.

Sprice had an infectious enthusiasm for life and all its gifts which could not help making him popular. Coming from an intellectual and cultured family, he was a man of many parts and a wide range of artistic interests. I remember most of all his passion for music, and the way he used to play *Mr Bach Goes to Town* on his clarinet, a lock of hair standing up on his brow above the flushed and ardent face.

There was one evening in *Maidstone* I shall never forget. I think Sprice's boat had returned from patrol in the morning; at any rate we had some special reason for celebration that night, and we got very merry in the wardroom before the bar closed, after which about half a dozen of us, including Sprice, Tony Johnson, Iwan Raikes and myself, retired to Sprice's cabin to accompany his clarinet with various instruments. In the middle of it all, the curtain was swept aside; the figure of Bertie Pizey stood in the doorway with all the icy severity of a displeased Commander S/M. The discords died away. "Captain S/M wants to see you all in his cabin. The whole lot of you. And you are to bring those instruments of torture with you." Tails between our legs, we trooped after him to the Captain's Cabin. There stood Captain Barney Fawkes in his pyjamas. "How do you expect me to sleep with that filthy row going on?" he said. "If you must make such a bloody awful din, for heaven's sake come and make it in here and we'll have a party." And to our astonishment he meant it. Drinks were produced and for nearly two hours the party continued, with Barney Fawkes and Bertie Pizey making as much noise as the rest of us. It was a wonderful evening.

With all our amusements, time passed quickly in Gibraltar. And after a few days for embarking stores and painting the submarine dark blue, *Saracen* was sent off on a short working-up patrol along the Spanish coast towards Barcelona. Here we

could expect to see no enemy ships, but plenty of neutral merchant-ships on whom we could practise dummy attacks and
in doing so acclimatise ourselves to Mediterranean conditions.
Indeed, nothing particular happened on this patrol, and we returned to Gibraltar more impatient than ever to get into the
fray. This time leave was given to half the ship's company.
The ratings went off to the submarine rest camp above the
town, and Chiefy Stevenson and I spent three civilised days up
at the officers' rest-flat in part of the old Naval hospital, with
magnificent views over the harbour and Algeciras Bay. When
we returned to duty we found *Saracen* under orders to join the
Tenth Submarine Flotilla at Malta.

Between June 1940, when Mussolini entered the war, and
September 1943, when his fleet surrendered, our submarines
based on Malta and Alexandria, and later Beirut and Algiers,
sent more than one million three hundred thousand tons of
enemy shipping to the bottom of the Mediterranean. This was
achieved in the face of great hazards and at the grievous cost of
forty-one of our boats.

The full story of our submarine offensive in the Mediterranean would require a large volume to itself and is outside the
scope of this narrative. At the time when *Saracen* left Gibraltar
to join the Malta flotilla, the long-drawn-out battle was at its
height. The island had just survived the most critical months
of its history. Earlier in the year the Germans had become
seriously anxious about their seaborne supplies to Rommel in
Africa, and had increased their air attacks on Malta to such frequency and violence that from the end of March until September it had been untenable as a base for surface ships. Admiral
Cunningham had been forced to withdraw his cruisers and
destroyers to Alexandria, leaving only submarines and aircraft
in Malta to continue the attack on Rommel's supply route.
This period of siege was a desperate one in the Mediterranean
sea war. The magnificent way in which the Maltese population
stood up to the bombing, which caused so many casualties and
blasted large sections of Valetta to heaps of rubble and stone, is

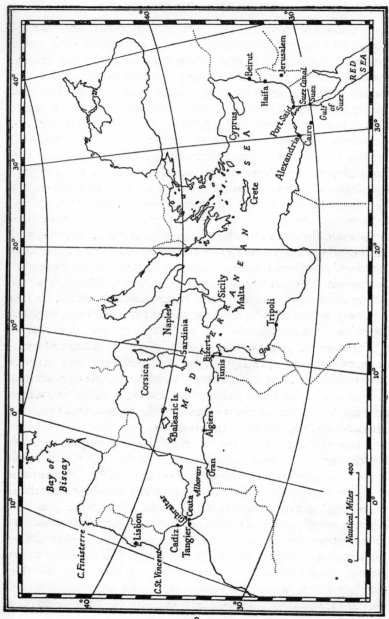

Bay of Biscay

C.Finisterre

C.St.Vincent

Lisbon

Cadiz

Tangier

Ceuta

Gibraltar

Alboran

Oran

Algiers

Balearic Is.

Corsica

Sardinia

Naples

Tunis

Bizerta

M E D I T E R R A N E A N   S E A

Sicily

Malta

Tripoli

Crete

Cyprus

Alexandria

Cairo

Port Said

Suez Canal

Suez

Gulf of Suez

RED SEA

Haifa

Beirut

Jerusalem

Nautical Miles

0

400

now famous in history. The submarines themselves had no peace between patrols and in harbour were obliged to spend much of the working day submerged to avoid the rain of bombs. Attempts to get convoys through to the island with badly needed supplies were for a time unsuccessful. Food began to run short. But at all costs petrol and ammunition had to be brought in to keep the defending Spitfires in the air, and there was only one solution. Five of the larger submarines of the First Flotilla based on Alexandria—*Cachalot, Parthian, Porpoise, Regent* and *Rorqual*—had been adapted for the purpose, and had been bringing in these vital supplies since the middle of 1941. This underwater transport service became known as "the magic carpet." With petrol filling a proportion of their fuel-tanks, fresh-water tanks, and even main ballast tanks, with one section of battery removed and every available storage tank crammed with ammunition, these unspectacular but highly inflammable cargo-carrying missions between Alexandria and Malta must have been a nightmare, especially since the Italians had been laying a lot of mines at this time. However, they did the trick: in one month alone the "magic carpet" delivered to Malta over 84,000 gallons of petrol, 83,000 gallons of kerosene, twelve tons of mail, thirty tons of general stores, six tons of munitions and over a hundred passengers. And in spite of all these difficulties and distractions, during the first six months of 1942 our submarines sank fifty-four merchant ships, two cruisers, eight U-boats and a destroyer.

Meanwhile the air defence of Malta had improved sufficiently to allow surface forces to return to the island, and in this same month of September 1942 Rear-Admiral A. J. Power was able to re-establish a cruiser squadron and two destroyer flotillas based on Valetta. Cargoes of petrol and food were also now being brought in by the two fast minelayers *Manxman* and *Welshman*, whose unusual speed of nearly forty knots enabled them to run the gauntlet of the most vulnerable stretch of the journey under cover of darkness. But supplies were still desperately short, and every submarine going through to Malta had to fill itself up with as much as it could carry, regardless of discomfort, so long as the fighting efficiency of the ship was not impaired.

During the last few days before we were due to sail from Gibraltar we used our ingenuity to discover ways of cramming stores into every corner of the submarine. One of the fresh-water tanks and two of the internal trimming tanks were emptied, opened up and filled with tinned food. Boxes of assorted engine spares, torpedo detonators, ammunition fuses and more tinned food covered the deck space in the torpedo-stowage compartment and paved the whole length of the passage-way as far as the control-room. We also had a surprise packet to deliver to Malta, nothing less than a "human torpedo," similar to an ordinary torpedo but with a detachable warhead and adapted to take two men sitting astride in diving-suits; some of these weapons were at this time being assembled in Malta with the object of attacking the Italian naval bases.* *Maidstone*'s engineers came down and erected a long steel con-tainer on our casing, just abaft the bridge, and after dark on the night before we sailed the mysterious object was lowered into it and boxed in. In a mild attempt to deceive curious eyes while leaving harbour, and later when entering Malta, we covered this erection with a canvas hood bearing the words "DANGER—PETROL."

With all this multiplicity of extra stores on board, I began to get worried about the trim. My slide-rule could not cope with the problem, so I gave up trying to calculate the answer and decided to rely on rule of thumb. When all the stores were on board I looked at her from the outside to see how she floated; and then had water pumped out of her until the surface water-

---

* Four months later, in January 1943, two of these human torpedoes, each manned by an R.N.V.R. officer and a rating, succeeded in penetrating the strongly defended Italian base at Palermo. One of them sank the cruiser *Ulpio Raiano* and the other inflicted severe damage on an 8,500-ton transport. Lieutenant R. T. G. Greenland, R.N.V.R., and Sub-Lieutenant R. G. Dove, R.N.V.R., were awarded the D.S.O., and Leading Signalman A. M. Ferrier and Acting Leading Seaman J. M. Freel the C.G.M. We must not forget that it was the Italians who showed the way in this extremely hazardous form of submarine warfare when, in December 1941, they got into Alexandria harbour and put the two battleships *Queen Elizabeth* and *Valiant* out of action for several months.

line looked about right. Finally I took out another ton of water to be on the safe side, and arranged with the Captain to carry out a trim dive as soon as possible after leaving harbour.

Approaching Malta in the dark at the end of our uneventful thousand-mile passage, we had no difficulty in finding the place. From some distance off we could see that a heavy air-raid was in progress, and the flying tracer, the bursts of ack-ack and enemy starshell, punctuated by the ground flashes from exploding bombs, were more effective than any navigational beacon. Because the enemy had been laying mines, we lay off to the south of the island until daybreak, when two minesweepers met us and led the way along the swept channel round the east coast. Even before we reached the harbour mouth an air-raid warning came over the W/T, and in accordance with standing orders we submerged to periscope depth in the swept channel until we got the all-clear signal from our escorts. As we drew near the entrance to Grand Harbour we began to see evidence of the heavy damage which Valetta had suffered in two years of almost constant air attack. But though more than half its houses had been wholly or partly demolished, the embattled city still retained its ancient character: the fortress walls sloping down to the water's edge, the myriad flat-roofed buildings mounting to the horizon, with here and there the gentle protuberances of domes and towers, all white or pink or sand-yellow against the blue sky.

The submarine base was not in Grand Harbour but in Marsumascetto Creek immediately to the west of it, so, leaving the imposing Fort St Elmo on our port hand and keeping the town of Sliema to starboard, we proceeded up the creek with our white ensign flashing in the sun and the seamen standing smartly to attention on the fore-casing. A small group of Maltese children standing on the spit of land under the walls of the fort warmed our hearts by raising a great cheer for us as we swept past. A minute or two later we were turning to starboard into the creek where the submarines lay, each berthed on the end of a floating cat-walk. There was no depot ship here, and all the workshops, stores and living accommodation were housed in the partly-blitzed sandstone buildings we could see strung out along the edge of the creek. Old friends and new faces were waiting to greet us as we glided quietly in to our berth, and presently we were stepping ashore and finding our way to the wardroom mess, a large, bare, stone-flagged room on the ground floor of a colonnaded building, with a flight of uneven steps leading up from the water.

I cannot remember anything quite like the Malta submarine base at this time. The shortage of food was a continual reminder of our beleaguered situation, though we fed like fighting cocks by comparison with the civilian population of the island. The enemy air bases in Sicily were only sixty miles away. Earlier in the year the bomb damage had been considerable, and the repair workshops had been kept going only by miracles of improvisation inspired by the Engineer Commander, the cheerful and imperturbable Sam Macgregor. Although the air defences had by now improved considerably, the air-raid warning still sounded several times every day. We got a preliminary warning from the ringing of a cloistral hand-bell, the signal for putting the smoke-screen into action. Besides the smoke canisters along the shore, each submarine in harbour had one placed ready on the casing fore and aft. In a few minutes a dense white fog would spread over the creek and the submarine base; the acrid fumes stung the eyes and the nostrils long after it was all over. Sometimes through a gap in the smoke-screen we caught a glimpse of the air battle going on high over our heads.

But if the enemy was uncomfortably close, by the same token our boats did not have far to go to find targets, and in those days it was unusual for a submarine to return to harbour without having struck some blow at the enemy's supply line. In the first six months of this year, under the strategical direction of its Captain S/M, "Shrimp" Simpson, the Malta flotilla had sunk fifty-four merchant-ships and thirteen warships.* Unhappily,

* Shrimp's Intelligence was so uncannily prescient and accurate that we began to suspect him of having a private telephone line to Rome.

a month before we arrived in Malta the flotilla had been stunned by the loss, on his last patrol before going home to refit, of the most successful C.O. of them all, Lieut.-Commander M. D. Wanklyn, who in the previous year had added to his D.S.O. the first submarine V.C. of the war, and who had in the *Upholder* sunk something like a hundred thousand tons of enemy supply and transport ships, besides three U-boats and a destroyer. Wanklyn I was too late to meet, but some of those I now met in the wardroom were men whose exploits were already famous: "Tubby" Linton of the *Turbulent*, for instance, Dick Cayley of the *Utmost*, and many others. Ben Bryant, still bearded, was here with *Safari*, building a new reputation for aggressive action surpassing even that of his *Sealion* days. Lumby found several C.O.s in the flotilla who had done their perisher course with him: McGeoch, Stevens, Crawford, Bromage. And here were two other R.N.V.R. First Lieutenants: Mike Tattersall, genial, ruddy, very popular and remarkably efficient, and the Canadian Freddie Sherwood, whom I had relieved when I had joined *Sealion* and who was now Ben Bryant's Number One in *Safari*. Shortly afterwards Sprice followed us in *P.45* from Gibraltar, making four of us anxious to know what chances R.N.V.R. First Lieutenants had of doing the C.O.'s course.

Because targets were frequent and torpedoes quickly expended, patrols from Malta tended to be short. It was nothing for a submarine to return to harbour with empty tubes in less than a week. My memories of *Saracen*'s Malta patrols are a little confused. At first we were out of luck. I remember one patrol in the shallow waters of the Gulf of Gabes, where the coast of Africa takes its sharp northward turn away from the Libyan desert towards Tunis; here I think we sank a small supply ship, but I am not sure. Another time we spent a week off Naples, with Mount Vesuvius and Capri tantalisingly in sight through the periscope all day, but here I fancy we were unlucky in our targets. By the middle of October we were back in Malta, making the usual preparations for going to sea again within four or five days.

Gradually we became aware that something out of the ordinary was in the wind. Boats returning from patrol completed their normal overhauls, reloaded with torpedoes, ammunition, fuel and stores, and then found themselves waiting beyond their normal time for sailing orders. It became clear that we were being held in readiness for some important and widespread operation. Commanding Officers, burdened with their secret knowledge, became unusually withdrawn from their First Lieutenants. As more submarines came in, the tension of anticipation and speculation in the overcrowded messes mounted like a fever. The smoke-screen drill was tightened up so as to make sure that reconnaissance planes from Sicily could draw no conclusions from the sight of so many boats in harbour.

At last one morning Mike Lumby told me to be ready to sail at dusk that evening for a billet he could not divulge. We had been ready for sea for so many days that there was little to do but embark fresh provisions and personal kit. At midnight we were steaming through the scented night over a calm sea on a north-westerly course. By the next morning most of the submarines would be on their way to their secret stations, and the Maltese would wake to find Marsumascetto Creek nearly empty. Two days later we were on our billet, a few miles off Cape St Vito on the north-west tip of Sicily. That night as we patrolled on the surface recharging our batteries, signals began to come through giving details of initial successes in a new Eighth Army offensive at El Alamein. The news seemed to be no surprise to the Captain, and in the wardroom we assumed this was the big event about which there had been so much secrecy. Lumby smiled but refused to discuss the matter any further, so we began to suspect there was more to come, particularly as we could not see what use we were to the Eighth Army in our present billet, a thousand miles from the battle.

A few mornings later we sighted a westbound Italian submarine on the surface. After a short attack at close range, during which Lumby said he could clearly see the smiling faces of the Italian officers on the bridge, he blew the enemy to pieces with three torpedo hits. From this submarine there were no survivors.

A few days later a wireless signal ordered us to shift patrol to a new position off the Gulf of Tunis and warned us of two enemy supply ships, escorted by two destroyers, approaching from the north to enter Tunis, the enemy's principal supply port into North Africa. We knew that the convoy had to pass through the position of another of our submarines to seaward of us. I was officer-of-the-watch on the morning the convoy was expected. Slowly sweeping the empty sea and sky with the peri-scope, my eyes were startled by the sight of the horizon erupt-ing silently into a shooting column of flame. I had time to cry, "Captain in the control-room!" before the slower-travelling sound-wave hit our pressure hull with a dull clang. We guessed McGeoch to the north of us had bagged one of the enemy, and sure enough when first masts and then hulls began to appear above the horizon we could see the two destroyers but only one merchant-ship. An hour later they reached us. The Captain

fired four torpedoes, going deep to avoid the destroyers at the same time, and we listened for the bangs. After too long an interval there was a muffled explosion which might have been a torpedo or a depth-charge. As soon as he dared, the Captain brought us back to periscope depth; a quick look round showed him a stern view of the merchantman going strong for Tunis with black smoke pouring from his funnel. One destroyer, however, had disappeared. Mortified at missing the main tar-get, we had to be content with the minor success, and crept quietly away while the remaining destroyer zig-zagged around looking for us. Over the air that night we reported one destroyer sunk and a merchant-ship missed, and the signal came back: "Not bad. Suggest you aim at the destroyer next time."

It must have been about now that our curiosity was satisfied at last by learning of the Allied landings at Algiers, Oran and Casablanca. Operation Torch was on. The submarines' part in it was to attack the Italian Fleet on their way from their home ports to the invasion areas. The Italian Navy, however, preferred to remain in harbour during this time of crisis.

We soon had visible evidence of the Germans' reaction. The sky became thick with flights of Ju-52s bringing troops into Tunis from Sicily. At first, in accordance with our usual drill, we went deep on sighting these aircraft, but they were not interested in looking for submerged submarines, and we stayed at periscope depth watching and recording this aerial charabanc service. The flights, sometimes including monster six-engined planes towing several gliders, would come in to land, take off again within half an hour and be back with a further load of troops two hours or so later. When they flew close enough we could see the troops sitting in their seats like passengers in a bus. This went on all day long for the rest of our patrol. As soon as he could the Captain got off a signal giving details, in the hope that a fighter patrol from Malta might be able to get in amongst them.

A few days after the Allied landings we were ordered to leave patrol and return to Malta. Shortly before midnight on the first night of our homeward journey, chugging along on the surface at eleven knots in misty weather, we nearly ran into two patrolling Italian E-boats. After an anxious fifteen minutes of surface avoiding-action we felt confident we had eluded them without being detected, but two hours later, as officer-of-the-watch on the bridge, I found myself far more frightened by a new enemy. The visibility had been poor all night, but now the sky grew appallingly dark, vision retracted to a circle of a few yards, so that I could barely make out the wash of our bow wave, and the air became heavy with threat. Ahead of us sinister snakes of lightning darted out of the blanket of dark and licked the surface of the sea. Watching the venomous deliberation of the storm's approach, I began to wonder what happens to a submarine when it is struck by lightning. If you can be struck dead under an oak-tree, why not surrounded by water and standing on seven hundred tons of steel? As the next fork of lightning plunged into the sea apparently less than fifty yards away and I heard, or perhaps imagined I heard, the sulphurous hiss of its extinction, a brutal fusillade of heavy hailstones burst in our faces. Feeling an absolute fool I called the Captain on the voice-pipe and told him that we were in the middle of a severe electrical storm, that the visibility was nil, and that in my opinion it would be advisable to dive until it was over. "All right, Number One," he answered, "if you think we ought to, dive." So we dived. Eighty feet down the hydrophone operator could still hear the noise of the hailstones hitting the sea.

It took me some weeks to live down my decision to dive because of a mere thunderstorm. But in spite of numerous arguments, nobody produced a final answer to the question: What *does* happen when lightning strikes a submarine?

Back in Malta we learned that we were to have ten days in harbour and then, after a short patrol, return to H.M.S. *Maidstone*, now preparing to leave Gibraltar and move across to the newly-captured port of Algiers, nearly five hundred miles nearer the scene of submarine operations.*

We said good-bye to Malta early in December. On a misty moonlight night shortly before Christmas, bound for Algiers after an uneventful patrol, we found ourselves to our surprise following two miles astern of another submarine, also westbound on the surface. We had just recognised the stranger through our binoculars as an Italian U-boat when he startled us by flashing a long and unintelligible signal. Lumby, thinking

---

* The popular belief that a depot ship re-fuels and re-stores her submarines at sea in enemy waters is a misconception. It would be foolish to expose so valuable a floating city of workshops, stores and technical knowledge to constant hazards of attack by air or submarine. Depot ships are designed for changing base quickly according to the strategic needs of the moment. At a few days' notice they can achieve a removal which a shore base would need months to complete. In doing so, of course, they run the risk of being attacked, and in fact, H.M.S. *Medway* had been sunk by torpedo while moving base from Alexandria to Beirut in June of this same year.

fast and hoping to delude the enemy into supposing us friendly, had the signalman on the bridge and told him to reply with a series of meaningless but rapid longs and shorts. The Italian was non-plussed but did not want to appear incompetent, so began his message again. We interrupted with the name of an Italian submarine chosen at random, and his flashing came to an immediate stop.

"Call him up again," said Lumby.

"What shall I make to him, sir?"

"Anything that comes into your head."

"Ay, ay, sir."

I suspected a sly grin on the signalman's face as he trained his Aldis on the enemy, and soon, listening to the clicking of the trigger, I realised that he was working through a remarkably comprehensive vocabulary of obscenities. It is not often given to any man in modern warfare to say exactly what he thinks of the enemy to his face, but this sailor certainly seized his opportunity. The situation was now so grotesque that we were all shaking with suppressed laughter. The Italian began signalling again, and through our glasses we saw that he was altering course towards us. "Down below!" said Lumby at once; "I'm going to dive and have a go at him." We scrambled down the conning-tower as the main vents opened, and in just over half a minute we had submerged, hoping that the enemy would not realise we had done so. In the dimly lit control-room we closed up to attack stations. The Captain searched on the enemy's bearing, but owing to the loss of light through the many lenses in the periscope it was not until two minutes later that he could make out the dim shape of his target. The Italian came on exasperatingly slowly, no doubt puzzled at our disappearance. Then, with less than ten degrees to go before the firing angle came on, Lumby lost sight of him, and in spite of a thorough periscope and listening search on all bearings we could not find him again. Our intended victim had come to his senses at last and dived. A pity; if it had come off it would have made one of the best submarine stories of the war.

VII

RECALLED HOME

We arrived off Algiers harbour on Christmas morning 1942, spruce in dazzling tropical whites reserved for the occasion, and buzzing with the anticipatory excitement of a new and reputedly exotic landfall. Through the sunny haze we began to make out the white buildings of the town, the villas on the hills behind, and finally the unmistakable outline of H.M.S. *Maidstone*, newly arrived from Gibraltar. We flashed our identification, and immediately the signal came: WELCOME TO ALGIERS. MERRY CHRISTMAS. ALL SHORE LEAVE IS CANCELLED. This struck us as a somewhat unseasonable greeting, but it turned out that Admiral Darlan had been assassinated the day before and no one knew how the local French were taking it; luckily there were no violent reactions, and by evening leave was restored.

News of far more interest to myself awaited us—a signal from Admiral Submarines in London recalling me to England for my Commanding Officers' Qualifying Course. Another officer in the flotilla, Tony Spender, an old friend from my submarine training class, had received similar instructions, and passage to England had been arranged for us in a cruiser leaving Algiers in a few days' time. When we worked out the dates we realised this would give us only two days' leave at home before starting the course. Spender conceived a better idea. For the last few months he had been First Lieutenant of *P.219*, the submarine commanded by Jewell which had carried out important "taxi" assignments for the Americans. In October they had landed General Mark Clark near Algiers for his secret conference with Giraud's representatives; they had also recovered him successfully. A few days later they picked up General Giraud himself after his escape from France and eventually

transferred him to a seaplane for onward transport to Eisen-
hower in Gibraltar. Through his new American friends Spender got in touch with the pilot of a Flying Fortress leaving for
England in three days' time and persuaded him to take both of
us as passengers. Captain S/M threw up his hands in resigned
horror. Air-passenger transport was frowned upon by the
authorities at the moment; too many high-ranking officers had
been lost in air travel recently; and had not Mr Churchill said
only the other day that submarine commanding officers were
worth a million each? Barney Fawkes, too busy to argue, finally
said it was all right with him provided he knew nothing about
it. Gleefully we completed our packing, and I said good-bye to
Lumby and everybody in *Saracen*.

[Some months later, while covering the landings in Sicily,
Saracen was heavily depth-charged and forced to the surface,
so badly damaged that the crew had to abandon ship and
surrender as prisoners of war. Lumby correctly stayed in the
control-room to the last and opened the main vents himself to
make sure the boat did not fall into enemy hands, climbing out
of the conning-tower just in time.]

On the appointed day Spender and I presented ourselves at
the Maison Blanche airfield outside Algiers. Except for the
runways, the field was a marsh of mud after the recent rains.
The surface was criss-crossed with narrow roadways of heavy
wire-netting; over these we rattled and bounced in our bor-
rowed car, trying to find our American friends. We found them
in a distant corner leaning despondently against one of the
plane's monster wheels just as a fine rain began to fall. One of
the starboard engines was giving trouble and a pessimistic
mechanic had already been working on it for two hours. The
weather report from Gibraltar was bad, indicating low ceiling
and poor visibility. Even if the engine was repaired quickly,
we had to wait for an important passenger whose time of arrival
was uncertain. We spent the rest of the day hanging about in
damp futility. By evening the weather showed no signs of improvement, no word had come from the V.I.P., and the defec-

tive engine was still out of action. Miserably we collected our
bags and returned to Algiers to find a bed for the night. We
were determined not to return on board *Maidstone*; we should
lose face if we did, and Captain S/M might have changed his
mind. At the quayside we found a merchant-ship that was being used as accommodation for passing naval personnel, and
gave our ships as *P.247* and *P.219*, omitting the fact that these
mystic numbers were submarines; otherwise we should have
been packed off to our mother ship for the night. We discovered later that our instinct was right. Our failure to arrive
at Gibraltar that afternoon had been reported, and there was
now a tremendous flap on in *Maidstone* because no one knew
whether we had crashed on our way or were still in Algiers.
Luckily we knew nothing of this, and spent the evening cheer-
ing ourselves up at the bar.

We ate an early breakfast and waited gloomily for the car
that had been promised to take us back to the airport. The
cloud ceiling seemed lower than ever, and by the time the car
arrived, an hour late, we had resigned ourselves to the prospect
of an ignominious return to *Maidstone*. To our surprise, when
we reached the Flying Fortress all four engines were warming
up with a most reassuring roar. Moreover, the weather report
from Gibraltar was perfect and the very important person had
telephoned to say he would be at the airport within the hour.
Thirty minutes later a car drove up and out stepped a Captain
R.N., whose name I forget, followed by General Browning, who
was later to command the airborne forces at Arnhem but now
came fresh from the Tunisian front. We all climbed in, the
pilot taxied to the start of the runway, the roar of the engines
grew louder, the ground raced away beneath us and we were up
and away.

The General and the Captain travelled in the rear of the plane.
Spender and I were by this time well acquainted with the pilot
and navigator and had been accorded the privilege of sitting up
with them in the nose. We followed the African coast until it
dipped away southward and left us flying over the blue Mediterranean on a course slightly south of west.

A few hours later the navigator announced that we shouldn't be long now, and started looking out ahead for recognisable land. "That's it," he said at last, pointing to a rocky peninsula just visible towards the misty horizon, and the pilot began losing height. Spender and I looked, looked again, then looked at each other. The rock we were aiming at was not the shape we remembered, and it was jutting north, not south. Anxiety struggled with good manners. Presently we could make out another rock coming dimly into view to the north-west, and this time there could be no mistaking the leonine contour of the Rock. Certain now that we were right, we called the navigator's attention to the real Gibraltar. He was not perturbed. "I guess you're right. Steer thirty-five degrees right, Cap'n." Thus we saved ourselves and General Browning from landing at Ceuta and being interned in Spanish Morocco for the rest of the war.

Landing on Gibraltar aerodrome in a Flying Fortress is one of the most terrifying sports in the world. The airstrip runs east and west across the narrow isthmus which joins the Rock to La Linea on the Spanish mainland. During the war an extension was built out into the sea at one end in order to accommodate the Fortresses. Even so, these large machines had to touch down within a few yards of the start of the runway to avoid falling into the sea at the other end. We made one dummy run westward over the airfield to test for wind drift, then swung to port and circled the Rock, looking down on the familiar landmarks of the town strung out along the lower slopes, the harbour full of cruisers and destroyers, and the old naval hospital up on the hill which had been our rest-camp six months ago. Passing Europa Point, and the water-catchments on the eastern slopes, we came full circle and straightened up once more for the airfield. Our shadow grew larger over the blue water in which we had bathed so often, the eastern wall of the runway raced up to meet us, and suddenly it seemed a stupid moment to die. But it was a perfect landing, and a few minutes later we were standing gratefully in the sun on solid tarmac, under the Rock's great northern cliff.

Arranging to return to the airport at seven o'clock the next morning, Tony Spender and I begged a lift into the town in an R.A.F. brake and went cheerfully to report ourselves to the Senior Officer Submarines. Now the storm of official wrath burst over our heads, originating (we were told) from no less a person than Admiral Cunningham himself. We were presented with a signal informing us that we were not, repetition not, to proceed further by air but were to wait for the *Scylla*, the cruiser in which our passage had been originally booked. The *Scylla* was not due in Gibraltar for two days. Our Fortress landed in England the following evening without us.

In the end we still beat the original schedule, and saw a bit of unexpected fun on the way. *Scylla* was routed well out into the Atlantic at an economical cruising speed, bound for the Clyde north about Ireland, but we were only one day out from Gibraltar when a Sunderland flying-boat sighted a German blockade-runner making for the Bay of Biscay, and Admiralty ordered *Scylla* to intercept. We altered course to the north-east and despite the rough weather increased to an uncomfortable speed which brought the spray crashing over the cruiser's bridge. The interception was a model of air–sea co-operation and pin-point navigation. We found the enemy merchant-ship in bad visibility as dusk was falling on the second day. An hour later we would have missed her in the night. Two shells from *Scylla* were enough to persuade the enemy to stop and lower her boats. It was decided to sink her by torpedo. The two sub-mariners among the spectators took a mean delight in the fact that the cruiser's first torpedo at the sitting target was a miss. The second ran true and blew a hole in her amidships, and as we turned away northwards in the gathering dark the stricken ship heeled slowly over and sank.

This diversion had brought us almost on to a direct route for the Irish Sea, and when *Scylla* dropped anchor off Greenock she was two days ahead of schedule. Spender and I caught the night train to London for our four days' leave. On a desolate Sunday evening in the middle of January 1943 I arrived at Portsmouth, and took the familiar diesel ferry from *Vernon*

H

steps over the harbour to *Dolphin*. Here, drinking sherry in the comfortable wardroom before dinner, I found Spender and other old friends, including Mike Willoughby, Freddie Sherwood, Phil May and Jimmy Launders. We were all about to learn how to be submarine commanding officers. Mike had achieved the rare, and I believe unique, distinction of being called to this course within eighteen months of entering the submarine service.

VIII

"PERISHER"

At one time the course on which we were embarked had been called the Periscope School; hence the grimly humorous contraction "Perisher." Now it was officially the C.O.Q.C., or Commanding Officers' Qualifying Course, but by tradition we were still known as the perishers.

For the first fortnight of the six-weeks' course the perishers lived in H.M.S. *Dolphin* within the walls of Fort Blockhouse, the formidable peninsular bastion at the entrance to Portsmouth Harbour which looks southward across the busy waters of Spithead, beyond the island martello-towers of Horse Sand Fort and No Man's Land Fort, towards the green Isle of Wight. Its eastern wall flanks the swift tides of the harbour mouth; on the north it faces across to the sheds and slips of Camper and Nicholson's yacht-building yards, and is separated from Gosport by the muddy channel of Haslar Creek. It is in this creek that the submarines lie, berthed alongside the concrete jetties which have been built out from the walls of Fort Blockhouse over the shallow water. The only land approach to the Fort is by the road which runs along the narrow isthmus between the sea and the creek and joins the Gosport mainland by Haslar Hospital. This geographical isolation gives to the place a pleasantly beleaguered air, which in wartime was intensified by the gun-emplacements along the sea road.

Every morning after an excellent breakfast we perishers walked out of the Fort's western gate and along the sea road, invigorated by the salty breeze and talking at the top of our voices, turned right past the huge tank where new submariners were trained to use the Davis Escape Apparatus, and came to a small brick building where we were learning how to carry out attacks on enemy ships. This was the Attack Teacher, an ingenious and elaborate "war game" which allowed us to make our elementary mistakes without fatal results to ourselves or anyone else.

It was built on two levels. The top floor, reached by an outside flight of steps, was the plotting-room. At the far end of it a travelling platform, with a small central turn-table to take the target model, ran out on rails through a window into the open air. The other end was occupied by a large white plastic plotting-table, marked off in squares to a scale of a thousand yards (half a sea-mile) to the inch. The plotting of the attacks, and the operating of the machinery which controlled the target's movements, were performed by a team of charming and intelligent Wrens. On shelves around the walls stood fleets of small-scale models of ships of all the warring nations: battleships, cruisers, aircraft-carriers, destroyers, submarines; liners, cargo-steamers, tankers, tramps. The lower floor of the building represented the interior of the attacking submarine. Imagine for a moment that you are a spectator in this lower room and that it is my turn to carry out the next attack.

The circular white box in which I am standing represents the submarine's control-room, though in appearance it does not resemble one in the least. A periscope leads up into the plotting-room; its top window is covered for the moment because the stage is being set for the start of the attack. Out of sight upstairs, Commander Teddy Woodward, the instructor, is placing a new ship-model on the travelling target platform. As the attack develops, the target will move slowly in towards the periscope, turning on its platform in accordance with the gradually changing relative bearing of the submarine. Its movements are pre-arranged by Commander Woodward before the start of the attack, and these are automatically repeated on the plotting-table. My own tactics also will be plotted on it by the Wrens, following the orders I give up the voice-pipe.

Around me in the room below, my fellow perishers are waiting to take their turn at the various duties which, when I get a boat of my own, will be carried out by my officers. One of them stands by me to read off bearings and range-angles as I set them on the periscope, and to help me identify the target from the various ship-recognition manuals at hand. Another operates the fruit machine, into which he will feed the information I give him about the enemy's bearing, inclination, mast-head height and range-angle, and in return will translate these data into the enemy's true bearing, course, range in yards, and distance-off-track. This information in turn will be passed to the navigating officer, whose job is to chart the progress of the attack and work out the target's speed.

Suddenly a Wren's voice in the voice-pipe at my ear startles me into action.

"Control-room, control-room. You are a T-class submarine on patrol in the North Sea. Submarine's course one four five. Are you ready? *Start the attack*." I repeat "Start the attack" as a signal to the stop-watches, and at once order "Up periscope." The top lens is now unmasked to represent the raising of the periscope, and looking into the eyepiece I find myself confronted with the urgent sight of the *Scharnhorst* coming straight at me, or a merchant-ship I cannot for the moment identify, or perhaps a U-boat whose angle-on-the-bow is impossible at that range to judge. I must take action at once. How am I going to get into an attacking position?

It was to the answering of this question that most of our thoughts were to be devoted for the next few weeks. Hour after hour we spent in the Attack Teacher every day, taking turns to do the attack or form a different part of the attack team. We started with simple attacks where the target maintained a steady course from beginning to end, and graduated by easy stages to more difficult attacks on zig-zagging targets. Sometimes, if you had kept the periscope down for too long during the closing stages of a hectic attack, you would suddenly hear the most appalling crashing and banging overhead; this was the plotting-room gleefully dropping lead weights on the iron roof of the control-room to indicate to you that you had been rammed by your target. At the end of each attack we all walked up the steps to the plotting-room to see whether the target had been sunk and to have one's tactics pulled to pieces by Teddy

Woodward. On a bad day you might have a run of unsuccessful attacks; and your gloom would increase when you remembered that these model attacks were carried out in perfect visibility, with no rainstorms to blot out your target, no breaking waves to obscure your view, and none of the navigational anxieties you were liable to have when operating in shallow water. If you made a mess of it in ideal conditions, when there was no question of anyone's life being at stake and you could consider the problem academically, what disasters might you not be responsible for when you were trying to do the same thing in earnest? Many times during this period did I wonder if Teddy Woodward had already decided I would not make the grade.

Our last day on *Dolphin*'s Attack Teacher provided some hilarious comic relief. It was as though the Marx brothers had been let loose in the plotting-room. Targets did the most astonishing things: proceeded backwards, turned upside down, stopped still, or disappeared altogether. We made Teddy Woodward do an attack, and set him an appallingly difficult one which ended with the target bursting into flames before he had a chance to fire. Finally the Wrens had their turn, while the perishers worked the machinery and did the plotting; some of the girls had achieved a remarkable grasp of the essentials of the game.

After that we packed our bags and Teddy Woodward took us north to Rothesay on the Clyde estuary for the sea part of our training.

We were billeted ashore in the Glenburn Hotel, but had to be on board *Cyclops* for breakfast. Every morning we dressed in the cold dark and caught the early boat off to the depot ship. The cheerless February dawn was breaking by the time we had finished our meal and trooped down the gangway on board the submarine allotted to us for this part of our course. This happened to be our old friend *Sealion*, to the great delight of Mike Willoughby, Freddie Sherwood and myself, old sealions all. Since I had left her in Blyth she had done two more patrols in the Bay of Biscay with Douglas Lambert in command and Mike as Number One. After all her arduous service it was sad to see the faithful war-horse relegated to the hack work of a training flotilla. She was now temporarily commanded by Lieutenant Verschoyle-Campbell, the youngest officer ever to achieve submarine command.

We took it in turn to act the part of Captain each day, to get used to the routine of taking the submarine to sea, diving and surfacing her in the exercise area, and bringing her back alongside the depot ship in the evening. I forget who it was who had the doubtful privilege of being the first Captain for the day, but it was probably Phil May, as he was senior perisher. While he gave the orders for letting go for'ard and aft, man-œuvring the motors to swing our stern out and then go ahead, changing over from the motors to the diesels and then settling down to a steady speed and course for the exercise area—all this under the anxious eye of *Sealion*'s real Captain and the critical eye of Teddy Woodward—the rest of us gathered at the after end of the bridge and told stories until the increasingly chilly wind drove us below to the cosy wardroom. Here, sitting comfortably round the table, the hanging lamp swaying gently as *Sealion* began to feel the slight swell from the more open waters of the Clyde estuary, we got out the poker dice and started in on a fierce school of Liars. Steadily the throbbing diesels drove us towards the exercise area in Inchmarnock Water, between the isles of Bute and Arran. Less than an hour after leaving harbour, the order was passed through the boat for "Diving stations in five minutes' time." The telegraphs clanged the order "Slow together" to the engine-room, and the pounding beat of the sixteen cylinders died away to a murmur. Soon the cry of "Diving stations" sent the crew hurrying past us along the passage-way to their posts, the telegraphs rang down "Stop together: out both engine clutches," and silence descended. To us, still sitting idly in the wardroom, it seemed delicious to be passengers for a change and to hear the preparations for diving going forward in this gentlemanly manner; fresh from operational patrols, we were used to diving without warning on the

klaxon hooter.* Now, as the raucous blare of the hooter gave
the diving signal through the submarine, we watched the wardroom depth-gauge creeping round until it was steady at 30 feet
and then without comment carried on with our game of dice.
The surface swell was left behind and all motion ceased. The
only sounds were the quiet words of the First Lieutenant giving
his trimming orders in the control-room, the humming of the
ballast-pump emptying a little water from one of the trimming
tanks in obedience to those orders, the voice of the navigating
officer taking a set of land-bearings through the periscope for a
navigational fix, the ringing of the telegraph bells passing
orders to the motor-room as the First Lieutenant became satisfied with his trim and was able to reduce down to the slowest
speed, and the rattling of the dice in the pot as one of us prepared to throw a full house. It was very peaceful and comfortable. We waited for the target vessel to appear.

It was not long before the order was passed to us: "Close up
for the first attack." We made our way to the brightly lit control-room. The target had been sighted passing Cumbrae
Lighthouse and had now altered course towards our diving
position. Phil May was already at the periscope watching for
the target vessel to hoist the attack flags. The rest of us prepared to carry out the attack routine that we had grown so accustomed to on the Attack Teacher. The fruit machine up
against the control-room's forward bulkhead, alongside the
helmsman, was familiar enough, and the navigational plot presented no new problems, except that you had to learn by painful experience which pipes and valves were liable to crack you
on the head as you crouched over the chart-table. Only the man
at the periscope, waiting to make his first attack, was faced with
an element of novelty.

An hour or so later the first attacks were over and it was my
turn to take the periscope. The others went for'ard to the
wardroom to continue the game of dice, and I was left to watch
the target vessel finish her run to the edge of the exercise area

* The term "crash dive" I never heard used by a submariner in wartime. On
operations every dive was what the R.A.F. and the Press call a crash dive.

before turning round for the next attack. Almost automatically, the first thing I did as I took over the periscope was to have a rapid all-round sweep to satisfy myself that we were not running too close to the rocky shore or being approached by any stray vessel that happened to be wandering through the area. I swept rapidly across the green shores of Bute, noted that the rocky outcroppings were at a safe distance, swung past the entrances to Loch Fyne and Kilbrennan Sound, and continued along the steep shores of Arran, which rose nearly three thousand feet to the imposing summit of Goat Fell. The only ship in sight apart from the target was an outward-bound merchantman steaming down the main channel of the Firth of Clyde, some four or five miles away. Completing the circle I came back once more to the target, still going away to the eastward and by now rather difficult to see against the land. My heart was pounding: I was no longer in the Attack Teacher, but in a real submarine containing fifty-odd men, with thirty feet of salt water over our heads, and the target was not a wooden model a few inches long but a live, solid ship—H.M.S. *White Bear*, a large raking motor-yacht with handsome lines that had been taken over by the Navy in wartime as a submarine target and escort vessel. For a moment I was seized by a sensation of panic, now that I was faced at last with the immediate translation of theory into the three dimensions of solid reality. In the Attack Teacher we had been able to concentrate almost entirely on tactics. Now Teddy Woodward would be watching us to see how we carried out our tactics in practice, how we used the periscope, how quickly we made our decisions and how we turned them into precise orders, how we made use of the instrumental aids at our disposal, whether we were likely to lose our heads in an emergency, and above all whether we were liable to run the submarine into dangerous situations through failure to judge time and distance. Waiting for *White Bear* to turn, I felt horribly uncertain of myself.

Suddenly I realised that the space between her masts was opening out, and a few seconds later I could see the full length of her. She was turning. In as calm a voice as I could muster,

I gave the order, "Attack team close up." As Teddy Woodward came aft into the control-room, closely followed by the other perishers, I had one more all-round sweep, to give myself a final reassurance that I had plenty of room to manœuvre in. Bringing the periscope back on to the target's bearing, I saw that she was now pointing almost straight at me, and that the attack flags were jerking up to her yard-arm. I said, "Stand by to start the attack," hoping that my voice would not betray my excitement, and then . . .

"Start the attack! The bearing is . . . *that*. Range . . . *on*. I am three degrees on his port bow. . . . Down periscope, starboard thirty, sixty feet. Group up.* Full ahead together." As I gave the orders, Teddy Woodward had one quick look through the other periscope to check up on my estimations and see that the situation was in hand. Then the periscopes hissed down into their wells, the helmsman swung the wheel over and reported "Thirty of starboard wheel on, sir," the telegraphs clanged their urgent message to the motor-room, the planesmen turned the hydroplane control-wheels so as to plane down to the required depth, watching the needles on the depth-gauges in front of them swinging, slowly at first and then faster, from 32 feet to 50 feet, at which depth they began to correct the dive and steady her at 60 feet. The submarine shuddered as the propellers forced her great bulk through the solid water at nine knots. My attack had begun.

I walked over to the fruit machine, noted the range and distance-off-track, chose my course for running out, and gave the helmsman the order to steady on that course. Suddenly I noticed, to my surprise, that I was quite calm. It all seemed much easier than it had on the Attack Teacher. The familiar submarine control-room was all round me. In the Attack Teacher, the dummy control-room had been circular, and it had sometimes been difficult to remember which way we were

---

* "Group up" is an order to the motor-room to move the "grouper" switch to put the batteries "in parallel" and so apply more power to the motors. When the batteries are "in series" for slower and more economical speeds, they are "grouped down."

pointing: we were then what was known as "lost in the box." Now I found I did not have to perform mental acrobatics to visualise the relative positions of myself and my target. This discovery was very stimulating.

After two minutes' running out at speed I ordered "Group down, slow together," and shortly afterwards, "Periscope depth." The hydrophone operator reported distant propeller noises on the expected bearing of the target. We planed up towards 32 feet. At about 35 feet I ordered "Up periscope," and was looking into the eyepiece of the small low-power periscope as the top lens broke through the surface into daylight. One quick sweep all round to see all clear, and then down periscope. Over to the large high-power periscope, train it on to the target, take bearing, range, angle-on-the-bow, and down periscope. "What's my distance-off-track?" "Distance-off-track is nine hundred yards." "Starboard thirty. Half ahead port. Give me a course for a 110 track." "Course for a 110 track is 325." "Right, steer 325." "Steer 325, sir." "Plot suggests target speed of nine knots, course 260." "Set nine knots. I'll give you another range. Slow port. Up periscope. Bearing *that*. Range *that*. Down periscope. What do you make the angle-on-the-bow, fruit machine?" "That makes the angle-on-the-bow 35." "Mmmmm . . . more like 45. No, leave it. Stand by the tubes. Enemy course and speed from the plot, please." Hell, I haven't had an all-round look for at least two minutes: I'll be getting a black mark from Teddy Woodward. "Raise the after periscope." Quickly sweep over the whole horizon. A small boat of some sort coming out of Kilbrennan Sound, miles away yet. "Down periscope." "Plot now suggests target speed ten knots, course 265." Last two ranges probably more accurate than the first. "Right, set enemy course 265, speed 10. Steer 330." Range getting too close now to use the big periscope. "Raise the after periscope. Bearing *that*. Down periscope. What's my D.A.? Stand by." A quick look through the periscope here from Teddy Woodward. "*What's my D.A.? Quickly . . .*" "D.A. green 9." "Right, up periscope. Put me on green 9. Down periscope. . . . Up periscope. On the D.A.

again, please. . . . Stand by. . . . Fire one. . . . Fire two. . . .
Down periscope. Carry on firing by stop-watch."

To save time between attacks we did not surface completely,
but planed up to show the conning-tower and thereby indicate
that imaginary torpedoes had been fired. *White Bear* flashed to
us by Aldis lamp what her course and speed had been at the
moment of firing, and our signalman read the message through
the periscope. I now handed over to Freddie Sherwood, pointed
out the small vessel I had seen entering the area during my
attack, and went for'ard to the wardroom. The white cloth on
the table, and the glasses and cutlery laid, promised an interval
for lunch after Freddie's attack. Meanwhile Teddy Woodward worked out the results of mine.

After the first few days the attacks became more difficult.
Target alterations of course were introduced and gradually developed into more complicated zig-zags. Finally two old destroyers were added to form an anti-submarine screen for the
target, and our attacks were made more exciting because we had
to dodge the nearest destroyer or dive under it. This part of the
course must have been an anxious time for Teddy Woodward—
and for Verschoyle-Campbell. The temptation to stay at periscope depth to the last possible moment, in the hope of evading
the screen and pressing home your attack, was difficult to resist,

but woe betide you if Teddy Woodward had to sound the emergency klaxon for going deep in a hurry before *you* did. Risks
were all right when an enemy target was at stake, but not while
training. In action, having once gone deep to avoid being
rammed by the target's escort, you would then have to judge
the moment for coming up again very accurately. Too soon,
and you would be hit by the destroyer or sucked to the surface
in his wash; too late, and you would miss your chance of attacking the target. In fact, so dangerous is this game that it was an
inflexible rule during training attacks that once the submarine
was forced to go deep it must stay deep until all vessels were
well past.

We had three strenuous weeks of these attacks. Some evenings we stayed out in the exercise area until dark and practised
night attacks on the surface; the conditions were particularly
difficult because Inchmarnock Water has land on all sides, and
it was hard to see *White Bear* until she was fairly close, especially in the bad visibility of the average northern winter's night.
But on most days we were back alongside *Cyclops* by dusk.

Ours happened to be the first perisher course to have Teddy
Woodward for instructor. He was very anxious to include an
extra week of attacks on fast modern warships as a final spur to
quick thinking, and had arranged to fly us north to Scapa Flow,
the main base of the Home Fleet. Before catching the plane
from Donibristle, we spent a night in Edinburgh. My memories of that evening are fragmentary; what none of us could ever
understand was how the real live goose got mixed up with our
luggage and after various adventures in the North British Hotel
spent the night in Phil May's bedroom. My hangover the next
morning was the worst I can remember, and it was not improved by an alarming incident as we were about to take off
from the airport. We were all packed into the same plane, a
twin-engined D.H. Flamingo; the pilot taxied to the start of the
runway, opened the throttle, and we were half-way across the
airfield, nearly airborne, when the port engine stalled. The aircraft lurched violently and screwed itself to an abrupt stop. We
sat speechless while the pilot restarted both engines, grinned

cheerfully and informed us he would try again. At the second attempt exactly the same thing happened. This was too much. We got out hurriedly, and Teddy Woodward persuaded some-body to transfer us to two separate aircraft.

At Scapa we found the cheerful Favell waiting to put his sub-marine *Trespasser* at our disposal for the week's programme. For four days we carried out attacks on fast destroyers in the somewhat constricted area of the Flow itself. At once the value of these attacks was obvious; the speed at which everything happened was bewildering after our leisurely attacks on *White Bear*. But we soon adjusted ourselves, and on the last day went out into the deep water to the westward of Orkney to attack main units of the Home Fleet through a destroyer screen. This was exciting. I have a memory of looking through the periscope at the start of my attack and seeing, magnified four times by the high-power lenses, the battleship *King George V* perhaps three miles away pointing her bows straight at me, her massive turreted structure dipping ponderously to the ocean swell, cleaving the sea with a snorting of foam and coming on with irresistible deliberation—a sight I shall never forget.

The next day we flew south again. The course was over. One of us had been failed; the rest went on leave to await our appointments. A week of idleness, and then this telegram: APPOINTED P.555 IN COMMAND. REPORT CYCLOPS A.M. 23RD MARCH.—FLAG OFFICER SUBMARINES.

IX

MY FIRST COMMAND

COMMANDER JACKY SLAUGHTER roared his customary greeting as I entered the *Cyclops* wardroom, ordered me a drink, and proceeded in his genial, blustery manner, with his unfailing mastery of the spoken word—sacred, profane and secular—to outline my programme for the next few weeks. *P.555* was at Campbeltown, and I was to take over command of her from Jeremy Nash. The usual time allowed for turning over was two or three days; I was to be allowed a week because I was R.N.V.R., and because *P.555* was an old American submarine differing in several important features from any boat I had known before. It happened that the retiring Captain S/M of the Flotilla, Captain Edwards, was paying a farewell visit to Campbeltown the following morning, and I was to be on board the old Dutch destroyer *Z.5* at 0930, ready to take passage with him.

A fresh south-wester was getting up as we set off in the morning. Even in the shelter of Arran the shallow-draught *Z.5* rolled uneasily to the swell, and when we turned the corner by Pladda to shape a course for Campbeltown the motion threatened to have its usual effect on my stomach. Not wishing to let Captain Edwards see my weakness, I kept out of his way in the fresh air on deck until we opened up the entrance to Campbeltown harbour and came into calm water. At the quayside Commander Corfield-Jenks, the resident Senior Officer Submarines, was waiting to welcome his superior officer and conduct him on his farewell tour of the local Naval establishments. Reporting myself to him briefly, and learning, as I expected, that *P.555* was out on the usual day's exercise until the evening, I escaped from the formalities, dumped my kit and went off for a solitary, windy walk round the coastline past

Davaar Island. Shortly before six I was back on the quay. The surface vessels from the exercise areas were already entering harbour. They were Admiralty trawlers and converted steam and motor yachts which had been fitted with asdic gear, and now took classes of officers and ratings to sea for anti-submarine training. I watched them secure to their various berths, and then looked out across the water, waiting for the submarines to appear round the point.

P.555 came in first. Turning gradually in a wide starboard sweep, she was approaching with an impressive air of confidence and efficiency. I could see at once that she was larger and faster than the old H-class boats, of which most of the Seventh Flotilla was composed. The seamen were already on the deck-casing in the usual harbour-stations rig of bell-bottoms and white jerseys, hauling out the berthing wires and ropes from their stowage inside the casing. Among the men on the bridge I could now make out the figure of Jeremy Nash, tall, erect, concentrated on making a good approach. With enough way on, he stopped engines and glided in until he was nearly opposite his berth, going astern on his motors to halt her exactly where he wanted her, almost parallel to the quay and only a few feet off. Heaving-lines shot out, the bow and stern lines were secured, the spring wires followed, and with a touch ahead on his inside screw and a touch astern on the other, Jeremy snugged her in and came neatly alongside.

Not until he had passed the order, "Fall out harbour stations, finished with main motors," did Jeremy look up to where I was standing. "Hullo, Teddy. Didn't expect you till tomorrow. Come aboard and have a drink." I walked over the narrow plank, and as I stepped on to the submarine's deck I received, for the first time, from the young Sub-Lieutenant on the casing, the salute due to me as a commanding officer, and was so taken aback that I almost forgot to return it.

The fore hatch had now been opened. Absurdly conscious of the appraising eyes of the sailors on deck, I lowered myself into it, and at the foot of the iron ladder found myself in the torpedo-stowage compartment. Here was red-headed Jeremy

Nash to greet me and lead me aft to the tiny wardroom just for'ard of the control-room, to be introduced to Fitzgerald, the First Lieutenant, tall, fair of hair and long of face, with a mouth and jaw that were beginning to impose an appearance of responsibility on a boyish turn of humour. "How do you do, sir," he said, very correctly, as we shook hands. I felt an odd sensation of being an impostor; I had never been called "sir" by an officer before, and here was I presuming to be commanding officer over a Lieutenant of the regular Navy who would normally have been senior to me by virtue of his straight stripes, even though I beat him on length of submarine service.

Jeremy now produced a bottle of gin from the wine-locker. Fitzgerald excused himself to go aft and supervise the starting of the main engines for the usual evening's battery charge. A new face appeared in the wardroom doorway. "Come in, Pilot, and meet your new Captain." I shook hands with Tait, a shy, dark Sub-Lieutenant who spoke with the soft voice of a New Zealander and was one of the first of more than twenty R.N.Z.N.V.R. officers who served in submarines during the war. As Jeremy filled our glasses, the boat began vibrating to the rhythm of the diesels starting the battery charge, and presently Fitzgerald reappeared, followed by Ellis, the R.N.V.R. Sub-Lieutenant who had saluted me when I first came on board. The introductions over, we talked our heads off until the wardroom steward came to lay the table for supper.

We agreed at once that a week was far too long for our turn-over, and that my being R.N.V.R. had nothing to do with it. We planned to complete it in four days, Jeremy to retain nominal command for the first two days, and to stand by for the other two to make sure I had the hang of things. While we were peacefully dived during the day's exercises, we went together through the whole boat until I was satisfied that I understood the broad outlines of its machinery, its pumping and blowing systems, its electrical circuits, and its diving and surfacing peculiarities. At the end of the fourth day we made a signal to Captain S/M reporting that I had assumed command, and Jeremy packed his bags and returned to *Cyclops*.

At five minutes to eight on the fifth morning I climbed the ladder up the conning-tower to the bridge, Captain of my own ship for the first time. I lifted myself out of the upper hatch between the periscope standards and stepped on to the bridge deck. The morning struck cold; it was not yet fully light and there were no colours anywhere. Fitzgerald saluted me with a "Good morning, sir." "Good morning, Number One," I replied, and looked at the sky, which was grey and restless. "All hands on board, sir," went on Fitzgerald, making the usual reports; "fore hatch and engine-room hatch shut, main engines ready, hydroplanes tested, steering tested, telegraphs tested, singled up fore and aft."

I moved up to the front of the bridge, stood on the raised step and leaned forward over my folded arms because I was afraid the trembling of my hands would be noticed. A gabble of sound came up the voice-pipe, translated by Fitzgerald into "Main motors ready, grouped down, sir." I said, "Right, let go both springs." Fitzgerald lifted his voice to Sub-Lieutenant Ellis, in charge of the fore-casing party: "Let go fore-spring," then turned and sang out, "Let go after-spring." As the wires were let go from the quay and gathered inboard with much clangour and scraping, I looked aft to see if it was all clear for me to go out astern. One of the H-class submarines was already under way and turning, and would be clear in a moment. Ahead of me another H-boat was backing out of her berth round the corner; I must move now, or she would have turned and I should have to wait for her to pass. "Let go after-breast, let go for'ard," I said, and waited until the after-breast was clear of the water before giving my first motor order, to make sure it would not be sucked under and wrapped round the propeller. I heard Fitzgerald say, "All gone aft, all gone for'ard, sir," and then ordered, "Half astern port." The rating standing by the telegraph indicator on the port side of the bridge turned the handle, a bell answered dimly below, and at the same moment Fitzgerald, in a quiet, anxious voice, asked, "Obey telegraphs, please, sir?" I had forgotten to pass the important operative order to the motor-room. Angry with myself and feeling rather incompetent, I said, "Yes, obey telegraphs," and passed quickly on to the next order. "Starboard thirty, Coxswain." A slight vibration told me that the port screw was starting to go astern. Looking over the side, I could see its wash beginning to sweep forward. We started moving, and gradually the stern swung out from the quay. We were off.

At this end of the bay the water shoaled rapidly towards the opposite shore. To turn, you had to swing your stern out as far as you dared towards the shallows, and then make a standing turn in the ship's own length.* We had turned through about forty degrees when I judged we had gone astern far enough. "Stop port, group up, half ahead starboard." When we had lost sternway I reversed the wheel from starboard thirty to port thirty, and ordered, "Half astern port." We swung slowly on our own axis, the ship's head still turning steadily to port. Astern, the opposing screws churned the shallow water into a boiling froth. When I thought we could complete the turn by proceeding ahead, I stopped the port motor from going astern and gave the order, "In port engine clutch." As soon as "Port engine clutch in," was reported, I said, "Half ahead port," and a moment later a cough of water from the exhaust and a healthy throbbing aft told me that the port diesel was going ahead. I then changed over to diesel on the starboard side.

We steadied on our course for the first beacon marking the channel of the harbour entrance. A cable or so ahead of us, *H.33* was already turning to port on to the line of buoys marking the course for the open sea. Astern, the other two H-boats were still manoeuvring. I held on, before altering course, until

* The diesels could not go astern; therefore all complicated harbour movements were carried out on the more manoeuvrable electric motors. If you were unskilful at handling your ship and used more battery amps than necessary, you would be very unpopular in the motor-room and engine-room: all the wasted amps you drained out of the "box" during the day would mean a longer battery charge after returning to harbour at night.

I was well over to the starboard side of the channel, because I remembered going aground here two years previously, when *H.28* had cut the corner too fine on a falling tide and spent an embarrassing day in full view of the shore.

The berthing wires and ropes had now been stowed inside the casing. The seamen climbed up over the side of the bridge and down the conning-tower. Ellis came last, and reported the casing secured for sea. I hoped he was right: a wire or a rope breaking adrift at sea, perhaps while we were dived, might entangle a propeller or a hydroplane and cause a lot of trouble.

Once abeam of Davaar lighthouse we could lay a course for our exercise area. "What course, Pilot?" I asked as we emerged into the open water of Kilbrennan Sound, and Tait had the answer ready. "Course 078, sir." "Right, Coxswain, steady on 078." When the Coxswain was steady on the course, I put my mouth to the voice-pipe. "Control-room, stand by to take over lower steering."

"Ready to take over lower steering, sir."

"Take over lower steering, course 078."

"Lower steering taken over, sir. Steady on 078."

Relieved of his duty, the Coxswain went below. I turned to Tait. "Well, Pilot, I'm going to have my breakfast. Will you take over? Let me know when you reckon it's a mile to go before reaching the area." I took a final glance at the cheerless day, at the hills of Arran looming darkly ahead beyond the tumbling sea, and at the other submarines following us out of harbour to their various exercise areas. Satisfied that all was well for the moment, I lowered myself into the hatch and joined the others at a breakfast of eggs and bacon in the wardroom. So far, so good.

When the control-room messenger came along and reported, "One mile to go, sir," I returned to the bridge, rang down "Slow together" and gave the order to "Stream the buffs." The buffs were three small orange marker-buoys which we towed at the end of a long grass line while submerged, so that the asdic instructors in the surface ships could keep an eye on our position. The Second Coxswain threw the buffs well to leeward and paid out the grass line as they bobbed astern, keeping the line fairly taut so that its bight should not foul the propeller or the after-hydroplane guard; the waves being moderately rough, it was a job that needed some skill. An Admiralty trawler was now overtaking us. This was the asdic vessel for whom we were to act as "clockwork mouse," and presently he began flashing the exercise instructions: the duration of the dive and the course he wanted us to steer. We went to diving stations and changed over from the diesels to the motors. I told the signalman to flash "Ready" on the Aldis, and a moment later a large black flag was fluttering up to the trawler's masthead, the signal for us to dive.

"Clear the bridge," I said.

My heart was hammering as it used to before the start of a cross-country race. Tait and the signalman went below. I turned to the voice-pipe and said, "Black flag up. Take the time." Then I climbed down into the hatch, pressed the klaxon button just inside the conning-tower, pulled the hatch over my head, secured the clips, and arrived at the foot of the control-room ladder as the depth-gauge needles were passing the 10-feet mark. "Shut the lower lid. Eighty feet. Up periscope." I looked quickly aft to make sure the buffs were streaming clear, and saw them bouncing merrily in our wake. Then we were passing 32 feet, dipping the periscope under, and I could see nothing but green water. "Down periscope." Reducing speed, we sank gently into the depths . . . 40, 50, 60, 70 . . . and levelled sweetly off at 80 feet. All was well.

"Watch diving."

"Ay, ay, sir."

So began again for me the routine which had become so familiar two years earlier when I had been the junior officer in *H.28* in this same training flotilla: the daily procession out of harbour in the half-light, the run out to the exercise areas, the dive to eighty feet, surfacing at the end of two monotonous hours, diving again, surfacing again, diving, surfacing, six days out of every seven. Occasionally the monotony would be broken by unpredictable accidents which led sometimes to laughter and sometimes to grey hairs.

There was the time when, as we dived, the conning-tower began flooding because the voice-pipe cock had been left open,* and, as if this were not alarming enough, the deck anchor simultaneously broke loose and rattled out to the full length of its cable. Neither of these two mishaps had ever come within my experience before. The whole situation suddenly struck me as very funny: the submarine floating in mid-water, the sea gurgling into the conning-tower, the buffs ballooning up astern, and the anchor hanging down from the bow as if it was on the end of a watch-chain several fathoms long. Really it was too absurd, and I could not help laughing as I turned to Fitzgerald and told him to surface.

There was the time when we were surfacing at high speed for a practice gunnery shoot, and the E.R.A. at the blowing panel suddenly sang out that he couldn't blow No. 3 Main Ballast because the valve had snapped off in his hand, so that there we were with plenty of buoyancy for'ard but none aft,† the hatches already flung open by the gun's crew, the stern still under water, the sea perilously near to spilling over into the conning-tower hatch, and myself not daring to reduce speed lest our stern drop still further. We managed to rectify the situation before long, but it was nasty while it lasted.

There was the time when, for some reason or other, all the bow-caps to the tubes were opened without my knowledge while we were on the surface (we carried no torpedoes in the tubes in this flotilla), and when we dived we were consequently terribly heavy for'ard, and only pulled her up at 150 feet blowing everything.

And there was the evening when, returning to harbour after the day's exercises, I overshot our berth, owing to a stupid

---

* In all British submarines the voice-pipe went direct from the bridge to the control-room, and it did not matter if the bridge end of it were left open, since the hull cock in the control-room was always shut on diving. One of the innumerable peculiarities of *P.555* was that the voice-pipe had a branch leading into the conning-tower. I forgot to shut the bridge cock, and the signalman forgot the one in the tower. Hence the flooding.

† *P.555* had only three main ballast tanks: most British submarines have five.

mistake of my own on the telegraphs, and crashed through a row of fishing-smacks lying side by side in the berth ahead of us. Ropes and wires parted in twanging confusion, startled heads appeared out of companion-ways, and I saw my career as a submarine commander coming to an ignominious end. When the chaos was sorted out and we were safely secured in our own berth, I nerved myself to go aboard the fishermen to make my apologies to their respective skippers. I found them all in conclave over the bottle, blissfully unaware that anything unusual had happened. Much relieved, I was able to gloss over the incident when reporting it to the Senior Officer Submarines, and got clean away with it.

Life was brightened for me during April by the arrival in Campbeltown of Tony Spender with his H-boat and of Freddie Sherwood with a lease–lend American submarine similar to mine. My own boat *P.555* had long ago been dubbed the State Express after the well-known brand of cigarettes, but Freddie's *P.556* was a chronic sufferer from machinery breakdowns and had come to be known as the Reluctant Dragon.

As always in this flotilla, my crew was continually changing. Before the end of April both Fitzgerald and Tait left us, as planned, to join Jeremy Nash in his new U-class submarine. I was reluctant to lose them, but they were replaced by Geoff Stuart as First Lieutenant and Brian Mills as Navigator, and these two officers impressed me so well that I decided to ask for them if I was ever given an operational command.

By the end of May I was growing very impatient with the monotony of our non-combatant activity, and when, early in June, we were sent north to Tobermory to carry out more "clockwork mouse" operations, even the wild beauty of Mull and the inner Hebridean islands failed to subdue my irritation.

Nevertheless, the exercises were more interesting here. The surface ships were new frigates and corvettes in the last stages of working-up before going out to escort the Atlantic convoys, and they required the more advanced types of asdic exercise which allowed us to dive without buffs and to steer whatever courses we liked. This gave me a welcome chance to practise evasion tactics and pit my wits against my pursuer. On these occasions I would try every dodge I could think of: ordinary zig-zags, constant-helm weaving, short bursts of high speed—always trying to discover which of my stunts would prove most baffling to him. Success was evident if five or ten minutes passed without our hearing him go over the top of us, and finally would come the sharp crack of a small underwater charge, indicating that he had lost us and wanted us to reveal our position by firing a smoke-candle.*

At last, in the middle of June, the signal I had been hoping for arrived, appointing me in command of "Job No. J. 3067" at Cammell Laird's, Birkenhead. This, I knew, would be an S-boat, similar to *Saracen*, and it was exactly what I wanted. Singey Anderson came up to Tobermory to relieve me, and after two or three days for turning over to him I was ready to go. As I had to get up very early to catch the steamer to Oban, I said good-bye to the crew and my officers the night before, and asked Number One to arrange for a couple of the seamen to row me ashore to the steamer pier in the morning. In the haggard hour of dawn I washed and dressed as quietly as possible in my cabin so as not to disturb the others. I climbed up the conning-tower and down on to the casing, and there I was surprised to find that the boat waiting alongside was manned by my three officers. As they rowed me ashore I felt deeply moved by this traditional but unexpected compliment, by the inevitable sadness at leaving the ship which had been my home, by the beauty of the land-locked bay at that early hour, with the trees dropping steeply to the water's edge, and by the sight of the trim steamer waiting to take me off on the first stage of my journey south to my brand-new submarine.

* This is a small canister which, when fired by compressed air from a "gun" fitted in the pressure hull, rises to the surface and gives off a white smoke. Smoke candles are also used as part of the surfacing drill in these exercises, two being fired with a five-minute interval between them, to indicate the submarine's surfacing course and enable the surface ships to keep clear.

PART TWO

H.M. SUBMARINE "STORM"

Keel laid down 23 June 1942
Launched 18 May 1943
Commissioned 9 July 1943
Tonnage: Surface 830
            Submerged 930
Length: 217 feet
Beam: 23·6 feet
Draught: 14·3 feet
Engines: Two Admiralty-pattern
  8-cylinder Brotherhoods, each
  engine generating 950 h.p. at
  full power
Motors: Metro-Vickers

X

BUILDING

It was a sweltering morning in late June when I walked once more through the entrance gate to Cammell Laird's. I was so eager to see my new command for the first time that instead of going straight to the Submarine Office I went down the yard towards the main basin to have a look at her. I found her secured alongside the south-eastern wall in the same berth which *Saracen* had occupied less than a year ago.

Her name was *Storm*. She lay in the dusty water, riding high because she was still very light, unmistakably a submarine from the shape of her long, rounded pressure hull and the tapering bulge of her ballast tanks, but still, it seemed, a long way from completion. The massive bronze periscope standards were in position, and the three-inch gun was already mounted; but the periscopes themselves had not been shipped, parts of the casing were still a framework of bare ribs with gashes of red oxide paint, the jumping-wire was not yet rigged, and the bridge structure was only half finished. The usual electric leads snaked fore and aft along the casing and down every hatch, supplying current for temporary lighting and power for the welders and riveters. Wooden beams secured along the water-line as protective fend-offs served also as footholds for the men working on the curving tanks. Among the overalled figures swarming everywhere I could distinguish several faces I remembered from the previous summer. And standing there in the sun beneath the great travelling crane, looking down with a bursting pride at my new ship, with my back to the engine-testing sheds and my ears full of the familiar metallic symphony of hammering and riveting, I felt almost as if the intervening year of voyages and excitements had never been.

A slightly-built man with sandy hair and a bowler hat detached himself from a small group by the fore-hatch and came towards me over the gangway. I recognised Mr Morgan, the Ship Manager, genial co-ordinator of all this methodical confusion. We stood together watching the bustling scene and discussed the new features of the S-class design since the previous year. *Storm* differed from *Saracen* especially in having radar, air-conditioning and an Oerlikon gun. But another important modification was causing an unexpected delay in the programme. Instructions had come through from Admiralty only that week to convert one of the main ballast-tanks to carry oil fuel, and so increase the submarine's cruising range by some hundreds of miles. This news confirmed what I had already heard from Jacky Slaughter in *Cyclops*: that all new-construction submarines were now destined for the Far East, where the distances from base to patrol area were immensely greater than anything we had yet experienced.

Presently, postponing closer inspection of my exciting new toy for the moment, I went off to see if I could find my Engineer Officer. I knew that his name was W. H. Ray, and that he had recently been promoted from Chief E.R.A. to warrant rank at an unusually early age, but I had not yet met him. Climbing the steps to the Submarine Office, I hoped we would take to each other. It was rather important that we should. I walked down a short corridor past glass-fronted cubicles until I came to a door marked H.M.S. STORM—ENGINEER'S OFFICE. Someone was sitting inside in his shirt-sleeves tapping slowly at a typewriter. I opened the door and walked in.

The long bench running down one side of the room was covered with blue-prints, engineering diagrams, bottles of ink, packets of stationery, rubber stamps, signal pads, and sundry boxes of stores and spares. A small safe occupied one corner of the floor, and several wooden cases of tools and other stores were neatly arranged against the wall. On a peg hung an officer's cap and the uniform jacket of a warrant engineer. The man at the desk stopped typing as I entered, and stood up diffidently. He was tall, younger-looking than I expected, and had a large, handsome head covered with tight curls.

"Ray?" I said, and introduced myself as his new C.O.

It was obvious that he had not heard who his commanding officer was going to be. I saw his eyes drop to the wavy stripes on my sleeve, and could not help noticing the flicker of dismay that passed across his face. But he recovered in the instant, came forward and shook hands with a polite smile.

This was not a very good start. In a way, I could understand his point of view. He had been standing by *Storm* for something like a couple of months. He had ferreted around inside her when she was still on the stocks, hardly more than a shell. He had seen her launched, watched her gliding down the slipway to take the water with a great splash and lie wallowing like an empty barrel until the tugs took her and towed her into the basin where she now lay. And then during the last month he had seen the installation of the main motors and the main engines and great batteries, and the construction of the maze of pipes for the compressed-air system, the low-pressure air system, the pumping and flooding system, the telemotor oil system and all the intricate wiring of the electrical circuits. He had climbed inside every internal trimming-tank, fresh-water tank, oil-fuel tank and store tank, and knew intimately each hole and corner of the submarine, not only from the engineering drawings but from personal inspection. *Storm* was his great pride. And now, instead of the man of iron he had subconsciously been hoping for, they had sent a kid of an R.N.V.R. Lieutenant to drive his precious submarine around the sea. He felt all the natural antagonism of the professional for the amateur.

However, there was nothing I could do about it for the moment. Time would have to show whether his fears were justified, and meanwhile there was plenty to do and talk about. He gave me a summary of the present state of the building programme, some of which I had already gathered from Morgan. We looked at the drawings of the new radar mast and the mechanism by which it was raised and lowered. He roughed out on a bit of paper the details of the conversion of No. 4 Main Ballast into a fuel-carrying tank. But I soon grew anxious to have another look at *Storm* herself. I suggested we go down to the boat and have a look through her internally, and we walked down together, the Chief beginning to thaw a little by now. We stood for a moment looking at *Storm* from the wall, then crossed the gangway on to the casing and clambered down through the fore-hatch. The heat below, with the sun beating straight down on the pressure hull overhead, was stifling. It was not easy to move about, dodging between the men working in the confined space, and picking our way over the bare steel decks amongst the coiled wire, lengths of piping, tool-boxes, welding leads, and a hundred other obstacles. The temporary lighting threw a harsh glare over the confusion and cast gaunt shadows into the curving recesses. My heart sank when I saw how far everything was from completion. I simply did not believe that the mess could be sorted out in the six weeks which Morgan had assured me would see the work finished. "They'll never make the date, Chief," I said as we stood looking round the control-room, but Chief, who knew what had already been accomplished since the launching a month ago, was content with the state of affairs. "She'll be ready on time," he said.

We climbed up the bronze ladder through the conning-tower and emerged on to the half-finished bridge. Standing there I tried to project myself several months ahead and imagine the submarine on the surface at night, patrolling off an enemy coast, with the bow lifting and dipping to the swell. By that time she would have acquired a past and a familiar personality of her own. Now she was still a composite of steel parts, in-animate and separate, not yet co-ordinated to a common pur-pose. History would not begin for her until the moment she moved in the water under her own power.

On the official Trial and Completion Programme was an item which read: "Tuesday, Aug. 10th. 6.00 p.m. Leave Basin for River (High Water 7.41 p.m.). Carry out manœuvring trials. On completion proceed to Tower Wharf."

August 10th was just over six weeks away.

"I can't believe they'll make it," I said again.

But they did.

The last few weeks were a hectic time for us, too, and a re-petition of my experience with *Saracen* the year before: order-ing and checking thousands of items of stores, engineering stores, navigational stores, Second Coxswain's stores, and finally victualling stores; supervising trials of various working parts, torpedo-loading gear, hydroplanes, steering gear, anchor gear, voice-pipes, the alignment of gun-sights, the installation of the two periscopes (I had to reject the first high-power peri-scope on account of two spots in one of the lenses, but the next one they put in was a beauty), and numerous other items of machinery and equipment; organising the crew into watches and training them in their special duties; playing the old game of persuading the dockyard to pander to our fads over small de-tails in the ship's fittings. The crew arrived in batches, the key ratings first. When I received a message saying that the Cox-swain and all the seamen would be arriving shortly, I thought it about time I had the rest of my officers to look after them, and sent an urgent signal to Captain S/M 5 asking for Geoff Stuart and Brian Mills from *P.555* to join me as soon as possible as First Lieutenant and Navigator. As Torpedo Officer he sent me a young man I had not come across before, Lieut. R. G. Wade, R.N.V.R., an insurance salesman in private life and with almost no submarine experience. Stuart and Mills had not had much more, and by comparison Chief and I felt like horny old veterans.

We commissioned on July 9th, and gave the usual crowded party inside the boat. I sent a signal inviting Admiral Sir Max Horton, a submarine hero of the First World War, Admiral Submarines at the beginning of the present war, and now in Liverpool as Commander-in-Chief Western Approaches. He replied that he could not come to the party but would like to pay a visit to the submarine two mornings later. This was even better. He arrived in a large car driven by a very beautiful Wren officer. After going through the boat both he and the beautiful Wren sat and talked with us in our wardroom for half an hour. He told us several stories of his submarine adventures in the North Sea in the previous war. On one occasion he had bottomed in 150 feet after being persistently hunted by the enemy. He had turned in to sleep, leaving one of his officers on watch in the control-room. Some hours later he woke up feeling something was wrong; he thought he detected a slight movement of the boat. He went into the control-room and found the depth-gauge still reading 150 feet; he tapped it, and to his horror it swung round to zero. "Up periscope," he roared, and sure enough they were sitting on the surface in broad daylight on a flat calm sea with not a thing in sight. Now, as I well knew, Max Horton was the dynamic force behind the gigantic effort to defeat the U-boats of this war, and on the threshold of turning the tide of the Atlantic battle. On parting he wished me good luck and said, "But you can thank your lucky stars you're not a German submarine."

At ten minutes to six on the evening of August 10th I was standing on the completed bridge, leaning over the side and watching my sailors on the casing preparing the wires for letting go. The eleventh-hour rush of storing ship was over. The last few days had been like the final movement on a telescope lens that turns the blur into sudden focus. A fortnight ago an appalling amount of work seemed still to be done, but Cammell Laird's had wrought their usual miracles. In her smart coat of navy grey, with her number *P.233* painted in man-high white figures on the side of the bridge, and with a new white ensign flying, *Storm* at last looked like one of His Majesty's submarines. It was thrilling to hear the familiar reports coming up the voice-pipe to Number One, and the *ting-ting* of the telegraph bell replying to the testing orders from the bridge. The ship was quickening into life.

There was no ceremony, but everyone was conscious of the Occasion. I think even Chief found it difficult to sound matter-of-fact when, for the first time, he came up from below and reported to me, "Main engines ready, sir." A tug was waiting in the middle of the basin, standing by in case anything should go wrong. The gate had already opened for us, and a slight swell from the river had come in to stir the sleeping water. On the wall beside us a small bunch of the dockyard men, who had been putting finishing touches at the last moment, were staying behind to watch the first venture of the ship they had built. The compulsory pilot was on the bridge with us; and so was Morgan, no doubt anxious that the ship should acquit herself well, and that her new Captain would not damage her by crashing the basin wall. I was indeed acutely aware of my responsibility for this fantastically complicated ship which had cost a year's work and over £300,000 to build, but that only made the moment more exciting. I felt strangely calm and confident.

We were all ready. At exactly six by my watch I gave the orders, "Obey telegraphs. Let go aft. Let go for'ard." The dockyard wires were lifted off the bollards and fell into the water to be drawn up by the men on the wall. "Port thirty, Coxswain." We had been secured with our port side to the wall and our bow pointing away from the river. We should have to swing our stern right out into the middle of the basin and make a standing turn before we could go ahead through the gate. I gave my first movement order:

"Slow astern port."

Until we were clear of the basin and well out in the river, I should not be using the diesels, and all our first manœuvres would be on the electric motors. "Port motor going astern, sir," reported the telegraphsman, and looking aft I could see a ripple growing in the water between us and the wall. Then the wall began sliding gently past. We were under way.

By going slow ahead starboard and half astern port, with my wheel hard over to port, I got her going slowly astern with her tail swinging steadily out, and she came round, as docile as a horse that knows its master, until she was pointing straight at the middle of the open gate.

"Stop port. Midships. Slow ahead together."

When you have a small gap to negotiate it is wiser not to con the ship by helm orders, but to leave the steering to the man at the wheel. "Right, Coxswain," I said, "take her straight through the middle." Chief Petty Officer Wells was a stolid,

K

imperturbable sort of man with a twinkling eye, but I could tell by the way he answered "Ay, ay, sir," and lifted his burly head to watch his marks, that he was secretly pleased at having this confidence placed in him so early. We were plumb in the middle of the gap as we slid through it at about five knots, and then we were out in the Mersey. I took over control again with "Starboard fifteen," turning up river with the last of the flood.

I wish I could describe the exhilarating sensation of being in charge of a new ship that is slipping through the water under her own power for the first time. I stood on the raised step at the side of the periscope standards, observing the movements of other shipping, keeping an eye on the chart, enjoying the breeze on my face and excitedly aware of the great bulk of the submarine below me thrusting forward through the water, her lines no longer obscured by the clutter of dockyard paraphernalia. The river-front of cranes and scaffolding slipped past us to starboard, and presently we were off Rock Ferry and could see the Royal Rock Hotel, where we officers had been living. We shone our six-inch Aldis towards the hotel in the hope that Mr and Mrs Gladstone would be looking out for us, and then it was time to turn. Going astern on the inside screw, we swung hard to port until we were facing down river and stemming the flood-water. There was very little shipping about, so we decided to try the diesels. They started at the first attempt with no trouble at all, and we cheered and gave Chief full marks. We ran down river on the engines towards Alfred Lock, with the high buildings of Liverpool's water-front some way off on our starboard bow, then went on to the motors for entering the lock. There was a nasty eddy across the entrance, but the pilot had warned me about it and I was lucky enough to judge it exactly right. We came gently to rest against the slimy lock wall, and Morgan, greatly relieved, said, "Very nicely, Captain, very nicely." I blushed with childish pleasure. Passing through the lock we secured on Tower Wharf.

Here we spent three days while the de-gaussing experts covered us with rubber-insulated cables and passed electric currents through the hull to render us temporarily safe from magnetic mines. We took the opportunity to get all personal kit on board and clean the boat up generally. We were due to sail for the Clyde early on the morning of Saturday, August 14th, to join the Third Submarine Flotilla in Dunoon. The sloop *Cutty Sark* had already arrived to escort us up the Irish Sea.

It was not until the afternoon of Friday the 13th that the snag was discovered. During a final check on all moving parts, in preparation for the Trim Dive we were due to carry out as soon as we got to sea, it was found that the after hydroplanes had seized almost solid. It was vital that the planes should function correctly, as it is by these that a submarine is controlled while under water. The only possible explanation was that the hull-gland bushes, which contained some new type of packing, had swollen. To remedy this there was nothing for it but to put *Storm* into dry dock.

This meant our departure would have to be delayed a week. Dejectedly I went over to *Cutty Sark* to break the news to her C.O., and later sent off a signal to Captain S/M 3 at Dunoon explaining the situation. The worst of it was that the submarine was uninhabitable in dry dock, and we had all vacated our digs and hotel rooms. We had to make emergency arrangements for the crew's accommodation, as most of their rooms had already been re-let. The officers went back to the Royal Rock Hotel, where the Gladstones had thrown a farewell party for us only two days before. They made us welcome with their usual generosity and somehow managed to fit us in, but it was a miserable time of anti-climax.

A week later, on the morning of Saturday, August 21st, we got away at last, proceeding down the Mersey in the wake of *Cutty Sark*, bound for the Clyde. At the Bar Lightship we dropped the pilot, pressed on into the deeper water of the open sea, and began to make preparations for our first dive.

Morgan and three or four other Cammell Laird technicians were on board for the trip north. Before diving they took the precaution of making their usual "vacuum test." This consisted of shutting the conning-tower hatch * and running the air compressors for a few minutes until a partial vacuum was created inside the submarine. If the barometers showed this was still holding at the end of five minutes, it was proof that there were no serious leaks in the hull or round the lips of any of the hatches. So we stopped engines, kept way on with one motor going slow ahead, and while I stayed on the bridge with only the Coxswain and the Signalman, the rest of the ship's company were battened down below having their eardrums pulled out. We idled through the listless water like a ghost ship manned by an invisible crew. It was an odd feeling, standing there in the bright daylight and the cool salt air, with hatch and voice-pipe shut, cut off from contact with the fifty men sealed up in the hull below me. I sent Robinson, the Signalman, climbing up on the periscope standards to secure a large red flag to the after periscope in readiness for the coming dive. Presently an explosive roar in the voice-pipe told us the test was over. The hull cock in the control-room had been opened, and the air was forcing its way in through the narrow pipe to fill the vacuum. The hatch was flung open, and Morgan emerged to say the test had been satisfactory and everything was now set for the dive.

"Call up *Cutty Sark*," I said to the Signalman, "and make: AM ABOUT TO CARRY OUT TRIM DIVE, TOWING BUFFS, SPEED APPROXIMATELY FOUR KNOTS, SURFACING IN ABOUT TEN MINUTES." While this message was being flashed across, I called down the voice-pipe for Petty Officer Blight, the Second Coxswain, to come up on the bridge and stream the buffs. These, together with the red flag on the after periscope, were to act as markers so that *Cutty Sark* could watch our position, keep out of our way and know that we were all right. We had the three orange buoys on the end of a grass line long enough to reach the surface even if we got into trouble and stuck on the bottom. The sea being calm, the Second Coxswain had no difficulty in dropping the buffs astern with the grass line towing clear of the

---

* The only hatch open at sea, the others being always shut immediately before leaving harbour.

propeller-guards. Meanwhile we changed over from bridge steering to control-room steering.

"Message passed, sir," reported the Signalman. "And from *Cutty Sark*, sir, GOOD LUCK."

The great moment had arrived. I sent everyone below, shut the voice-pipe cocks (we had one each side of the bridge), and took a final look at *Cutty Sark*, now dropping back to take station on our port beam. Turning aft, I stepped down through the hatch. There was no hurry, for this was to be a dive in slow time. I had no intention of diving on the klaxon until the crew had reached a higher state of training. Pulling the hatch lid down over my head, I pushed home the long-handled clips and inserted the safety-pins. The conning-tower still smelt of fresh paint. Descending the ladder I was aware of a pleasurable excitement that was quite different from the anxiety I had felt when I dived *P.555* on my first day in command.

In the control-room the bright lights shone warmly on the new paint, the gleaming brasswork and the white jerseys of the men waiting quietly at their diving stations. The Signalman reached up and pulled the lower hatch shut with a hollow thump. "All set, Number One?" I said, and Geoff, his invariably white face looking paler than usual for the occasion, replied that everything was ready. "Raise the for'ard periscope." As we were still on the surface, the top window of the periscope was thirty-two feet above the sea, and I seemed to be looking down at the water from a tremendous height. *Cutty Sark* was now three cables away on our port beam; it seemed that the whole of her ship's company was lining the starboard rail to watch us submerge. By depressing the top lens I could see our own bow as far aft as the fore hatch. "Turn out the fore planes." The fore planes, unlike the after planes, were a few feet above the water-line, and on the surface it was usual to keep them folded in to avoid damage from pounding in rough seas. Through the periscope I watched them opening slowly outwards like a pair of entreating hands. Remembering our trouble with the after planes the previous week, I decided to try them out once more before we dived. "Test fore and

after planes, Number One," I said. I watched the fore planes
tilting from the "rise" to the "dive" position and then back to
"midships."

"Hydroplanes tested and found correct, sir," reported
Stuart.

"Right, are you all ready, Mr Morgan?"

"All ready, Captain."

This was it.

I said: "Group up. Slow ahead together. Open main vents.
Take her down to thirty feet."

Until we met the enemy there would be no tenser moment
for us than this first committing of our submarine to the deep.
But the sensation of diving was limited, for everyone else in the
boat, to what could be deduced from the movement of the
needles moving on the depth-gauges. Only I at the periscope
could look down at the submarine rippling through the water,
and, as the main vents banged open, see her slumping and
settling, the bow wave easing, the sea bubbling up into the free-
flood spaces of the casing and forcing the air out through the
perforations along the deck. It was as though I were mounted
on the back of a great sea-beast plunging into his familiar
element. Now the fore planes, tilted downwards like fins, were
biting into the water, throwing up their individual flurries of
spray, digging deeper, driving the submarine down by the
head, until the deck was awash and the sea, spilling over it, a
milky stream of disturbance, with little spouting fountains
thrown up by the last escaping pockets of air. At the next lift
of the almost imperceptible swell, the whole of the fore part of
the submarine was abruptly under water, the dark shape of her
swaying and dissolving into the sea's amorphous grey, the bow
wave dying and only the taut jumping-wire still cutting
through the water, but slipping down until it, too, was out of
sight. As the surface came gliding steadily up towards me I
felt a ridiculous impulse to hold my breath like a man caught
on a rock with the rising tide up to his nose.

I turned away from the periscope. A quick glance at the

depth-gauges and the hydroplane tell-tales showed me that Number One had everything under control. We were levelling off to the required depth as surely and confidently as an old campaigner.

Storm was a submarine at last.

XI

TRIALS AND WORKING-UP

AFTER surfacing we followed *Cutty Sark* all day and night up the Irish Sea. In the dark hours I slept only fitfully, remembering how *Umpire* had come to grief during her first night at sea. Chief's engines ran sweetly without a hitch, and at dawn we were an hour ahead of schedule, chugging slowly past Ailsa Craig into the Firth of Clyde, a little drowsy, pleased with our first run, and watching the daylight roll over the hills of Arran. Passing through the boom off Dunoon, we turned the corner into Holy Loch and joined the other submarines secured on both sides of H.M.S. *Forth*, in time for a comfortable breakfast inboard.

Storm lay alongside the depot ship all morning. After lunch we set off up the Clyde and entered the Gareloch for further diving trials. We still had the Cammell Laird representatives on board, this time including Mr Bremner, one of the directors, who had travelled up by the night train. We dived several times, and tested the hydroplanes at varying speeds. All was well, and the following morning we went down river to Inchmarnock Water for the full power trials. This was Chief's great day. For those of us on the bridge it was good sport tearing back and forth along the measured mile as fast as Chief could make us go, stop-watches in hand, waiting for the beacons to come into line. We achieved the specified 14·9 knots at 480 revolutions, and returned to harbour well satisfied. Back alongside *Forth* we squeezed into *Storm*'s little wardroom, and over a bottle of whisky and amid great good humour Mr Bremner and I formally signed the Hand Over.

We, Cammell Laird and Company Limited, Birkenhead, handed over J.3067, constructed by us for His Majesty's Navy, at four p.m. o'clock

this 23rd day of August 1943 off Dunoon. (Signed) for and on behalf of
Cammell Laird & Company Limited, H. BREMNER.

J.3067 has been received, without prejudice to outstanding liabilities,
from Messrs Cammell Laird & Company Limited, Birkenhead, this 23rd
day of August 1943. (Signed) E. YOUNG, Lieutenant, R.N.V.R., Commanding Officer.

Thus casually did I accept, on behalf of the Admiralty, the
latest addition to the submarine fleet. *Storm* was now entirely
ours. But there were to be many occasions later when we remembered Cammell Laird's and blessed the men who built us
such a stout, seaworthy and reliable ship.

We were expected to be ready for our first operational patrol
in ten weeks. The knowledge of this loomed over the future's
horizon, sometimes like an invitation and sometimes, when our
training seemed to be making no progress, like a threat. Before
we could be passed fit for operations we knew we should finally
have to undergo the test of Commander S/M's Inspection.
Commander S/M of the Third Flotilla happened at this time
to be none other than Ben Bryant, now beardless, fresh from
his successful commission in *Safari* in the Mediterranean. He
gave me a cheerful welcome as an old sealion, but left me in
no doubt that he was setting a hot pace for his submarines.

It was eight months since I had left the Mediterranean, and
it was exciting to be once more in an operational flotilla. For
the Third Flotilla was not only vigorously training the new-
comers like ourselves, but at the same time sending boats out
on patrol. Some of these were permanently attached to the
flotilla and slogged away at the Norwegian patrols, attacking
the Germans' coastal traffic and keeping a watching brief on the
Scharnhorst, whose very presence in a Norwegian harbour presented such a menace to the Russian convoys. Most evenings,
after the day's exercises in Bute Sound or Inchmarnock Water,
we returned to the depot ship and there mingled with submariners who had just returned from patrol or were preparing
for the next one. This was a valuable stimulus to those of us
who were still in the training stage, and gave the spur of imminence to our rehearsals.

I vividly remember talking to Hezlett on the day of his return from taking part in towing the midget submarines to Norway for their attack on the *Tirpitz* in Alten Fiord. Great secrecy had surrounded the whole operation. We knew the attack had been successful, that Lieut. D. Cameron, R.N.R. (whom I had got to know when we were doing our submarine training course together) and Lieut. B. C. G. Place, D.S.C., R.N., had managed to lay their explosive charges under the German battleship, that they and their crews had been taken prisoner, and that between them they had succeeded in causing enough damage to the keel to put her out of action for many valuable months; but none of us knew how the midget submarines, with their obviously limited range, had made the long passage across the North Sea. I now learnt that about half a dozen of them had made the trip, each towed by a T- or S-class submarine to within striking range of their target. Until they neared the Norwegian coast the crews had remained on board the parent submarines, leaving a substitute crew in the midgets. They had encountered stormy weather, and the towing itself had been a nightmare. One of the midgets had broken adrift and foundered in the heavy seas. Another had already been manned by its own crew when the tow parted in the middle of the night, unknown to the towing submarine, leaving them adrift and too far from Norway to complete their mission; by a fantastic chance one of the other submarines, running a little behind schedule, had come across them in the dark a few hours later and taken them in tow.

It was not until Cameron and Place were repatriated at the end of the war that the full story of what happened inside Alten Fiord was known. As soon as he dived for his approach up the fiord, Cameron had discovered his periscope was flooded and quite useless. He therefore decided to go in *on the surface*, and actually followed unsuspected astern of a small tug as it made its way through the various boom defences. Only when he was in full view of the *Tirpitz* herself was his purpose realised; as soon as the guns opened up on him he dived towards his target, estimating the distance, and in spite of depth-charging managed to lay his time-fused explosives under the battleship's keel. He scuttled his craft, and he and his one-man crew swam to the surface and gave themselves up. They were drinking coffee in the *Tirpitz*'s wardroom when the charges went off. (Imagine the agony of standing there trying to look unconcerned, knowing the explosion was due any second.) Place also succeeded in exploding his charges under the ship. The only other member of the expedition who managed to penetrate the inner defences, Lieut. H. Henty-Creer, R.N.V.R., was killed by depth-charges before he could get his craft under the battleship. Cameron and Place were both awarded the Victoria Cross.

Most of the new-construction submarines were destined, after training and one working-up patrol, for foreign stations. And as the days went by, more submarines completed their working up and left for the Far East, and new boats arrived fresh from the building yards to take their places. Some of these were commanded by men who had done their perisher with me. Jimmy Launders was already here with *Venturer*, Tony Spender arrived from Barrow with *Sirdar*, Mike Willoughby followed me from Cammell Laird's with *Stratagem*, and Freddie Sherwood, after a delay due to a battery explosion, joined us with *Spiteful*.

Early in our working-up period came the trial of the Deep Dive, the biggest test of *Storm*'s constructional soundness as a submersible craft. The orders were that we were to take her down to 350 feet. This was nothing like the depth she was supposed to be capable of withstanding; nevertheless it was impossible not to feel a little uneasy as we passed 100 feet for the first time and continued gently but deliberately into the depths . . . 150 feet . . . 200 . . . 250. . . . One submarine, in these very waters the previous year, had failed to reappear from her deep dive trial and had never been found. It was now that we became acutely aware that the plating of the pressure hull was only just over half an inch thick. As we continued sinking, Chief and his E.R.A.s moved about the compartments listening for creaks or spurting water . . . 300 feet . . . 320. . . . The pressure squeezing in on the hull must now be tremendous. Even at a depth of 100 feet there is a weight of twenty-five tons of water on every square yard. At 350 feet the total weight impinging on the whole pressure hull would be over 80,000 tons, or about the displacement weight of the *Queen Mary*.

We levelled off. "350 feet, sir," said Number One, and there was a general stir of relief in the control-room. I had, however, previously determined to go beyond the 350 feet— just for the hell of it, no other reason—so I threw a cold douche on the relaxed atmosphere by ordering "380 feet." The faces of the men were politely expressionless, but it was plain they thought the Skipper had gone off his head. As if to support them in this view, we had hardly begun moving on beyond the 350 mark when from somewhere over our heads there came a sharp crack which made us all start violently. By the way Number One turned his head towards me I could see that he now expected me to countermand the order. My own heart was thumping loudly, although in fact there was no cause for alarm. "It's only some part of the hull plating taking up," I said. "Keep her going." I knew it was quite a common occurrence: it had happened on *Saracen*'s Deep Dive. Secretly I wanted nothing more than to go straight back to the surface, but I had said "380 feet" and it must never be thought that the Captain had lost his nerve. So I continued leaning carelessly against the ladder in the middle of the control-room and watched the needle creeping round . . . 360 . . . 370. . . . The surface was now the height of St Paul's Cathedral above us. After this I knew the men would have even greater confidence in the toughness of their submarine. At 380 feet I said, "Right, take her slowly back to periscope depth," and the Deep Dive was over.

A few days later Tony Spender returned to harbour considerably shaken after *Sirdar* had performed an involuntary deep dive, to a depth greater than 380 feet. Submerging for the first morning exercise they had found themselves unusually heavy for'ard, and went plunging down out of control until they hit the bottom at some speed and a fairly sharp angle.

Their first attempts to surface were unsuccessful, and they realised they must be stuck in the mud. Finally, by pumping everything out, going full astern on the motors and blowing main ballast for all they were worth, they succeeded in extricating themselves. When they reached the surface they found mud clinging to the fore-casing as far aft as the gun platform. They were very lucky.

Another item on our programme was the depth-charge trial. The corvette exercising with us had to drop a live, full-size depth-charge at a range of 200 yards, a safe enough distance, but sufficiently near to disclose any serious weaknesses in the shock-proofing of lights or other comparatively delicate fittings. The secondary object of the exercise was to give the crew an idea of the noise to expect and help them realise that the enemy depth-charges they would later hear in earnest were perhaps not as close as they seemed. We dived to thirty feet, with the large red flag on the after periscope to mark our position, and the corvette ran in towards us, carefully judging her course so as to pass at the required distance. For my own satisfaction I took ranges on her through the periscope to check her movements, and when she was abeam of us I made the range only just over the 200 yards. I saw the deadly cylinder shoot out from the stern and drop into her wake. I was unkind enough to pass this information on to those around me in the control-room, and we all waited in a horrible suspense, with a vivid picture in our mind's eye of the beastly thing sinking in the water. When the explosion came it was more violent than I had expected. On surfacing I signalled to the corvette: MANY THANKS. VERY NOISY. GLAD I'M NOT A JERRY.

For our torpedo trials we went up to the top end of Loch Long, where the striking formation of the hills has made an undeviating stretch of deep water that is ideal for a torpedo firing-range. We spent several days in these romantic surroundings, and some of our wives and girl-friends came up to stay in Arrochar. For me, as Commanding Officer, life here was exceedingly pleasant. I lived in the comfortable hotel ashore, and all I had to do was to take *Storm* down to the south end of the firing-range, point her in the right direction, dive, fire off the practice torpedoes as required by the Range Officer, and return to the anchorage opposite the hotel. It was a full-time job for Wade, my Torpedo Officer, and his torpedo ratings, and Number One was kept fairly busy. But I shamelessly took full advantage of a Captain's privileged position, and as soon as the anchor was down at the end of each run I went ashore. I had a private arrangement with Number One that he would fly a large blue flag to indicate when the next salvo of torpedoes was ready for firing. But there was plenty of shore leave for everyone during those few days, and we climbed the hills under the shadow of The Cobbler, walked for miles along the wooded shores of the loch, visited Tarbert on the edge of nearby Loch Lomond, and one evening made village history by organising a great dance in Arrochar's church hall.

It was also here that I had my deserter.

He was one of our most junior A.B.s, a young lad not long in the service, and unfortunately not good at mixing with his messmates. After a while he had begun to imagine that they were all against him, and that the Coxswain had taken a dislike to him, though this had no foundation in fact. At any rate, one night at Arrochar when he was doing his turn as sentry during the middle watch (midnight to four a.m.) he decided to desert the ship. First he wrote a note addressed to me: he was sorry to let me down but he couldn't bear his situation any longer, and furthermore it was no use my trying to find him, as he was quite capable of hiding in the hills for a long time. He left the note in a prominent position in the control-room, stepped quietly into the whaler we used as a liberty boat, rowed in the darkness up to the shallow water at the head of the loch, and disappeared into the night. There was a blustery wind, and it must have taken some courage. He was no seaman, for when we found the boat at daylight it was half on its side at the high-tide mark with the hook over in the mud and one oar still dangling in its rowlock; the other had floated away and vanished. After breakfast we discovered that he had taken his sentry-go revolver and some ammunition. I telephoned the news of his disappearance to *Forth*, and the machinery of the law was set in motion. I was very depressed all day by the desertion. It disturbed my complacent belief that *Storm* was developing into a reasonably happy ship's company. I felt that it must in some way be my fault, and that I should have realised something was up with the lad. But it came as a surprise to everyone. "He's always been a bit queer, you know, sir," was the nearest I got to a solution from the for'ard mess. It gave me an uneasy feeling that day as we exercised down the loch: all the time we were on the surface I imagined our deserter perhaps watching us from the steep slopes of the nearby shore. He was armed, and if he was off his head it might occur to him to take a pot shot at me on the bridge.

Some days after we had left Arrochar and returned to *Forth* in Holy Loch, he was brought back. He had eventually reached home, where his mother had sensibly made him give himself up at once. When he stood before me at the defaulter's table he was very contrite but had little to add, by way of explanation, to what he had said in his note. I had no option but to bring him up before Captain S/M, and he had to suffer his inevitable punishment of several days' detention in a naval prison. After his release I was faced with the problem of what to do with him. The best solution for him, and for his messmates, would have been to get him transferred to another submarine, but this I was not allowed to do. Unless I was prepared to state categorically that the man was unsuitable for the submarine service, I must make the best of my doubtful number and not try to unload him on to some other unfortunate C.O. So I had to take him back. But the arrangement was not a success: the stigma of his desertion remained, and set him inevitably apart. Unfortunately it was not until we were on our way out to the Far East that I managed to exchange him for a spare-crew seaman from the Beirut Flotilla.

We carried out the routine noise trial on a special range in Loch Goil, opening out of Loch Long. As we turned into the loch I dived while still out of sight of the shore station and amused myself by trying to approach the noise range undetected. Unfortunately Lieut.-Commander Percy had heard by telephone that we were on the way, and guessing at our little joke, picked us up on his hydrophones long before we popped to the surface opposite the recording hut. For the Noise Trial we had to secure to buoys, bow and stern, sink to periscope depth and run all the various machines throughout the submarine in turn. The sounds were picked up on the submerged hydrophones near the shore, transmitted to an amplifier in the recording hut, and scientifically measured. Thus we could discover whether our machinery was up to the required standard of sound-proofing and what it was essential to stop if we were being hunted by the enemy. Finally the submarine had to make several dived runs at varying speeds, using each screw in turn and then both together. Owing to the narrowness of the loch it was necessary to surface at the end of each run and go astern back to the starting-point. For all these tests the submarine's C.O. could, if he wished, go ashore and listen to the amplifiers himself. I was very keen to do this, although it would mean leaving Number One in charge of the ship and responsible for diving and surfacing her several times. I remembered what a kick it had given me last year when Lumby had gone ashore for *Saracen*'s noise trial and left me in temporary command, and I could see how enthusiastically Geoff responded to my proposal. So I sat in the little hut anxiously watching my submarine dive and surface, horrified at how much could be heard on the amplifiers.

The noise trial took all day, so we stayed in Loch Goil for the night, leaving in the morning when the light was just beginning to catch the tops of the hills. And in the near-darkness I made a terrible mistake that might easily have had fatal consequences. To keep the crew on their toes I was by now often diving the submarine at unexpected moments, and this morning as we proceeded down the loch I said, without warning, "Clear the bridge," followed close on the look-outs' fingers into the tower, pressed the klaxon button and shut the hatch. We were already submerging by the time I reached the foot of the ladder. Suddenly the telegraph handles, untouched by anyone in the

1. S-class submarine (*Seawolf*) leaving harbour.

2. "The sea rolling along the bulging curve of our saddle-tanks."

3.Control-room of a T-class submarine (*Tribune*), looking aft towards the engine-room.
The for'ard periscope is raised, the after one lowered into its well. *Left:* the panel of lever

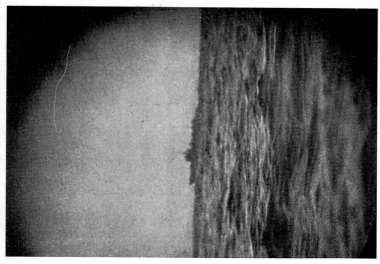

9 and 10. Photographs taken through the periscope of Commander Bryant's later submarine, *Safari*, in the Mediterranean. *Left*, a tanker he has just torpedoed. *Right*, enemy destroyer hunting *Safari*.

11(a). Ben Bryant

11(b). George Colvin

12. Torpedo-stowage compartment, or "Fore Ends." About a dozen men live, eat and sleep here at sea. Spare torpedoes can be seen in the racks to port and starboard. Note stores stowed in every available corner overhead; also the water-tight doors leading to the tube space for'ard.

13. Old L-class submarine beginning to dive. The patches of foam are caused by the air still escaping from the main ballast tanks. Note the gentle angle of the dive: a greater angle would bring the propellers too near the surface and reduce the submarine's speed of diving.

14. Nearly under, the periscopes, gun and top of bridge still visible.

15. Modern A-class submarine surfacing. Note the water draining off the gun platform, the bridge and the after-casing.

16. Underwater photograph of *Auriga*'s bridge.

17. First underwater photograph ever taken of a torpedo leaving the tube. Sent on its way by an initial burst of compressed air, the torpedo thereafter travels under its own power at a steady speed and depth.

18. T-class submarine (*Tribune*) taking in diesel oil from the depot ship after a patrol.

19. *Saracen* in Malta.

20. "The maze of pipes."

21. The galley, where all meals are prepared by electric cooking. The same food is served to the whole ship's company, officers and ratings. To conserve the battery and the oxygen in the air, most of the cooking is done when the submarine is on the surface.

22. *Storm* on her first run in the River Mersey, August 1943.

23. Going down, shutting the upper hatch. Note the drain holes which allow the water to run away when the submarine comes to the surface.

24. H.M.S. *Forth*, submarine depot ship. A floating factory, with torpedo and engineering workshops, crew accommodation, stores, "attack teacher" training, operations room.

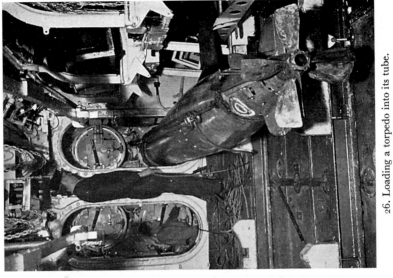

26. Loading a torpedo into its tube.

25. Unloading hammocks and kit-bags after a patrol.

Geoff Stuart   Author   Bill Ray

27. On the bridge of *Storm*, returning from the North Cape patrol,
November 1943.

28. A self-conscious group round the wardroom table. *Left to right:* Bill Ray, Brian Mills, Author, Richard Blake and Dicky Wade.

30. Brian Mills takes a bearing from the bridge.

29. Author.

31. Fisher joined later.

THE OFFICERS OF H.M. SUBMARINE "STORM".

32. Fleet Air Arm photograph of *Storm* approaching Trincomalee at the end of a patrol. The camouflage was designed to break up the shape of the submarine while on the surface at night.

33. Enlargement of part of the photograph overleaf, showing *Storm's* bridge with (*left to right*) the "bandstand" platform for the Oerlikon gun, the radar aerial (lowered), the periscope standards (with perched-up look-out), the upper hatch of the gun-tower, and the three-inch gun.

35. Able Seaman Brown at the Oerlikon gun. (View looking for'ard.)

34. Picking our Japanese prisoner out of the sea. (Page 278.)

36. Three stalwarts: Taylor (gunlayer), Evans (T.G.M.), and Greenway.

37. Boarding party investigating a schooner's cargo off Celebes (page 309). Fisher standing back to camera, the Second Coxswain walking aft.

38. *Storm* entering Haslar Creek, Gosport, on her return from the Far East.

39. Home again! April 8th, 1945.

Note: It was customary in wartime for submarines to fly the skull-and-crossbones flag, or Jolly Roger, on entering harbour after a successful patrol and on returning to England at the end of a commission. *Storm*'s Jolly Roger boasted a small bag compared with those of many other, more famous, submarines. The straight bars, top right-hand corner, represent torpedo sinkings; the crossed guns at top left indicate gun actions, the attendant stars showing the number of ships sunk; the dagger represents our "cloak-and-dagger" special operation; and the little schooner surmounting a row of dots was our own idea for indicating the results of the Celebes patrol.

control-room, turned violently back and forth as though operated by a poltergeist. For a moment we stared at them in un-
belief. Then I realised what was happening. "Blow all main
ballast. Surface. There's someone on the bridge." When I
opened the hatch I found myself looking up into the reproach-
ful faces of Wade and the Second Coxswain. They had been on
the fore-casing making their final check that everything was
properly stowed after leaving the moorings, and in the darkness
I had forgotten they were still there. It must have been a nasty
moment when they heard the main vents open and realised they
had been left up top, but with admirable presence of mind they
had run up to the bridge and moved the telegraphs to attract
our attention. The incident passed off with much laughter, but
the thought that I might have drowned them unnerved me for
some time.

We worked hard during these weeks. Of the seventy days
between our arrival at *Forth* and the end of October there were
only thirteen when we were not at sea. We spent a week in the
Irish Sea exercising with one of the newly formed convoy escort
groups of destroyers and frigates. They were exciting games
and left us plenty of freedom of manœuvre. In one exercise we
represented a U-boat patrolling on the surface; a scouting plane
picked us up on radar, came skidding down at us out of the sky,
forcing us to dive, and his wireless report homed the escort
group on to our diving position from several miles away. My
orders were to dive to a safe depth of eighty feet, but as I wanted
to see the fun I decided to stay at periscope depth as long as I
could. Manœuvring between the approaching hunters I was
lucky enough to penetrate their asdic screen undetected and
watched them sweeping on past me. Half an hour later, when
it was obvious they were getting no warmer, I could not resist
surfacing and signalling HERE I AM, submerging at once before
they had time to reply. The senior officer of the group no doubt
considered it a feeble joke, but at least it saved him a wasted
hour or two.

Later we were sent north to Scapa Flow. This was my longest voyage so far in my own ship, though the navigation was still

L

entirely coastal. Here we spent several days at the familiar, tedious game of acting as clockwork mouse for the benefit of the Home Fleet destroyers, but in return I managed to get in a number of fast practice attacks which helped to brush up what I had forgotten since my perisher. One morning I arranged for a gunnery shoot at a towed target; I intended to go through the usual drill of diving until the target was in range and then surfacing from deep as fast as possible, but when we emerged from the shelter of the islands into the Pentland Firth we saw that the sea for miles around was a boiling ferment; the flood was coursing headlong through the rock- and island-strewn channel between Orkney and Scotland, forcing the water into a cauldron of opposing tide-rips, welling up to the surface from submerged rock obstructions, and swinging round in erratic whirlpools. We dived into this maelstrom but hurriedly came up again when we found we were quite unable to control the boat under water, and continued the shoot on the surface, the gunlayer gaining the valuable experience of firing from an unsteady deck.

When we returned to the Clyde we were nearly at the end of our training. A few more days of intensive exercises—practising radar-shadowing and night attacks, wolf-pack tactics, beach landings, more gunnery, anti-aircraft defence and emergency drills to cope with every imaginable breakdown or damage—culminated in Commander S/M's Inspection. For this alarming ordeal, Ben Bryant came to sea with us for a day and put us through our paces, gave unusual orders without warning, even surreptitiously opened valves or vents so that the trim changed without our knowledge, and all the time he watched for any sign of inefficiency or slowness to respond to emergency. Luckily he failed to catch us out in anything serious, and we were passed fit for an operational patrol.

Ten weeks of living in close proximity had given the crew every chance of shaking down together. Each man gradually revealed his strength and his weakness. We learnt where we could safely put our trust and where further supervision would be needed. At the same time *Storm* was developing a corporate identity of which the men were dimly aware and already a little proud. And living day after day in our tiny wardroom I had got to know my officers pretty well. Geoff Stuart, my Number One, with his square white face and tip-tilted nose; desperately, sometimes almost ridiculously, keen; recently married; a little highly strung, but respected by the men for his energy and efficiency, and to me an entirely satisfactory First Lieutenant. Brian Mills, "Pilot," slenderly built, not very tall, fair-haired; in those days a little unsure of himself and apt to show an Irish resentment when criticised, but full of acute observation, quick to appreciate humour; a good navigator, and pleasant company in the wardroom. Dicky Wade, the only R.N.V.R. officer besides myself, who carried out his watch-keeping and torpedo duties with an unexceptionable but somehow resigned competence, as if he was still surprised to find himself in this queer outfit rather than at his proper business of selling insurance; and who was now worried because his wife was expecting their first baby at about the time we should be leaving for patrol. Richard Blake, a young sub-lieutenant, R.N., whom I have not mentioned before because he only joined us as an additional watch-keeping officer shortly before we sailed; a shy, well-mannered lad with a keen interest in navigation, who quickly fitted in with the others in the wardroom and later on in the commission performed yeoman service.

And lastly, but almost first in importance, Bill Ray. Chief had already, I think, got over some of the disappointment he had felt at our first meeting. So far, at any rate, nothing startling had happened to strengthen his apprehensions about my wavy stripes. Admittedly he must have been horrified at my extraordinary ignorance of the workings of the diesel engine, but early in our acquaintance I had confessed to him my innocence in mechanical matters, and insisted that whenever he had a defect to report he was to take pencil and paper and go on drawing diagrams until I understood exactly what was wrong and how it affected the operation of the ship. I knew it was no good my pretending to understand when I didn't; he would soon find me out and I should be made to look a fool. In fact he warmed towards me for my honesty, and in the end took pride in the improvement of his pupil. For my part I had soon been impressed by Chief's modest and unobtrusive efficiency. I always respected his point of view where the engines were concerned, and by the end of our training Chief and I had reached a state of mutual liking and confidence.

The opportunity for action was drawing closer. At the end of October the Staff Office told me that we had ten days to prepare for patrol and that I could give four days' leave to each watch. I at once went off on leave myself. When I returned I left Number One to see that the ship was got ready, and retired to the Staff Office to study the intelligence reports and find out all that was going on in the North Sea and up the Norwegian coastline. I talked to other C.O.s who had recently been on patrol, read their patrol reports, and generally began to get the feel of the operational situation.

I was due to sail on November 11th in company with *Seraph* (Lieut. I. S. McIntosh, R.N.) and *Seanymph* (Lieut. J. C. Ogle, R.N.). On the morning of the 10th the three of us were called to the Staff Office for our briefing.

XII

INSIDE THE ARCTIC CIRCLE

THE Staff Officer drew back the curtain which hid the operational wall-chart, and we studied the white expanse of empty sea stretching up from Scotland (looking very small in the bottom left-hand corner), past Orkney and Shetland, past the Faroes, past Iceland, into the Arctic Circle and beyond to Jan Mayen Island and Bear Island, with the jagged coast of Norway sprawling up the right flank until it reached North Cape and swung east towards the Barents Sea.* The Mercator gridlines of latitude and longitude, the submarine patrol areas precisely outlined, the known and suspected minefields blocked in and neatly shaded with red pencil, the routes to and from patrol drawn in exact, variously coloured lines—all combined to make our particular war seem like a gigantic paper game; a game in which the enemy's moves were hidden and could only be shrewdly guessed; a game in which there were no winds, no stormy seas, no wet and weary men struggling to keep to route and schedule without sight of sun or star for days on end, only straight lines drawn on paper, and pins for pieces—the coloured pins which represented the positions of our submarines at 0900 that morning.

He was pointing to the top of the chart and telling us where our respective patrol areas were to be. Ogle and McIntosh were allocated neighbouring areas along the Norwegian coastline in the approximate latitude of Tromsö. I imagined my billet would be somewhere further south, perhaps out of sight of land in the middle of the North Sea where I was unlikely to run into enemy anti-submarine activity. I was surprised to learn that I was being sent to the most northerly patrol area

* See previous map on page 66.

of all, off North Cape itself, in the same billet where two years earlier *Sealion*, operating from North Russia, had spent a bleak and fruitless fortnight. At first I was mildly excited by the task of making the 1,500-mile voyage in each direction, but when I looked at the little huddle of pins clustered round Dunoon, saw the one marked *Storm* amongst them, and realised that I was responsible for getting that pin safely over the enormous distance to the top of the chart and back, I was assailed afresh by all my old fears.

For months my chief anxiety had been lest I should, on my first patrol in command, make a fool of myself through some avoidable navigational error or misjudgment. Disaster resulting from a mistake of this sort would not be forgiven by one's crew or by the Staff at home. It was true that I had in Brian Mills a navigating officer on whom I knew I could rely, and I had myself had a certain amount of practical experience of celestial navigation. But I had always been aware that with all the navigational data available there were moments of crisis when the Captain must make a decision, perhaps to disregard a doubtful star-sight because it ran counter to common sense, or to play for safety when approaching land in bad visibility after several days without a sight. When approaching a new patrol billet he must adjust the submarine's speed so as to be able to dive at dawn in the right position, and not so far out to seaward as to waste a day in getting close in. He must choose the best approach for keeping clear of shoal water and for early precise identification of the landfall. Suppose, I thought, I should fail to find my appointed billet among the thousand islands of Norway's coastline; suppose I should through stupidity or carelessness strand my ship on the enemy shore; or suppose on my return journey I should miss the pin-point of the Shetlands altogether and drift out into the Atlantic with empty fuel-tanks? * I was more worried over possibilities like these than I was about encountering the enemy, and it struck me as ironical that on my first patrol in command I should be making the longest voyage of my life.

---

* *Seawolf* very nearly did this when returning from Russia early in 1942.

Meanwhile there were more immediate things to concentrate on. We were to be escorted by H.M.S. *Breda* as far as Lerwick. The Dutch submarine *K.14* would also be sailing in company with us, detaching at Scapa. During our surface passage up the west coast of Scotland we were to burn stern lights at night to facilitate station-keeping. At Lerwick we were to top up with fuel and then sail independently for our respective patrol areas. We were to travel all the way on the surface, not diving during daylight hours, as I had always done before; this comparatively new policy was a little more risky, but would reduce the time of a long passage by two or three days. Between us we agreed not to use radar within sixty miles of the Norwegian coast, except during an actual night attack, since it was known that the Germans had a method of detecting radar transmissions.

The wind was rising as we made our way down the Clyde the following day, and when we turned the corner by Ailsa Craig it was clear that we were in for a rough passage. All that night and the next day a northerly gale whipped itself into a state of fury and flung the sea in our faces. But as we battled our way north past the lonely islands with their magical names—Islay, Skerryvore, Tiree, Coll, Muck, Eigg and Rhum, Benbecula, Shiant, and the rest—I felt, as I had often felt before, that no harshness from sea or wind could ever shake my belief that this is surely the most beautiful and enchanting place in the world. On the second evening, passing through the Minches, we found ourselves in more sheltered water, but at dawn Cape Wrath lived up to its name with a vengeance. We skirted the northern edge of Scotland, passed through the Pentland Firth, where *K.14* broke off and went in to Scapa, and leaving Orkney to port pressed on north-eastward into the unending gale. Fair Isle slipped past us unseen in the driving rain and spray.

At last, towards evening, we sighted Sumburgh Head, the southward-reaching arm of the Shetlands. When it was abeam of us we knew we should be in Lerwick within a couple of hours. If the gale had been westerly the land would now have given us protection, but the wind had gone into the north-east and it was a lee shore that we had on our port hand. There was so much water about that in the darkness there seemed no difference between rain and sea. It swirled round our feet and into our boots as each wave fell roaring over the staggering bridge. It stung our cheeks and whipped our eyes, ran down inside our collars, forced its way into our gloves and trickled down the inside of our sleeves whenever we raised our hands to peer into the angry darkness ahead. Somewhere beyond our thundering bow were *Breda* and the other two submarines suffering the same discomforts.

We had not seen the stern light ahead of us for so long that when the blood-red stutter of an Aldis flashed at us through the watery night it seemed appallingly close. A signal was coming down the line to us. Robinson, our Signalman, was an expert and the message was short, but it cost him ten minutes of desperate concentration to read it through the curtains of wave and spray. PROCEED INDEPENDENTLY INTO HARBOUR was the signal from *Breda*, thus relieving us of our theoretical station-keeping.

Noss Head appeared at last, an abrupt blackness right ahead, and we were able to turn in towards the entrance to Lerwick harbour. Luckily the lights were burning for us; somehow we groped our way in and found the benediction of sheltered water. A lamp flashing from the shore instructed us to anchor as convenient. The conventional word struck us humorously as we nosed slowly in, seeking a berth, for the small harbour was very full, the wind-pressed ships tossing and jerking at their cables. There seemed to be no space left. Finally I edged in as near to the windward shore as draught and nerve would allow, dropped the anchor and paid out cable until we lay close to a bucking corvette. We made four attempts before I was satisfied, and altogether it took us an hour. Twice we swung too near the corvette, and once we dragged, and each time the shivering men on the fore-casing had to heave in the anchor, and all my orders from the bridge had to be passed by messenger, as no voice could carry against the deafening wind. It was midnight before we were able to call it a day and drop, exhausted and frozen,

down the conning-tower into the light and warmth below.
Standing blinking in the control-room I called for the Coxswain
and ordered him to make a special issue of rum to the bridge
and anchor parties. In the wardroom we opened up the wine-
locker and knocked back a large tot of whisky all round. The
cook had not wasted the last hour, and we were soon stuffing
ourselves with a steaming hot shepherd's pie, our first good
meal for twenty-four hours.

It was a discouraging start. All our bridge clothes were sodden; much water had come down the conning-tower into the
control-room; half the crew had been ill with sea-sickness, and
my own stomach had been in a state of scarcely suppressed re-
bellion ever since we turned the corner at Cape Wrath. After
topping up with fuel in the morning we were due to sail again
after lunch, and for all we knew this gale was going to last for
days. Even here in harbour our situation needed vigilance, and
the weary watch-keeping officers must split what remained of
the night into anchor watches, with the motors held in readiness
for an emergency move.

I turned in and was asleep in a few minutes.

After an early breakfast we upped anchor and proceeded
across the gale-whitened harbour to secure alongside a small
tanker. Leaving Chief in charge of fuelling operations, I
assembled the hands in the control-room below and with the aid
of a chart explained to them where we were going and what we
might possibly expect to see in the way of enemy aircraft, U-
boats, patrol craft and targets. There was an astonished murmur from the men when they saw how far north our billet was.
There was no danger now of the secret going beyond the submarine itself, and I had long ago decided that whenever possible
I would keep my crew informed of what was happening. I felt
they had a right to know, because their own lives were at stake;
and I was sure that if the look-outs were constantly aware of the
situation they would always believe in the possibility of sighting something at any moment and consequently use their binoculars with intelligence (half the battle in looking out). Some

submarine C.O.s did not agree with this policy on grounds of security, but I am sure it paid dividends in look-out efficiency.

The wind had backed to north and increased in violence by the time we slipped from the oiler at ten minutes past one. *Seraph* and *Seanymph* were not sailing until the evening, and we envied them their few extra hours of rest. The moment *Storm* stuck her nose outside Noss Head the gale sprang at her as though it had been lying in ambush. We gritted our teeth and butted into it. Three miles off the land we dived to catch a trim, not having done so for three days. The movement was so lively at periscope depth that we had to take her down to eighty feet. Even at that depth the sea rocked us gently like a cradle; normally you would expect to find absolute calm below periscope depth, but if rough weather has lasted for several days, as it had on this occasion, the wave motion is perceptible sometimes down to a hundred feet, particularly in shoaling water. When Number One was satisfied with his trim, we surfaced into the mountainous sea, and as first out of the hatch I took the brunt of the wall of foaming water which shattered itself on the bridge before we had gained full buoyancy. In the next two hours so much sea poured over us that all our five pairs of binoculars were flooded and rendered useless. By working all night, Cottrell, the E.A.*, managed to take them all to pieces and make four of them serviceable by morning. Meanwhile we kept look-out with the naked eye.

Soon after nightfall, about seven o'clock, we were sitting at table in the wardroom, trying to make the best of a scratch meal of corned beef and boiled potatoes, when a heavier sea than usual came cascading down the conning-tower, followed by a heavy thump and a painful sensation in our ears. Realising what had happened, I ran into the control-room and moved the engine telegraphs to STOP. The weight of the last wave had knocked the upper hatch shut, with the result that the engines had pulled half the air out of the boat, causing an uncomfortable vacuum. The sea was tumbling out of the voice-pipe into the control-room

---

* Electrical Artificer. Cottrell was an ingenious inventor of gadgets and a universal handyman.

like flood-water through a drain, and for a moment it seemed as
if we must be completely submerged. (Afterwards Brian Mills,
who was officer-of-the-watch on the bridge, assured me that we
were.) When the voice-pipe was clear I called up to see if they
were all right up top, and Brian's spluttering voice reported that
no one had been washed overboard. We then opened the
hatch and (to quote from my Log):—

1905   Went slow ahead. Tried increasing to 280 revolutions, but the
       sea threatened to repeat hatch-shutting performance. Decided to
       remain at slow together until sea moderated.
2007   Muckle Flugga [northern tip of the now invisible Shetlands]
       abeam by dead reckoning. Altered course to 019°.

15th November

0055   Gyro compass defective as a result of the heavy rolling. Steered
       by magnetic compass. Seas still short and steep, continually break-
       ing over bridge. Remained at slow together throughout the night.
1035   Sea appeared to be moderating. Increased to 340 revolutions,
       making good estimated 7½ knots. Gyro now seemed to be steady
       about 10° off magnetic and nothing seriously wrong. Magnetic
       compass too jumpy owing to violent pitching and rolling, so re-
       verted to steering by gyro. Sun azimuth in the late afternoon con-
       firmed gyro settled down and correct.
1636   Increased to 400 revolutions, making good 10 knots. Sea still
       moderating.

16th November

0107   Increased to 420 revolutions.
0740   Dived for trim and exercised emergency drills.
0829   Surfaced. Proceeded at 420 revolutions, zig-zagging, making
       good 11.4 knots. Visibility excellent, except in snowstorms.
1358   Dived for unidentified aircraft sighted very far away on the eastern
       horizon on northerly course.
1430   Surfaced and proceeded.
2100   First star sight since leaving Lerwick. Bad horizon, but sight
       indicated position approximately 50 miles SSE of dead reckoning
       position.

I was now getting seriously worried about the navigation.
When you are out of sight of land, and the sky is so continually
overcast that you cannot check your position by observation of
sun, moon or stars, you can do no more than keep a careful plot
of your course and speed, make allowances for your zig-zag, for

known currents, for the over-reading of the Chernikeef log in rough weather, and for possible errors in steering—in other words, navigate by D.R. or dead reckoning. This we had had to do for over two days,* but I was staggered when this first star sight put us no less than fifty miles behind the D.R. It was an error of one mile in every hour since leaving Lerwick. This meant one of three things:

1. We might have made a serious miscalculation in the D.R. But I went over the plotting again and again and could find nothing wrong; all possible allowances had been made.

2. Perhaps the star sight was entirely erroneous. Admittedly the horizon had been very woolly during the few minutes the stars were visible, and the five position lines when plotted were nowhere near passing through the same point. But a rough average gave a clear indication that we were a long way astern of our D.R.

3. We might be experiencing an adverse current. The information in the Admiralty pilot gave no indication of a south-going current at this time of the year. Perhaps the prolonged northerly gales had created a surface current. If so, to account for the fifty-mile error we should have to assume an average current of at least one knot.

I comforted myself by hoping for a good star sight in the morning.

Soon after midnight we received a signal from Flag Officer Submarines with news for Wade. He himself helped to decode the signal, and there was great excitement round the ward-room table as the message was gradually unravelled and found to announce the safe arrival of a son.

The day just starting was my own birthday, my thirtieth, and I took it as a good omen for the future of our navigation that when I went up on the bridge in the chilly hour before dawn, the paling sky was full of stars and the visibility excellent. To keep my hand in I decided to take a set of sights as well as Pilot,

---

* We were now just on the edge of the Arctic Circle, and in these high latitudes the autumn sun, even at noon, is too low on the horizon to be of any use navigationally. We had to rely on the stars, if any, at dawn and dusk.

and when the horizon had sharpened to a hard rim Brian Mills
and I were both on the bridge, busily shooting the stars before
they disappeared.

Taking a star sight in a submarine can be an uncomfortable
business in rough weather. You must wrap the sextant in a
towel when carrying it up the conning-tower, or the mirrors and
lenses will be soaked before you reach the bridge. And what
with dodging the spray, and bracing yourself against the violent
movement, and trying to catch the stars in the cloud-gaps, and
at the same time see the horizon between the leaping waves
(your "height of eye" in a submarine is only about fifteen feet),
it is a miracle sometimes that you get any useful result at all. In
the Arctic winter freezing fingers are an additional handicap,
but that is a difficulty familiar to all navigators in high latitudes.
In general the drill is much the same in a submarine as in
any other ship, although it is slightly complicated by the fact
that you cannot have the chronometer on the bridge. With the
sextant in your right hand, you adjust the vernier scale with the
fingers of your left. When you have the mirrored reflection of
your star swinging on the tangent horizon, you call out "Stand
by . . ." and when you have it exactly *on* you say "STOP!"
The officer-of-the-watch shouts "STOP!" into the voice-pipe,
and down below in the control-room the helmsman repeats
"STOP!" to the P.O. of the watch, who, leaning on the chart-
table with his eye on a chronometer, takes the exact time to the
second and writes it down. You then read off the star's angle
(its altitude) from your sextant, and call out the degrees and
minutes of arc; this information, too, is passed down to the
control-room. If you don't know what star it is (perhaps you
have only caught a glimpse of it through a hole in the clouds),
you take a bearing of it so that you can work out what it is from
the star globe afterwards. If you do recognise it, you sing out
its name. And what splendid names they are . . . Procyon,
Capella, Arcturus, Vega, Deneb, Sirius, Altair, the Pleiades,
Aldebaran, Betelgeuse . . . all wheeling in space through the
centuries with such precision that astronomers have forecast
and tabulated their movements for years ahead, enabling

navigators to reach out into the firmament from our spinning earth and pull down the information they need.*

It was a good sight we obtained that morning. When we had worked out our respective stars, Pilot and I found that our positions agreed within a mile, so we halved the difference and marked the spot on the chart with the time against it. This sight confirmed the existence of a strong current of two knots in a SSE direction. At last I felt I knew where I was. But my newly gained confidence was shaken only a few hours later when a message came down from the officer-of-the-watch to say that land was in sight to the eastward. I could not believe it, but when I went on the bridge I could see it for myself with the naked eye. The air was dry and bitter, and the visibility superb. And on the horizon was a low, jagged excrescence, blue with distance, but sharply outlined and not to be denied. Through my binoculars I could even see that the peaks were covered in snow. It was very disturbing. I took a careful bearing and went below to study the chart.

The land was obviously the highest point of the Lofoten Islands, but if our morning sight was correct it was ninety miles away and ought not to be visible. And then I remembered the cold dry January of 1941 when I was in *H.28* exercising off the Isle of Mull in weather exactly like this: the air brittle, frozen, marvellously clear, when the comparatively warmer sea water caused a shallow layer of moister air which acted as a lens for the creation of fantastic mirages—buoys transformed into tall spars which shrank as you neared them; masts and funnels

* For the benefit of those who are as ignorant of celestial navigation as I was before the war, the principle is briefly as follows: You think you are in a certain position in the middle of the ocean, say X. By looking up tables you can find out how high above the horizon any star should be, seen from that position, at the time you take your sight. With the sextant you measure what the height-angle of the star actually is. If the actual height is greater, that means you are nearer the star than you thought you were. Calculation from the tables will tell you how far. Let us assume you find you are ten miles towards the star, which is, say, due east. On the chart you draw a line eastward from position X. You mark off ten miles along this line. Here you draw a second line crossing it at right angles. You are somewhere on this second line, which is known as a "position line." Repeating the process with other stars you should finally have several position lines all of which pass through the same point. This point is your "observed position."

stretching and contracting like pistons; distant islands lifted above the horizon when they ought to have been invisible.

This last phenomenon was repeating itself now. And when we took our star observation that evening, in apparently ideal conditions, the refraction so raised the horizon itself that when we had worked out the sight, the position lines, instead of passing through a single point, formed a pentagon measuring roughly ten miles in each direction. This time Blake had also taken a sight, and the three of us separately got the same result. So we pencilled a spot in the middle of the pentagon and said, "We're there!" Later we were to experience the same trouble with refraction in the Red Sea.

After this we had no serious difficulty with our navigation. All the officers got into the habit of taking sights whenever they could; Blake in particular was showing great promise as a navigator. Every evening at star-time the wardroom was a scene of intense mental activity. Two of us would be methodically working through the calculations on the stars we had just taken; the others would be assisting by identifying the stars from the star globe, or reading out the required information from the *Nautical Almanac*, or finding the logarithms from *Inman's Tables*, and the excitement grew as we plodded through to the result. Intercepts of less than half a mile were greeted with sceptical cheers. Even Chief began to take an interest, and although he never actually wielded a sextant himself, he nevertheless got a rough idea of the principle of the thing and could find his way about the tables without any trouble.

We pressed on northwards, and the Pole Star climbed steadily higher over the northern horizon. The weather was brilliant, bitterly cold but crisp and invigorating, and the nights were ablaze with moonlight and stars and northern lights. The wind continued fresh, but the sea had settled down to a long, comfortable swell. We recovered quickly from the rough handling we had endured at the start of the voyage. Nobody was seasick any more. And in the evenings the messes buzzed happily with argument and noisy games of uckers.

We were not without our moments of alarm. One early morning when it was still dark, the control-room messenger, changing the recognition flare on the bridge at the appointed hour, let it slip from his fingers; in trying to catch it he accidentally yanked the string and set it off, and it fell sputtering down the conning-tower. At the noise of the crash we tumbled out of our bunks and found the control-room ablaze with vivid light and acrid smoke. I turned to my drawer for a glove, but Number One, braver than I, picked up the flaming cylinder with his bare hand and holding it by the base scrambled up the tower and hurled it into the sea. The engines soon sucked the fumes out of the boat, but we knew that in the darkness the flare must have been visible for miles around when it went over the side, and for the next half-hour we felt as conspicuous as a burglar who has inadvertently sneezed.

It must have been the following night that for the first time since becoming a captain I had my dreams shattered by the dreaded call of "Captain on the bridge!"—felt the plunge of alarm in the pit of my stomach, sprang out of my bunk (fully dressed and booted as always, with binoculars slung round my neck), blundered into the control-room and climbed the tower, fighting my way out of the mists of sleep, in an agony of apprehension at what I might find when I reached the top. Stumbling out into the bitter night air, I saw from the wheeling sky that we were turning rapidly to port. Number One was passing helm orders down the voice-pipe . . . "Midships . . . steady." I moved up beside him. "What is it, Number One?" He said he had seen a splash in the water and a streak of phosphorescence coming straight at us; it might have been a torpedo, but he couldn't be sure; perhaps it was only a large fish. We were now making directly for the spot. We stared through our binoculars, sweeping ahead of us and on either side of the bow. But we saw no dark shape against the muffled horizon, only the empty and indifferent sea. After a few minutes we swung back to our original course. Almost certainly it had been a porpoise leaping; but it might not have been, and Number One had done the right thing. "Turn end-on the quickest way," was my

Standing Order for torpedo sightings, and: "The officer-of-the-watch is to call me for all enemy sightings and at any time if *in any doubt whatsoever.*" I never lost an opportunity of impressing on my officers that I would prefer to be called to the bridge a hundred times in the night, no matter how trivial the occasion, rather than be called too late. There were times in later patrols, especially after a succession of anxious nights, when I found it difficult to live up to my own precepts; to be called out on a false alarm just after I had dropped into a sleep for which my brain had been screaming for forty-eight hours was absolute torture, and it was often as much as I could do to tell the officer-of-the-watch that he had been right to call me.

By midday on the 18th we were approaching the position where we were due to turn in towards North Cape. During the morning I had half expected to see *Venturer* on her way out from the billet—we were relieving her—but there was no sign of her, and at 1300 we swung round on to our easterly course. In fact an hour earlier *Venturer* had sighted *us*, seen the top of our periscope standards emerging over the horizon and immediately dived to carry out a dummy attack on us. I knew nothing of this until I met Jimmy Launders on our return to *Forth*, when I was considerably mortified at finding our look-out efficiency thus shown up. At the time, however, unaware that we were under observation and being used as a practice target, or of how lucky we were that *Venturer* was not an enemy submarine, we zig-zagged blithely on our way.

1300   Altered course to 090°. Ceased radar watch in view of approach to coastline.

1520   Star sight. Position 71° 03′ N. 18° 56′ E. Still being set to the south. [Our morning sight had indicated a set of no less than three knots, but I decided to ignore this in running on my D.R. and turn in towards the coast too early rather than too late, to make sure of hitting Norway *somewhere.* I did not want to run the risk of missing it altogether and passing to the northward of North Cape.] Altered course to 079° to regain route. Slowed to 10½ knots and increased zig-zag to delay arrival on billet until shortly before dawn.

2030   Land sighted bearing 110°. This was shortly afterwards identified as the northern tip of Söröy. More land appearing gradually, some of it white with moonlit snow.

M

2248   Obtained rough land fix. This put us closer to Söröy than ex-
       pected, indicating slight set in towards the coast. Further fix at
       2351 confirmed this. Altered course to north to gain latitude of
       patrol position. Land fixes now giving fairly accurate positions.

We had made our first landfall. It was a commonplace, of
course, and it would have been a disgrace not to have done it,
but we had crossed 1,500 miles of empty ocean and found the
right place, and I have to admit that our arrival was a tremendous relief to me. And at 0350 in the morning, the 19th, we
entered our patrol area, with two hours to spare before it would
be time to dive. It was bitterly cold and there was a short, uncomfortable sea which from time to time jumped up and slapped
a handful of icy spray over the bridge. The moon was bright,
and we patrolled up and down its track so as to present as small
a silhouette as possible to any enemy that might be down moon
of us. At six o'clock we dived, went to eighty feet because it
was still too dark to see through the periscope, and moved slowly
in towards the enemy-occupied coast.

Two hours later we came quietly up to thirty-two feet and I
made my first periscope examination of the patrol area.

It was an uneventful patrol. We had nothing very interesting
to look at. There was a brooding sullenness about this frozen
extremity of Norway, the most northerly tip of the whole Euro-
pean continent, over 250 miles inside the Arctic Circle. The
land was all black cliff or white snow, with high mountains
rising sombrely behind the coastal fringe. Blinding snowstorms came sweeping off the land without warning and were as
suddenly gone. Sometimes these sudden falls of snow made
startling changes in the appearance of the landscape, but in
general the left- and right-hand edges of the islands were so
clear-cut that position-fixing was easy. Some days the off-shore
wind knocked up a bit of a swell which made depth-keeping a
little difficult, splashed the periscope, and provided good practice for the planesmen and watch-keeping officers.

Hidden round the corner to the south-west, not very far
away, was the port of Hammerfest. The numerous islands

formed a natural screen behind which the Germans could move their ships unobserved. But if they wanted to send the *Scharnhorst* to attack our Russian convoys, she would have to break out through one mousehole or another. One of these mouseholes was the gap we now spent the brief daylight studying with great interest through the periscope. If the *Scharnhorst* chose to emerge here, our job was to sink her if we could, or, failing that, report her by W/T to the Admiralty. Between us and the nearest land was an area marked on our chart as "German declared minefield," and we were to patrol just outside this area, entering it only for the chance of an attack.

One night we thought our chance had come. We were on the surface charging batteries, patrolling slowly up and down about two miles outside the minefield, and keeping end on to the moon, which appeared fitfully between the clouds. Blake was officer-of-the-watch. We were playing a game of uckers in the wardroom after our supper when the night alarm buzzer sounded. As I made for the conning-tower I heard the helmsman repeat, "Hard a-starboard, sir. Captain on the bridge!" This could only mean a target. When I reached the bridge we were swinging round towards the land. Through my binoculars, I could certainly see a black shape standing out distinct from the mainland: its outline was not clear, but if it was a ship it was a very large one and it was steering in a north-easterly direction. "All right, Blake, I'll take her," I said. "Stand by to take bearings." I altered to port to close the target's estimated course as rapidly as possible, and rang down for FULL AHEAD TOGETHER. In a few seconds we were thundering through the water. "Stand by all tubes." My hands were trembling with cold and excitement. Presently I realised the target was getting no closer. Blake was taking frequent bearings and passing them down to Pilot below, but they were changing very little and, oddly enough, moving aft instead of ahead, as I would have expected of a fast target. Pilot now called up the voice-pipe to warn me that we were about to enter the declared minefield. I asked him what the plot suggested, if anything, and he answered, "Well, sir, the bearings are changing very little, but they all seem to go through one of the small islands." This confirmed what I had already begun to suspect. I ordered SLOW TOGETHER and altered course to starboard to point once more directly at the target; it was soon obvious that it was absolutely stationary, and in fact now much less distinct than it had been. Regretfully I concluded that some trick of lighting, from the moon or the northern lights, had momentarily lit up the snow on the mainland and left the island in darkness, standing out sharply from the background. I ordered, "Fall out diving stations," and we returned to our patrol line and our game of uckers.

Apart from this false alarm and the sighting, on two successive nights, of distant searchlights sweeping the sky in the direction of Hammerfest, absolutely nothing happened to break the monotony of the patrol. However, I was well content with this. The ship's company were getting used to the daily routine of a submarine on war patrol, and for my part I was able to learn gradually to delegate responsibility to the officer-of-the-watch, to relax in the wardroom and in my bunk, to sleep with only a small part of my mind listening for "Captain on the bridge!"

Here is a typical day's routine on this patrol:

About 0600. Word comes down from the bridge to "tell the Captain it's beginning to get light." I am woken by the P.O. of the watch and go up on the bridge, where I can see the faintest paling of the sky to the eastward. Glancing round at the dark land to reassure myself that we are still roughly in position, I pass the word for "Diving stations." After a careful look round the whole horizon through my binoculars I go below, leaving it to the officer-of-the-watch to dive the boat, for I want my officers to practise diving her on their own as often as possible. In the still darkened control-room the men are waiting at their diving stations. The diving-klaxon sounds twice, the look-outs come clattering down the ladder, and as we start diving I listen up the tower for the sounds of the hatch shutting and the clips going home. The officer-of-the-watch descends, and stands by to take over the depth-keeping from

Number One and complete his watch. We glide down to eighty feet. It is all very peaceful, now that the engines have stopped and there is no longer the gale of icy air whistling down the tower: no sound but the occasional hum of the pumping motor. We go into "watch diving" routine. It will be two hours before it is light enough for periscope work (there is a long twilight in these northern latitudes), so we stay at eighty feet for the time being. Telling the officer-of-the-watch to call me at ten to eight, I retire to my bunk. All the hands not on watch follow my example.

0800. We come up to periscope depth and I have a good look round, get the feel of the weather and visibility, check one or two land bearings, and then leave the periscope to the officer-of-the-watch. He keeps the boat moving slowly up and down the five-mile patrol line I have marked on the chart, taking a land fix every half-hour. As it is now daylight we can make the compartments look more cheerful by switching on full lighting. Meanwhile breakfast is up, and I return to the wardroom and join the others at the rather unappetising meal. Admittedly, our chef has to cook for fifty men in a galley half the size of the kitchen of a small modern flat, so it is perhaps unfair to expect him to produce the subtleties of French cooking. But if only he could manage to introduce a little variety into his meals! Breakfast is quite his most devastating effort. The tinned bacon always turns out moist and flabby, swimming in a tepid sea of wet tomatoes (also out of a tin). The coffee, made from coffee essence and condensed milk, is of course undrinkable, but of course we drink it. Toast is all right, because we make it ourselves in an electric toaster, and we have plenty of butter and marmalade.

Breakfast to lunch. Sleep—punctuated, for me, by occasional visits to the periscope to see how things are going. The watches continue to change every two hours as usual.

Lunch. Usually cold corned beef or spam, with boiled potatoes and pickles, chutney, tomato ketchup or anything you fancy in that line. After lunch more sleep, or reading, or writing up the log.

About 1430. It is beginning to get dark already. I go to the periscope and have a final search of the snowbound coastline until I can no longer see. We go deep and retire to seaward, since I do not wish to surface too close to the land while the moon is up. We darken the control-room and the neighbouring wardroom, using red bulbs only. We have tea at about 1600, and everybody begins to wake up.

About 1650. I stick my head round the corner and tell the officer-of-the-watch to order "Surfacing stations in five minutes' time." The order is passed by telephone to the various compartments. Although there is no difference between "surfacing stations" and "diving stations" I like to make the distinction because it warns the look-outs to get dressed in warm clothing and lets the engine-room department know the diesels will be required. Presently I hear the order "Surfacing stations" passed through the boat. Meanwhile, over my sweater and old uniform trousers, I am putting on my Ursula suit, my balaclava and my fur-lined leather seaboots. I loop my binoculars round my neck, give them a final polish, check the focusing, drop the anti-splash lid over the eyepiece, pull on my woollen gloves and go into the control-room. We are in complete darkness except for a little glow of light to illuminate the depth-gauges and the bubble. McIllmurray, the asdic listener in the corner, reports, "No H.E., sir." We come up to periscope depth and I have a rapid look all round in low power. It is all a shapeless black except where the moon is reflected on the water. We alter course towards it to reduce our silhouette on surfacing.

"Stand by to surface."

Robinson opens the lower lid. I order, "Down periscope. Surface!" and climb the ladder with the look-outs at my heels. Up here in the dark tower I feel horribly cut off from my ship's company. Far away below me, as it seems, I hear Number One giving the surfacing orders, and the clang of the telegraphs calling for more speed, and then the hiss and roar of the compressed air exploding into the ballast tanks. In the pitch darkness I pull out the safety-pins and release one of the hatch-clips.

Number One is now at the foot of the tower, calling up the depths. "Twenty-five feet, sir . . . Twenty feet . . ." I ease off on the final clip because, although the hatch is still well under water, there is a bit of pressure in the boat and I want to start getting rid of it as early as possible . . . "Fifteen feet . . ." We are beginning to roll a little now, and I can hear the sea crashing over the top of the bridge as it breaks surface . . . "TEN FEET, sir!" I jerk back the long clip-handle, the pressure roars up past me (and I hang on to the ladder for a moment, for a C.O. was once blown clean overboard on surfacing and never seen again), the hatch swings up and open, and I heave myself out of the tower. The bridge deck is still a-swirl with escaping water, and a shower of cold, salty drips falls from the periscope standards. The fresh night air strikes dizzily at the starved lungs. I move quickly to the front of the bridge and open the voice-pipe, glancing rapidly round in the darkness to make sure we haven't surfaced under the nose of a patrol vessel. This is our most vulnerable moment. The look-outs and the officer-of-the-watch have followed me out of the hatch and are now searching their

allotted sectors through binoculars. I start with the most dangerous sector, right astern, since it is from that direction that an
enemy would have us silhouetted in the moon's path. We are
still moving silently ahead on the motors, altering course either
side of the moon on a pre-arranged zig-zag. We are not yet at
full buoyancy; our casing is a half-tide rock over which the sea
breaks and recedes in a smother of foam. After the stale atmosphere we have been breathing the air has at first a strong and
almost unpleasant smell, as of a mixture of salt, seaweed and
rotting shellfish, a tang so strong that some nights we think
there must be a large dead sea-creature trapped in the bridge
casing.

After five minutes' concentrated search we have seen nothing; all is well. I turn to the voice-pipe: "Control-room—start
main engines." On getting this order Number One knows it
is safe to run the blower for more buoyancy, to start the battery
charge and the air compressors, to go into "patrol routine" and
pass the eagerly awaited orders, "Carry on smoking. Up
spirits." I probably don't stay long on the bridge. When I am
happy about the situation in general, I hand the ship over to the
officer-of-the-watch, with any special instructions I may consider necessary, and go below.

Evening. This is the best time of the day. Supper is dished
up at about half-past seven, and because it is hot and we are
feeling hungry we enjoy it greedily. We have soup followed
by cooked meat (out of the cold store) or something like
sausages or steak-and-kidney pudding out of a tin, with potatoes and greens of some kind (usually tinned peas, towards the
end of the patrol), finishing up with perhaps a treacle pudding,
or spotted dog, or tinned fruit. After coffee we continue to sit
round the table in the dim but rather cosy red lighting (red because it is the colour least harmful to night vision). Now is the
time when cigarettes and pipes are lit up, and we settle down to
passionate games of uckers or liar dice. The fresh air, after the
day's dive, has stimulated our brains, and we have the comfort
of a solid hot meal inside us. On the deckhead over the table
the open electric radiator glows down at us through the drifting

tobacco smoke. The hanging lamp sways with the motion of the ship. Sometimes we feel disinclined for games, and just talk about anything under the sun: the chances of seeing a target, the war in general, where *Storm* will be this time next year, where we should like to live when the war's over, the delights and perversities of women, memories of childhood, pubs we have known, cars, night clubs in foreign ports . . . Eventually there comes a pause in the talk, and someone yawns and says, "Well—I'm for the hay." Chief stubs out a cigarette with long, nicotined fingers and goes off to the engine-room to see how the battery charge is getting on. I go up top for another breath of fresh air, and, wishing to relieve myself, move to the after end of the bridge and use the "pig's-ear" built there for the purpose. Standing there I look down at the sea swirling over the ballast tanks and past the sputtering exhausts, at the blunt-ended after-casing shining wetly in the moonlight, at our wake bubbling and dying away, and across the water at the gloomy coastline with its patches of snow making the irregular pattern of a deliberate camouflage. After a little while I take a couple of land bearings and go below to check our position on the chart. In the wardroom I probably find Chief smoking yet another cigarette. If we are in the mood, we sit and continue talking for a time, speaking quietly so as not to disturb the sleepers in their bunks. Shortly before ten o'clock, when the watches are due to change, I put the electric kettle on and make four cups of cocoa; one for the officer-of-the-watch, who will be coming below in a moment, one for his relief just going on watch, one for Chief, and one for myself. I turn in about eleven, pull the side curtain across the head of my bunk, and in a couple of minutes I am asleep.

The next thing I know is the P.O. of the watch shaking me and saying, "From the bridge, sir; it's beginning to get light."

The patrol was unusually short. We were astonished, on the evening of the 21st, to receive our recall signal, instructing us to withdraw from the area two hours after midnight on the following night. Thus we had only four days on the billet. By daylight on the 22nd we were well out of sight of land and making for home on the surface. We had fine weather almost all the way, a gentle following wind, calm seas and stars every dawn and dusk. On the evening of the 26th we received a signal telling us that Muckle Flugga light would be switched on for us during the night, and at four o'clock in the morning we picked up its loom flashing on the starboard bow. By ten o'clock we were in Lerwick harbour. We left that same afternoon, and reached the Clyde two days later, having logged 3,500 miles.

We had spent our patrol in the latitude of 71° North. Less than three months later we were to be sweating in the tropics within four degrees of the equator. In the midst of the gales of a Scottish winter it required an effort of imagination to turn our thoughts to the preparations for living and working and fighting in Far Eastern waters.

XIII

PASSAGE TO CEYLON

WE left Holy Loch the day after Boxing Day. When we let go and started drawing away from the depot ship Geoff Stuart's white face was up there among the officers and sailors leaning over the rail to see us off. To my great regret, and I think also to his, I had been obliged to leave him behind. It was clear that by virtue of his seniority he would soon be due for his perisher, and it seemed a pity to take him out to Ceylon only to have to send him all the way back as soon as we got there. Far better to let Brian Mills take over as First Lieutenant immediately so that he could settle down in his new capacity during the passage out, rather than make the change on the eve of our first Far Eastern patrol. I had therefore felt it was fairer to everybody to let Geoff transfer to one of the home-operational submarines. But he never did his perisher, and I never saw him again; a few months later, while he was on leave, he and his wife died together in a tragic accident.

As Brian Mills had got married only a fortnight before we sailed, it was perhaps the best possible thing for him that his mind should now be occupied with his new and increased responsibilities as Number One. Fortunately I had in Richard Blake the ideal man to take his place as navigator; Blake's ability had been proved during the North Cape patrol, and he had already endeared himself to all of us. My officers were now as follows:

First Lieutenant:	Lieut. C. B. Mills, R.N.
Torpedo Officer:	Lieut. R. G. Wade, R.N.V.R.
Navigating Officer:	Sub-Lieut. R. L. Blake, R.N.
Engineer Officer:	Wt.Eng. W. H. Ray, R.N.

and this team remained unaltered, except for changes in rank and the later addition of Dicky Fisher, until our return to England sixteen months later.

We sailed down the Irish Sea in company with two other submarines—*K.14* (a Dutchman, also bound for the Far East) and Bannar-Martin's *Viking* (bound for Plymouth)—all three of us escorted by our old friend *Cutty Sark*. Soon after eleven o'clock on the morning of the 29th we were diving south of the Scilly Isles, and through the periscope I was having my last look at England in the shape of Bishop Rock. *Viking* and *Cutty Sark* were vanishing on the north-eastern horizon, making their way up Channel to Plymouth. To the north-west of us *K.14* was diving on a course diverging from ours; our orders were to make our separate ways to Gibraltar, submerging by day.

By New Year's Eve we were well out in the Atlantic, travelling due south. The day was noteworthy for the first appearance of what was to develop into the ship's newspaper. I began it as a daily bulletin in pursuance of my policy of keeping the ship's company informed of what was going on. Soon I grew more ambitious and included a summary of the war news as supplied by the wireless office, and presently I introduced a lighter note by posing quizzes and other competitions. Gradually its scope was widened to include contributions from anybody in the ship's company with a talent for writing or drawing. In the wardroom we had a large bunch of American magazines full of glamorous photographs of film stars in various stages of undress, and for a long time I was able to provide a popular "duty beauty" feature each evening by cutting them out and pasting them into the paper. Only one copy of each issue was produced, typed out by myself (I can type quite fast with two fingers of each hand) and then handed round the submarine from mess to mess during the evening. As the bulletins contained information classified as "secret" I made a point of recovering the issues after they had been circulated. Indeed, I still have them by me as I write, and looking through them again I find that the dog-eared and oil-stained pages, with their ephemeral, often schoolboy humour and their passing comments on the day-to-day life of a submarine at sea, recall the atmosphere of those days with an extraordinary vividness. I called the bulletin *Good Evening*, in deference to the printed daily news-magazine specially produced for the submarine service by the *Daily Mirror* and called *Good Morning*. I managed to keep it going for most nights at sea until we reached Aden on the homeward journey. It varied in length according to the energy of its editor, but often it covered both sides of a foolscap sheet in single-spacing. Sometimes, after a day of excitement when I had been continually on the go, it was a considerable effort to sit down in front of the typewriter and tap out the evening's issue, but from the complaints I received on the rare occasions when *Good Evening* failed to appear I knew that the energy put into producing it was not wasted.

Here are some extracts from my bulletins issued during the passage to Ceylon:

December 31st

K.14 is forty miles further west and a little north of us. She has been ordered to keep a look-out for an aircraft dinghy with British airmen in it, reported sighted on her route. Just to the south of us are some lifeboats carrying survivors from the three German destroyers sunk by *Glasgow* three nights ago. We have had no less than thirteen U-boats reported to us as being somewhere in the Bay of Biscay (look-outs please note). H.M. Submarine *Shakespeare* is on her way home and is expected to pass not very far from us tonight on an opposite course.

January 1st

We have so far had no star sight since leaving England but by D.R. we have now passed the Bay of Biscay. Considering the time of year, and the Bay's reputation, we have been extraordinarily lucky with the weather.

We are just over 100 miles due west of Cape Finisterre. We received our onward route to Gibraltar last night, and from about midnight to-night we steer in a bit towards the Portuguese coast to make a point about twenty miles off Cape St Vincent on the evening of the 5th. After that we shall be on the surface the rest of the way.

To-night's disposition signal indicates sixteen U-boats either inward or outward bound. Positions are very approximate, and some may easily be encountered on our route.

January 2nd

Star and sun sights have confirmed our D.R. position within a few miles. We are 120 miles west of the coast of Portugal. Any time now the look-outs should be able to smell the scented breezes coming off the land. The First Lieutenant sighted a swallow through the periscope today, and yesterday afternoon the Engineer Officer sighted an old boot. These sightings have prompted the Navigator to believe that land can't be far away now.

January 3rd

Sorry I had to disappoint all you bloodthirsty pirates today, but we are not at war with Spain yet, and this is too early in my naval career to face a court-martial. Our "target" turned out to be the Spanish *Capitan Segarra*. She is in my list of neutral ships that are above suspicion as possible blockade-runners. Anyway, we went up close enough to read her name and make sure she couldn't have been a blockade-runner in disguise.

We are gradually closing in towards the Portuguese coast. It is just possible we might be able to see the glow of the lights of Lisbon tomorrow night. Ships encountered from now on are more likely than not to be neutral, though these will naturally have their lights burning, and any darkened ship is just asking for one of the T.I.'s death-dealing fish. And of course anywhere on the ocean these days we are always likely to meet U-boats.

January 4th

In the early hours of this morning we chased a lighted ship that turned out to be illuminated as a hospital ship. This was puzzling, since we have had no signals about our own hospital ship sailings, and even enemy hospital ships are usually well advertised to all shipping before sailing. We were unable to overtake her, and I saw no point in adding grey hairs to the Chief E.R.A.'s head by doing a full-power trial for the sake of a probably harmless ship. So I compromised, abandoned the chase and made a signal to Gibraltar reporting the ship. She was steering a course for England, so in all probability she was one of ours, but it seems odd that we weren't informed of a hospital ship expected to pass through our position.

January 5th

We have been patrolling today off Cape St Vincent, whose light we sighted during the night. Two aircraft, both ours, are all that has been seen through the periscope. After surfacing we proceed round the corner towards the Straits, passing Cape Trafalgar, and we should sight Africa about noon tomorrow. We shall, enemy aircraft permitting, be on the surface all the rest of the way into Gibraltar, where we are due to arrive tomorrow afternoon.

Gibraltar was not the same without *Maidstone*, but we enjoyed our two days there. I spent most of the time with my

young brother, who was then stationed on the Rock in an
R.A.S.C. unit, and when we slipped our wires in the early hours
of January 9th, he came down to the dockyard on his bicycle to
see us off.

Outside the harbour we joined a merchant-ship convoy
bound for Alexandria.* It did the heart good to see this armada
forming up in preparation for a voyage that would have been
impossible a year ago. There had indeed been a most extraordinary transformation in the Mediterranean scene since the
time when I arrived there in *Saracen*. The Germans had been
thrown out of Africa and Sicily and were now being pushed
painfully up the Italian peninsula. But there was still the possibility of attack from German aircraft based in the south of
France:

January 9th

The convoy route skirts the North African coast as far as Cape Bon,
after which it goes straight for Malta. Tomorrow afternoon we should
be off Oran. . . .

The dangerous time is dusk. The enemy may send out a dawn reconnaissance plane to spot the convoy, and in the evening just before dusk one
plane will shadow and then close the convoy, and home the bombers on.
We are setting radar watch at these periods, and hope to get warning by
picking up the shadowing aircraft. We are not allowed to dive while we
are with the convoy

January 10th

I apologise for the delay in producing today's *Good Evening*, caused by
a slight altercation with the enemy . . . Nothing very much happened.
About ten minutes before the attack started we had a radar contact to the
northward, range twenty-one miles, which we reported to the Commodore. This may have been the shadowing aircraft . . . The attack was
made from a very low level, and from different directions. The first ship
to open up was the corvette on the port wing of the escort, and a moment
later an aircraft was sighted coming in from the starboard beam through
the smoke screen which had been started fifteen minutes earlier. He flew
across and ahead of the leading line of ships, several of whom opened up,
including *Storm*. Our tracer was pretty close, and it was unfortunate that
the Oerlikon jammed after firing about ten rounds . . Two other aircraft were seen, and others fired at by ships in further sections of the convoy, but nothing else came near us.

* See previous map on page 98.

January 12th

Today makes me wonder what on earth newspapers do when there is absolutely no news at all. The news is that the sea is blue and that Africa still bears Green 90. And we are still rushing along in the convoy at the terrific speed of six knots . . . If only Jerry would spring another air attack on us, I might have some meat for tomorrow's *Good Evening*.

January 14th

At the moment of writing we can see Malta immediately to the south of us, and at the same time the high coast of Sicily is just visible to the north. The distance is only about sixty miles . . . At six o'clock in the morning we leave the convoy and proceed independently. We should reach Beirut some time on the 20th.

January 17th

There still seems to be a misconception that we carry limitless fresh water. On many days during this trip the consumption has been *twice* as much as it should be. Just because we have been told to arrive in Beirut by the morning of the 20th, it does not follow that we may not at any time be diverted to carry out an emergency patrol on the way. We should look rather stupid if I had to send a signal saying "Sorry, but we've used up all our fresh water." Rationing of water is a nuisance to everybody, but unless the consumption is considerably reduced voluntarily from now on, rationing will have to be introduced. One day our lives may depend on having enough fresh water

January 19th

We are due to arrive at 0645 in the morning. Whether we do so exactly then or not depends on (a) the weather, (b) the Navigator's mathematics, (c) the idiosyncrasies of the helmsmen, (d) the good will of the Chief E.R.A. and finally (e) the keenness of the First Lieutenant to get ashore . . . A mail will close for censoring at 2100 tonight.

Beirut gave most of us our first smell of the East and our first sight of a camel outside a zoo. In the six days we spent there we had time to carry out some minor engine repairs, paint the ship dark green (the standard colour for Far Eastern waters), and enjoy ourselves ashore. Beirut was the home of the First Submarine Flotilla; originally this flotilla had operated from the depot ship H.M.S. *Medway* in Alexandria, but when the Middle East situation deteriorated in the shadow of Rommel's advance, the *Medway* (reputed the finest depot ship ever built) was sailed for Haifa; she had hardly left harbour when she was torpedoed and sunk. In a remarkably short time an alternative base was built ashore in Beirut and the flotilla was able to continue its good work. But later the improving situation steadily reduced the opportunities for attack, and at the time of our arrival the base was on the point of packing up and transferring to Malta to amalgamate with the Tenth Flotilla. However, life ashore was still full of opportunity for pleasure. If you wanted to get outside Beirut itself you had the choice of ski-ing in the Lebanese mountains or driving to Damascus or Jerusalem. I chose Jerusalem, and spent two days in the Holy Land; passing through an orange-grove I discovered the glory of an orange eaten straight off the tree.

We left Beirut on the 27th, put into Haifa to spend a day in the floating dock scraping the ship's bottom, and on the 29th sailed for Port Said. We immediately found ourselves struggling against head winds. Before midnight we received a signal diverting us to search for possible survivors of a Wellington bomber believed to have crashed in the sea. In the violent seas it was a hopeless task, but using our six-inch Aldis lamp as a searchlight we devoted four hours to a systematic search which covered an area of 160 square miles. Lit up in the beam of our searchlight, the spume came off the sea like smoke. At four o'clock in the morning we abandoned the search and pressed on. The wind was still piling the water up towards the Palestine coast, and when dawn broke we faced an endless vista of toppling mountains and reeling valleys, the shortest and steepest seas I think I have ever seen—hardly the popular conception of the Mediterranean seascape. The search for the Wellington had already put us behind schedule; the weather delayed us still further and it was not until nearly midnight on the 30th that we dropped anchor off Navy House in Port Said, completely exhausted.

The Suez Canal pilot, coming on board at the unexpectedly early hour of 0515, roused us out of a groaning sleep. We forced ourselves to harbour stations and set off through the canal, reached Suez that evening and anchored off Port Tewfik.

At the crack of dawn we were under way again and making a start on the 1,500-mile-long passage of the Red Sea.

February 1st

We are now travelling south in no uncertain terms. Every day should be noticeably hotter. We cover, on the average, four degrees of latitude every twenty-four hours. Half way to Aden we cross the Tropic of Cancer, which (in case you don't know) is the most northerly latitude at which the sun is ever directly overhead, i.e. on midsummer's day in the northern hemisphere. Those of you who have been through the Red Sea in the middle of the northern summer will know that it can be hellishly hot here. We are lucky to be passing through while the sun is still south of the Equator.

By the third day it was so hot, and the sea so calm, that we put into operation a routine that would have been madness in almost any other stretch of water in the world at this time. Because the Red Sea was a sort of no-man's-land between the German war and the Jap war, we were not likely to have to dive in a hurry, and we were therefore able to open the fore hatch and the engine-room hatch during daylight to allow a stream of fresh air to flow through the submarine. Each morning we stopped engines and piped the hands to bathe, with a look-out posted and the Oerlikon manned as a precaution against sharks. Once we saw a dorsal fin flapping lazily within a hundred yards of us only five minutes after the last man was out of the water. On two successive days we rigged up a target on the fore deck, and the various messes competed in a revolver-shooting match which ended in a victory for the E.R.A.s, the wardroom team being badly let down by myself with one of the lowest individual scores recorded.

One night we had to take drastic avoiding action to avert head-on collision with a northbound United States merchant-ship; not only was she, by our reckoning, on the wrong side of the swept channel, but when I altered to starboard to show my red light she turned to port towards me and forced me to go hard over; I had to turn a full circle to get out of her way.

February 6th

We are now racing down the narrow straits of Bab-el-Mandeb leading out into the Indian Ocean. At Perim the straits are only ten miles wide

. . . We are due to rendezvous with our escort, the trawler H.M.S. *Loch Melfort*, at 0800 in the morning at the entrance to the Aden swept channel. Incidentally, once we get out of the Red Sea we must return to serious business. Jap submarines have been operating off Aden.

We met the *Loch Melfort* half an hour ahead of schedule, and by ten o'clock *Storm* was secured alongside the Boom Defence Jetty in Aden. Here we spent three agreeable days waiting for the arrival of the submarines *K.14* and *Tantivy*. On the 10th we all sailed together for Ceylon, remaining in company and under escort until we were clear of the Gulf of Aden. We had a voyage of nearly 2,500 miles ahead of us.

February 11th

We remain in company for another two days. At the moment we are steering east along the Gulf of Aden; soon we cut down between the island of Socotra and the African mainland. It behoves look-outs to be on the top line from now on: at least one Japanese submarine has been operating in the vicinity of Socotra, and there may well be others.

Warning: I have said it before, and I say it again—IT IS ESSENTIAL TO BE CAREFUL WITH FRESH WATER. The moment the daily consumption reaches 100 gallons or more, rationing will be introduced.

Health in the tropics : The first essential is to keep the body as clean as circumstances permit. This may seem difficult when I tell you in the same breath to conserve the fresh water, but it is perfectly possible with care and trouble. The next point is: don't go on wearing the same filthy clothes day after day. As far as possible wear white, or at least khaki that will show the dirt—it's fatal to go on wearing dirty old overalls. If you have been sweating a lot, wash it off, or at least wipe it off with a handtowel; if you don't, the salt which your sweat has pushed out of your pores will begin to irritate the skin. Try to avoid drinking too much water or tea—it only gives your body more liquid to get rid of, and thus leads to more sweating.

February 12th

Tonight we shake the dust of Africa off our heels, leaving the island of Socotra to the north.

Health in the tropics (continued): Wear clothes that are as loose as possible. Don't have tight belts, for instance—tightness prevents ventilation of your perspiration and creates an ideal breeding-ground for prickly heat. Wear your shirt *outside* your shorts; it doesn't look so smart, but it aids the circulation of air round the body. The best garment of all is a sarong. Failing that, a towel tied in a loose roll at the waist.

February 13th

The escort leaves us at 0130 in the morning, *Tantivy* diverges to the northward, *K.14* carries straight on, and we diverge to the southward. From that moment on we return to a proper wartime routine. The holidays are over. The Jap is a clever and determined enemy, and his tentacles reach out far and wide, even to the Arabian Sea . . .

Today's health hint: Last year a ship arrived in Aden, having come through the Red Sea at the height of its summer. Three stokers had flaked out in the boiler room from heat exhaustion. The M.O. asked the Captain what he'd done about them. "Oh," he said, "we got 'em up on deck, dipped a bucket over the side, gave 'em all a good drink of sea water, and then sent 'em back down below on the job. They were as right as rain." This story points to a true medical fact. Heat exhaustion is caused by the body losing all its salt through perspiration. The absorption of salt, either in solid or in liquid form, has an almost immediate effect in a case of heat exhaustion. The answer is—eat plenty of salt.

February 15th

Today's health hint: The M.O. in Aden assured me that well-tanned people never suffer from prickly heat. Moral—get as much sun as possible. During the present day surface-running two extra hands are allowed on the bridge at a time. Not only your skin but also your whole health benefits from a reasonable amount of sunning. ("Stokers, get up them stairs"—Engineer Officer.)

February 17th

Well, you asked for it. The fresh water consumption for yesterday was up to 120 gallons, which is 50% more than it ought to have been. Fresh water will now only be on between the hours 0630–0830, 1130–1230, 1530–1630 and 1830–2000.

February 18th

Our destination now is not Colombo, as we thought. We are being met by an escort on Sunday afternoon (the 20th) and taken round to Trincomalee on the eastern side of Ceylon.

February 19th

We are due to rendezvous tomorrow afternoon at 1530 with *Tantivy* and our escort, the Italian sloop *Eritrea*, a very fine-looking steamer to judge from her picture in *Jane's Fighting Ships*. We then have 300 miles or so to Trincomalee.

Keeping a rendezvous with another ship in the middle of the ocean is even more exciting than making a landfall. A ship is such a small dot on the chart; even stationary islands are sometimes hard enough to find. Two ships, two chances of error; and perhaps, if the weather is unkind, no sights and poor visibility. As it happened, on the 19th we had no sights at all; luckily the sky cleared in time for our star sight on the morning of the 20th—luckily, because we discovered we had been set a few miles to the north of our route and were able to alter course to the south-east in plenty of time. We knew from W/T signals that *K.14* was going into Colombo on her own; *Tantivy* had come up on the air the previous evening to report that she had been delayed and would be two hours late at our rendezvous. We, however, looked like being on time, and from about 1400 onwards we had no lack of volunteers as extra look-outs. I felt as excited as anybody; for it was my first experience of trying to find a ship at sea so far from land. I felt oddly conscious of the other navigator plotting his way towards us. The sea was calm, the sky bright, and the horizon clear. At ten to three there came a shout from the look-out stationed high on the periscope standards: "Mast bearing Red 20, sir!" and a moment later we could all see it, a pin-point steadily rising over the curve of the blue sea. We began calling her up on the six-inch Aldis with the appropriate recognition signal, and twenty minutes later·we were in company with her, exchanging chatty signals, admiring her handsome lines, and noting with surprise that she was still flying the Italian ensign. We zig-zagged astern of her in the vicinity of the rendezvous position to await the arrival of *Tantivy*. Rimington was as good as his word: at 1715 *Tantivy* was observed approaching from the north-west, and by the time dusk had twitched its mantle over the sky we were in line ahead and zig-zagging towards the southern point of Ceylon.

At dawn the island was well in sight on the port hand, and all that day as we came gradually round to a northerly course we could see Adam's Peak rising to its misty summit several miles inland. We ploughed through a sea of shining glass in which sleepy whales lay below the surface like waterlogged hulks. (Sam Marriott in *Stoic*, a few days ahead of us, had run smack into one of these slumbering whales and bent his bow so badly that he had to go into Colombo dry dock for repairs.) At

night the exotic smell of the island hung softly on the balmy
air. The following noon we began closing in towards the coast,
came into green water, and by tea-time were examining through
our binoculars the jungle forest which came everywhere down
to the shore. At 1800 we passed through the defence boom at
the entrance to Trincomalee harbour, a magnificent and extensive natural anchorage for the Eastern Fleet which was being
built up under the Commander-in-Chief, Admiral Sir James
Somerville, in preparation for an offensive against the Japanese
Fleet. In port were the battleships *Queen Elizabeth*, *Valiant*,
and *Renown*, the aircraft-carrier *Illustrious*, one or two escort
carriers and some destroyers. But our eyes were drawn first
towards the large ship moored in the bay to the left of the entrance, the submarine depot ship *Adamant*, newest of her kind.
I had last seen her, still unfinished, on the stocks at Harland
and Wolff's shipbuilding yard in Belfast in the early part of
1941, and now here she was, the mother ship of the Fourth
Submarine Flotilla, queening it in Trincomalee harbour with a
trot of T-boats and S-boats on each side of her. However, it
seemed there was not room for both *Tantivy* and *Storm* at the
moment. She flashed a signal ordering *Storm* to berth on *Wu
Chang*, which I correctly took to be the queer-looking Chinese
river-boat moored a cable or so away.

Wu Chang, though small and ancient, had one great advantage: she was built for the tropics. After dinner that evening
we sat drinking our port on the open poop deck, looking across
the bay and the lights twinkling in the still water (for the nearest
Japanese air base was so far away that there was no need of a
black-out) and speculating on the dark mysteries of the jungle
shore. The smoke from our cigars scarcely wavered in the
breathless air. We felt pleasantly tired after our strenuous journey: we had wasted little time on the passage from England,
having done it in less than two months. I had been over to
Adamant's Staff Office as soon as we arrived, and ascertained
that we could expect about ten days in harbour before we should
be needed for patrol. Chief had some repairs to carry out which

required the partial dismantling of the engines; he had in fact set the duty watch of E.R.A.s and stokers on the job already. But this evening we leaned back in our creaking wicker chairs and relaxed comfortably; we felt we could take things easy for a few days. The Chinese steward was kept busy supplying us with rounds of drinks. I was in a contented mood, and it seemed to me, looking round at my officers, that we really got on with each other remarkably well. Mills was shaping satisfactorily as Number One, Blake had done his stuff on the navigation and possessed a delightful sense of humour all his own, Wade was still perhaps something of an unknown quantity but had given no cause for complaint, and Chief and I, after our unpromising start at Cammell Laird's, were already extremely good friends. I felt very happy.

It was after eleven o'clock when a signal rating came seeking me with a message that my presence was urgently required in Captain S/M's cabin. Such a summons at this late hour was disturbing: either I had done something wrong or unusual events were afoot. Standing up in the stern of the little motorboat which took me across to *Adamant*, I tried to pull my rather fuddled thoughts together.

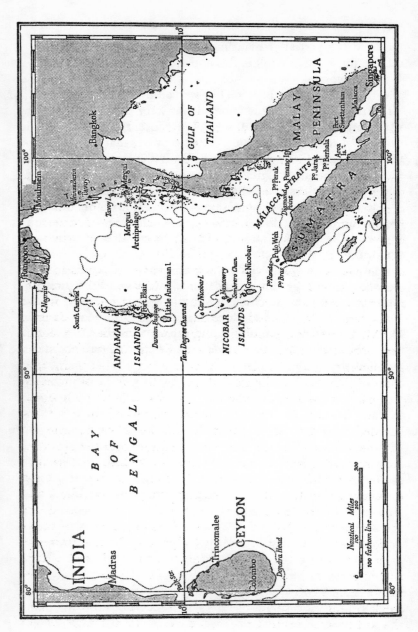

XIV

IN THE NARROWS : MALACCA STRAITS

In the depot ship all was stir and bustle. The passage-way between the Captain's Cabin and the Staff Office was busy with
the coming and going of submarine C.O.s and their navigators,
depot-ship officers and messengers from the wireless office. I
nearly bumped into Verschoyle-Campbell, who had been in
command of *Sealion* when I did my perisher and was now
C.O. of the submarine *Stonehenge*; he did not recognise me, but
strode past with the far-away look of a man setting forth on a
crusade. It was the last time I ever saw him. I tucked my cap
under my arm, knocked at the Captain's door and went in.

Captain S/M, Fourth Submarine Flotilla, was Captain
H. M. C. Ionides, popularly known as "Tinsides." He had
been ashore when I came on board earlier in the evening, and I
had never met him before. He sat at a large table studying a
chart of the Malacca Straits and was in the middle of dictating
a signal to a messenger, who took the words down on a signal
pad and hurried off. By the Captain's side stood the tall, trim-
bearded Staff Officer, Commander Clarke, R.N.V.R., whom I
had met earlier. The Captain moved a finger over the pencilled
areas marked on the chart and discussed with him whether submarine A would be able to shift from Area 1 to Area 2 in time
to relieve submarine B. As I stood waiting respectfully I was
able to study this man under whom I would be operating for
the next few months. He was still in his daytime rig of open-
necked shirt and shorts, and had obviously been working at
high pressure for the last two or three hours. He had a large
and impressive head with greying hair cut rather short, eyebrows permanently raised in an expression of mild surprise, and
small bright eyes surrounded by innumerable little wrinkles,
the sort of wrinkles that add charm to a smile and severity to a

rebuke, and come from past suffering or long periods of intense concentration.

Suddenly he was aware of me, and looked up to see what I wanted. Clarke came to my rescue. "This is Young, sir; just arrived with *Storm* this afternoon."

"Ah, yes," he said, in his soft voice, "I've got a bit of a shock for you. We have just received information that leads us to believe the Japanese Fleet may be planning a sortie through the Malacca Straits at any moment, and I need every submarine I can lay my hands on to plug the gap. I would like you to sail for patrol tomorrow. Can you do it, do you think?" And he leaned back in his chair, watching me and summing me up.

I had to think quickly. I should dearly have liked to give without hesitation the answer he wanted. But I had a mental picture of Chief's engine-room, already stripped down for repairs, and asked if I could possibly be given one more day. He did not disguise his disappointment, but when I gave him details of the work to be done before we could be fit to sail he agreed to postpone our departure for twenty-four hours.

I left him and returned to *Wu Chang* to break the news to Number One and Chief.

The first enemy ship to appear in *Storm*'s periscope was a Japanese submarine.

We had dived in the Nicobar Channel before dawn that morning, after an uneventful three-day surface passage of 900 miles, with a further 550 miles to travel to reach our patrol billet in the narrows of the Malacca Straits. It was still the calm season of the north-east monsoon. When we dived we had not yet made a landfall, but on coming to periscope depth at first daylight we sighted the low-lying, palm-fringed southern extremity of Great Nicobar Island on the expected bearing of NNE. Nothing of note happened during the day until, at three minutes to four in the afternoon, just as we were sitting down to tea in the wardroom, we heard an exclamation from Blake at the periscope. "Captain, sir!"

In three seconds I was at his side. "An object in the water,

bearing Green 20," he said as I took over the periscope, and at
the same moment the asdic operator reported "diesel H.E. on
the bearing."

The object in the water was the conning-tower of a westbound submarine, a grey-green box lifting and dipping to the
gentle swell.

"Sound the alarm," I said.

He was a long way off, over two miles at a rough guess, and
we were already nearly on his beam. There was not much time.

"Group up, full ahead together. Hard-a-starboard. Sixty
feet. The bearing is *that*. I am eighty degrees on his starboard
bow . . . Bring all tubes to the ready . . . Give me a course for
a 120 track."

I was speeding up to our full under-water speed of nine knots
to close the range, and going deep to avoid disturbing the surface water. After three minutes I slowed down and came back
to periscope depth, to find that my target had altered course to
starboard and put me in a slightly better position. He was difficult to estimate on because the casing was hidden by the swell;
the periscope scale made the range at this point 3,400 yards, but
to my eye it still appeared over 4,000. The chances of a hit on a
submarine at that distance were not very good. I decided to
make one more effort to close the range, and went to sixty feet
for another burst of speed. Coming back to thirty-two feet I
put *Storm* on a firing course and waited for the firing angle to
come on.

"Stand by."

At this stage of the attack I was raising and lowering the periscope every few seconds. I could see the enemy a little more
clearly now. He was one of the large Japanese ocean-going submarines of over 1,500 tons, with a 4·7 inch gun mounted fore
and aft of the conning-tower, and he had a small square of white
painted at the foot of the tower.

He had only a little way to go before coming on to the firing
angle, when I suddenly realised he was altering course away.
Cursing, I brought the ship round to port to get on to a new
firing course. By the time the helmsman had steadied I knew

that the range was opening rapidly, that, being well abaft his beam, I was now in a very poor firing position, and that if I fired the range would be even greater by the time my torpedoes had overtaken him. The temptation to take a long shot at this target—the dream of every submarine C.O.—was almost irresistible. But I had brought my torpedoes nearly a thousand miles with the specific object of firing them at the Japanese Fleet, and in view of the mounting odds against success I decided, with the greatest difficulty and reluctance, that it would be a waste of torpedoes to fire.

"Break off the attack," I said, and explained briefly to Number One why I had come to the decision. The news went through the boat in a murmur of disappointment. Through the periscope I continued to watch the unsuspecting enemy until he disappeared over the horizon towards the open water of the Indian Ocean. I blamed myself bitterly for having wasted time in trying to close the range. If I had steadied on a firing course immediately after the target's first alteration, I might have been able to fire before he zigged away again. Wise after the event, I realised I had made a mistake.

Full of gloom I sat down and prepared an Enemy Report, but decided to wait until later that night before transmitting it. If I surfaced to make the signal immediately the enemy Intelligence would probably guess their submarine had been sighted; moreover, I knew from the wireless disposition signals that none of our own submarines was in a position to make an attack on him. So we coded the signal, all ready for transmission after dark.

We surfaced at seven o'clock that evening, sent off my signal, and proceeded eastward, keeping well clear of the northern tip of Sumatra. There were so many of our own submarines coming and going through the Nicobar Channel that we had to stick closely to our prescribed route to avoid embarrassing encounters. Even so, while we were dived the following day, the asdic operator, Leading Seaman McIllmurray, heard propeller noises, "probably electric motors," passing down the port side. The visibility was good but nothing was in sight through the periscope. I told McIllmurray to transmit an asdic "ping" on the bearing, and after three shots he obtained a good echo at 4,500 yards (2¼ miles). If I had been certain there were no British submarines about I would have carried out a submerged torpedo attack, firing blind on an asdic plot; but knowing that *Tactician* was in the process of withdrawing from patrol I took no action. (It was, in fact, *Tactician*, as I confirmed later.)

That night, in *Good Evening*, I drew a map of the Malacca Straits to show our present route and the position we were making for.

Tomorrow morning we hope to sight the island of Perak, and then alter course south-eastward towards our billet. From now on we must expect to find patrol vessels—and, during our surface run tomorrow, aircraft. We shall quite likely have to dive for aircraft two or three times in the day. We should arrive stealthily on the billet in the early hours of the morning of March 2nd, the day after tomorrow. You will be interested to learn that *Tally-Ho*, making her situation report on her way home, has reported the sinking of one *German* U-boat and a medium-sized merchant vessel; also a midnight brush with a destroyer during which she suffered some damage to her main ballast tanks. She also reported the presence of numerous patrol vessels.

As *Tally-Ho* had been patrolling only just to the north of our appointed patrol position, it began to look as if we were in for an interesting time.

We saw only one aircraft the following day, and the look-out spotted him so far away that we had plenty of time to dive without being sighted. We also saw our first junk; owing to the distortion of mirage I thought we had a promising target, but as we closed the range her idly flapping sails took shape and revealed her for what she was. During the last night of our approach to the patrol position we had no alarms. That evening, as I leant over the chart-table to work out our speed for the night and make sure that we reached the billet at the right time, I could not help admiring the way in which submarine movements in this constricted sea-lane were organised by the Staff Office in Trincomalee. *Truculent* (Robby Alexander) was leaving my billet the same night; so my route was neatly diverted towards Sumatra to make me side-step her homeward route;

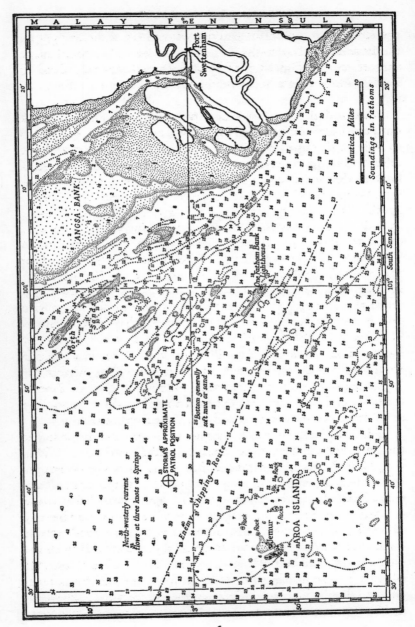

and since it was notoriously difficult to pin-point the navigation in my area, my route was also arranged so that I could make sure of my position by getting a sight of the small island of Berhala less than six hours before my arrival.

We dived at five o'clock that morning, three miles north of our patrol position by dead reckoning, and as usual went deep to wait for daylight, trickling slowly southward. Half an hour later we slid up to periscope depth. Finding nothing in sight I handed the periscope to Chief, who was now taking an occasional dived watch to give the regular watch-keeping officers a break. I was hoping soon to sight the little lighthouse on Jemur Island, the only landmark available to us for fixing. We were going to have some anxious moments over the navigation, I suspected. On the ordinary map the Straits look fairly wide at this point, but my study of the large-scale chart had made me familiar with the litter of invisible shoals and sandbanks which made the area an uncomfortably restricted one for submarine operations. In few places was there as much as forty fathoms of water, and the ten-fathom line would never be very far away. The whole stretch of water was so shallow that it would have been easy to strew it with mines; fortunately the Japs were short of mines, and our Intelligence knew it. Nevertheless I had a feeling that the area would begin to seem very small if we ran into serious anti-submarine opposition.

Chief had been on watch only ten minutes when he sounded the alarm for a distant object fine on the starboard bow. "What is it, Chief?" I said as I pushed him away from the periscope. "Can't make it out," he answered; "looks like three junks alongside a junk depot ship, if you ask me!" I could not at first make a better guess myself. I thought it might be a large ship heavily camouflaged, and then that there were several small vessels bunched together. It seemed to be changing shape all the time. Not until several minutes had passed did I realise it was the island we were looking for, considerably distorted by mirage. Jemur Island. We had arrived and we knew where we were.

Mirage distortion was to cause us much unnecessary anxiety

on all our Far Eastern patrols. Particularly annoying were the innumerable drifting logs and branched tree-trunks which abounded in these green waters, and which, besides being a constant menace to our propellers when we were on the surface, in daylight through the periscope assumed the most convincing shapes of submarines, submarine-chasers or junks.

Our next sighting, in the middle of the afternoon of this first day, was no mirage. Two masts were seen approaching from the south-eastward. Could this be the advance guard of the Japanese Fleet, so early in our patrol? I began to manœuvre into an attacking position, but as they approached and began to show their upperworks over the horizon I realised they were very small ships. One of them had the small bridge and funnel amidships and the low freeboard of a Jap submarine-chaser; the other, perhaps because he was distorted by mirage, looked at first like a small coastal merchantman of no more than 600 tons, but he was painted grey and had a small gun mounted on the fore deck, and I finally decided he must be some kind of converted anti-submarine patrol vessel. In any case, he was too small to be worth wasting a torpedo and compromising our position. The sea was as calm as a Thames backwater, and I dared use only the small periscope, showing no more than an inch for a second or two at each glance. I had passed the order for absolute silence through the boat, and we lay doggo and watched them moving slowly past as though we were holding our breath. Leading Seaman McIllmurray, listening on his asdic receiver, could hear no "ping" transmissions from the enemy ships. Probably they were equipped only with listening apparatus. There was something horribly sinister about their deliberate, watchful progress. I could see them so clearly that I was able to count at least ten depth-charges on the submarine-chaser's stern. But they drew past us at last and finally disappeared over the horizon to the north-west.

We were much encouraged by seeing these patrol vessels on our first day, and hoped they were the forerunners of bigger game to follow. Nothing is more depressing than to spend day after day on a billet without a sign of the enemy. Now at least we knew we were in a likely spot. However, except for the idle sails of two or three fishing-junks on the horizon, nothing more was seen that day. On surfacing after dark I was at once alarmed to find a black shape in the water less than a mile away. This was soon identified as another junk, but not wanting him to see us, I retired rapidly northwards to put him out of sight before starting the battery charge. It was always possible that these junks were less innocent than they seemed; it would have been easy to equip them with wireless transmitters, or even torpedo tubes. During this patrol we were constantly seeing them at night, and in misty weather they were a confounded nuisance, giving rise to many false alarms.

The strain of the nights was the most exhausting part of being in command. Some C.O.s learnt to sleep on the bridge, but though I tried to do so several times I never succeeded. During this first patrol in the Malacca Straits I had a strip of canvas slung between the side of the bridge and the periscope standards, and lay restlessly on my back watching the stars sway gently to the swell. Every few minutes the whole sky would spin slowly through thirty or forty degrees and I knew the helmsman in the control-room below was altering course on to the next leg of the zig-zag. I laid bets with myself, trying to estimate the time to the next alteration. Sometimes the helmsman was a little late on his zig, and I watched on tenterhooks until the heavens duly revolved again. Around me on the narrow bridge I could see the silent figures of the officer-of-the-watch and the three look-outs searching the horizon with their binoculars. Above me towered the periscope standards, and immediately aft of them the radar aerial, constantly turning; if it stopped I waited anxiously for it to begin turning again. I might doze off uneasily for a while, but then one of the look-outs' reliefs came clumping up the conning-tower ladder and I would start up, stiff, chilled, wet from the dew and frantic for proper sleep. In the end I gave up the struggle and slept below in my bunk in the wardroom. Even then one half of my brain was always on the alert for the cry of "Captain on the bridge!" After several nights on the billet my reaction to the urgent summons became almost automatic, and sometimes I have rolled out of my bunk feet first on to the wardroom floor, stumbled, still asleep, through the control-room and found myself standing on the bridge in the blackness demanding "What is it?" and unable to remember how I got there.

But on the nights when we were expecting trouble I did not turn in to my bunk. Part of the night I spent sitting alone in the wardroom. The red lighting cast an eerie, yet almost intimate, glow over the mahogany woodwork of bunks and cupboards and across the curtains which hid the snoring forms of the officers off watch. On these nights I sat at the table with my binoculars slung round my neck, smoking incessantly, sometimes reading, though the dimness of the light prevented too much of this, sometimes just thinking, sometimes dozing with my head on my arms, but always listening with half an ear. Sometimes I would get up and go over to the chart-table on the other side of the passage-way, to ponder over the chart of our patrol area for the hundredth time.

When I could stand my own company no longer I would go up top and stand on the bridge for an hour or so. How lovely they were, those balmy tropic nights. The gentle puttering of our diesels' exhausts mingled with the sighing of the sea washing along the ballast tanks. The stars danced in the water, and from the invisible forests of Malaya came faintly a breeze to seduce the senses, heady and laden with a thousand spices. By leaning over the side of the bridge I could look for'ard along the whole length of the narrow fore-casing to where our bow was shouldering the smooth water aside and stirring the plankton into a blaze of phosphorescence. Sometimes this was so brilliant that the whole water-line of the submarine seemed to be edged with a white fire that would surely have caught the eye of a low-flying airman. But the nights of moonlight were the worst for making us feel naked, and when half the sea was a shimmer of light we felt we must be visible for a hundred miles.

At last an almost imperceptible paling of the eastern sky would warn us of the approaching dawn. Day comes so swiftly in the tropics that the temptation to stay on the surface just a

little longer had to be sternly resisted. I would decide to dive,
thankful that in a short while I should be able to relax and sleep.

On the North Cape patrol I had always made the early morning dive on the klaxon, which meant rousing the whole ship's
company to diving stations. Now that the crew had reached a
higher state of training I saw no point in disturbing the sleepers
below when we could perfectly well dive the submarine gently
and in slow time with those men who were already on watch.
So I would go to the voice-pipe and order both engines to be
stopped. When the report came back, "Both engine clutches
out, main motors ready," I ordered "Slow ahead together,"
told the men on the bridge to go below and then, quite quietly,
passed my final order, "Open main vents, take her down." The
vents opened, expelling the buoyant air with a dull roar and
shooting fountains of spray on each side of the bridge, as
though I were in the middle of a school of young whales. As
we began to sink bodily into the water with a gentle bow-down
angle, I took a last look round the horizon, lowered myself
through the hatch and pulled the heavy lid down over my head,

shutting out for the next fourteen hours the surface world of air
and space and light. Descending the ladder into the control-
room I could hear the swirl of the water rising gently outside
the hull, and by the time I was standing on the control-room
deck we would be well on our way down to 80 feet.

Half an hour later it would be time to come to periscope

depth, and we planed up, the depth-gauge needles creeping round to 75 ... 70 ... 60 ... 50 ... and at 40 feet I would be looking through the eyepiece at pale green water which in a moment scattered into a little flurry of broken light as the top of the periscope broke through the surface. Nothing in sight but the brimming sea, the sky flooding with light, and the brown-and-green island with its lighthouse just visible to the south of us. "Down periscope." Then I would go to the chart-table, show the officer-of-the-watch the line I wanted him to patrol on, tell him what time I wanted to be called, and climb gratefully into my bunk. There I would lie for a while, sensitive to the least change in the angle of the boat, glancing sometimes at the small depth-gauge by my right elbow, hearing the occasional hiss of the periscope being raised or lowered in the adjacent control-room, feeling the humidity already rising, and watching the little beads of condensation beginning to form on the compressed-air pipes overhead. Then—deep, blessed oblivion until breakfast-time.

The submarine-chaser came back alone the next morning, and again we watched him circumspectly as he passed through our area. He disappeared to the south-east, but two hours later returned on an opposite course. What was behind all this? Was he going north to escort something coming south, or was this a routine patrol? Or a preliminary scouting in preparation for something big expected from the direction of Singapore?

But our hopes of a sortie by the Japanese Fleet gradually dwindled. Except for the usual junks and driftwood, and one aircraft flying south, we sighted nothing for four days.

One morning when we came to periscope depth at first light I was disturbed to find that our island was not in sight. For a moment I felt like a man in a rowing-boat off shore who suddenly looks round to find a fog has come up and blotted out the land. With no landmarks visible there was nothing for it but to navigate by the shape of the sea's bottom. I assumed the north-going current had been stronger than usual during the night, and set a course to the south. Switching on our supersonic echo-sounder we noted the depths every quarter of a mile, plotted them on tracing paper and then by trial and error discovered a corresponding line of soundings on the chart. The horizon was mistier than we realised, and when we eventually sighted Jemur Island it emerged out of a thin haze exactly where we expected it to be. This being my first experience of navigation by echo-sounder, I was interested to find how accurate it could be in shallow water.

I was still under orders to reserve one full salvo for large warships (i.e. six bow torpedoes—we carried thirteen altogether: six in the tubes for'ard, six reloads and one in the external stern tube). On the evening of the 5th, however, all submarines in the Malacca Straits received a signal cancelling this instruction. This showed that the Staff in Trinco were no longer expecting the Japanese Fleet to come our way, and left us free to fire at any worth-while target. The following day a special signal addressed to *Storm* indicated the possibility of a merchant-ship passing through our area in the near future. That night, instead of retiring north as usual for the battery charge, I remained close in, despite the many junks in the neighbourhood.

But it was not until the following night that anything came our way. Shortly after eleven o'clock the officer-of-the-watch sighted a dark shape to the southward, sounded the alarm, and in accordance with my night orders turned stern-on. When I reached the bridge and began examining the stranger through my binoculars I could not decide what sort of ship he was. There was moonlight, but also a mistiness in the atmosphere which blurred his outline. He was moving on a north-westerly course, and he certainly wasn't a junk. He could have been a medium-sized merchant-ship—perhaps the one I had been warned about—or he might have been something a good deal smaller at a shorter range, possibly a submarine or even, if we were unlucky, a submarine-chaser. Right up to the last minute I still thought he might be a merchantman. We should have to chance it. I altered course to port.

Closing in to attack, I ordered four tubes to be brought to

the ready, with alternate depth-settings of 8 and 12 feet, and decided to spread my salvo a little ahead and astern of my target to cover possible errors in my estimations. Our radar could not pick him up and appeared to be quite useless. I set the night sight on the side of the bridge to the firing angle and gave the preparatory order:

"Slow together . . . Stand by."

Looking along the bar of the sight, I waited for the dark smudge that was the enemy to move across into line with the luminous pointers. As the moment approached when I was to fire my first torpedoes in action I was disgusted to find that I could not control the shaking of my limbs. Only a length now separated the target's bow from the point of aim . . . now three-quarters . . . a half . . . (I could still change my mind, let him pass, continue our peaceful night patrol) . . . and at last only a quarter. I yelled the order down the voice-pipe.

"FIRE ONE!"

The submarine gave a little arrested lurch as the first torpedo slipped away. Still crouched over the sight, I waited until the enemy's bow had crossed the line.

"FIRE TWO!"

The black shape moved steadily on, unaware of the torpedoes racing towards him at forty knots.

"FIRE THREE!"

And when his stern had drawn just clear of the sight I sent off the last of the salvo.

"FIRE FOUR!"

I straightened up and looked right ahead along the line of fire. The torpedoes were running true and smooth below the surface; in the moonlight I could see a shimmering path of disturbance streaking out across the water like a vapour trail. I now had a wild desire to turn away and retire at top speed, but if I did so he might sight us as we turned and have time to avoid the torpedoes. So I gritted my teeth and held my course, feeling horribly conspicuous, although we had the advantage of the light. I trained my binoculars on to him again as he approached the line of fire: he was still on the same course and still unaware of our presence. But we were closer to him now than at any time since the attack started, and I suddenly realised, with a stab of dismay, that what we had fired at was, without any doubt whatsoever, a submarine-chaser less than a mile away.

To my horror he crossed the line of fire unscathed. As he did so he saw the tracks of the torpedoes and began turning towards us. I bent to the voice-pipe.

"Control-room, control-room. DIVE, DIVE, DIVE!"

The main vents opened and I turned to the men behind me and yelled "Clear the bridge!" While the look-outs were tumbling through the hatch I looked back over my shoulder at the enemy. Black smoke was pouring from his funnel; he was increasing speed and coming in for the kill. Cursing myself for having missed him, I jumped down into the conning-tower, slammed the hatch shut over my head, rammed home the safety clips, and descended rapidly to the control-room thinking hard of all the things I must do.

"Shut the lower lid. Hard-a-port. One hundred feet. Steady on course 130. Shut off for depth-charging . . . Pilot, how much water have we got here? . . . Let me know when we've been two minutes at this speed . . ."

So long as the enemy was coming in fast his listening apparatus would be ineffective; this was the time to use our own speed for getting as far away as possible from our diving position. On the other hand, high speed under water was expensive on the battery, and if the hunt lasted a long time we should need every amp we had. After two minutes, therefore, I reduced to two knots. At this speed our propellers were practically noiseless.

"Stop the fans. . . . Absolute silence through the boat."

The snag about going deep when put down by the enemy was that the increased sea pressure tended to squeeze the hull, reducing its volume and so making the submarine slightly heavier in relation to the sea density. The trim had to be adjusted, which meant running the rather noisy pump. This time, however, we were lucky, for on passing 80 feet our rate of descent was checked by an apparent increase in the sea density. At 100 feet we were able to maintain our depth without any change in the trim.*

Blake reported that we were in about 25 fathoms of water. We dropped gently down to 120 feet. In the red glow of the night lighting we waited, tense, silent, expecting to be depth-charged at any moment. Now that the air-conditioning fans had been switched off we began to notice the heat. Sweat oozed from our brows and trickled down from our armpits. I stripped off my shirt and stood in nothing but my khaki shorts, and some of the others did the same. I looked across the control-room to the port after-corner where McIllmurray was sitting, crouched over the asdic set, moving the pointer steadily round the dial and listening through his headphones with patient concentration. Presently he looked up.

"H.E. on Green 170, sir." The enemy was somewhere astern of us.

"H.E. increasing, moving left."

I altered course fifteen degrees to port, trying to keep the enemy right astern as much as possible, and moved over to the chart-table, where Blake had been plotting our movements, to see exactly where we were in relation to the surrounding shoals and decide on my tactics. At the moment I felt rather hemmed in; we were steering approximately ESE, whereas our way of escape lay roughly NW. My best plan was, quite simply, to work round gradually to a north-westerly course, trying at the same time to keep the enemy's H.E. behind us.

Exactly ten minutes after we had dived, McIllmurray spoke the ominous words which every submariner hates to hear:

"H.E. closing rapidly . . . Bearing Green 175, sir."

And then they came, two cracking explosions in quick succession, and the echoes rolled and tumbled for miles over the sandy floor of the sea and came back to us like the sound of a

---

* Density layers were a common, almost daily, occurrence in warm waters, and in the event of trouble it was useful to know how deep they were; so much so that it was a regular drill on diving in the morning to drop down until the layer was found. Another advantage of the density layer was that it helped to deaden sound and confuse the enemy's asdic.

spent wave falling back over shingle. The shock dislodged a few crumbs of corking from the hull above my head, but did no damage to the lights. I remembered my first experience of depth-charging more than three years before, and said:

"Not very close."

Number One's eyebrows went up, and the Coxswain, sitting stolidly at the after hydroplanes, allowed himself a sceptical grin. We waited.

This was what I disliked most of all, this silent waiting, wondering when the next explosion would come, and whether it would be nearer than the last one, and when it came taking it without a chance to retaliate, unable to do anything but creep quietly away, not knowing what the enemy was doing, the barometer of hope rising and falling with the asdic reports . . . "H.E. moving up the starboard side . . . H.E. decreasing on Red 130 . . . H.E. moving across the stern from port to starboard . . . H.E. increasing on Green 140 . . ."

Ten minutes later, although there had been no further depth-charges, McIllmurray had some more unpleasant news for us. He could now hear two vessels thrashing about astern of us, and it was clear that our submarine-chaser had been joined by another. We spent an hour of anxiety, listening to their movements, but growing more confident as the minutes passed without further explosions and the H.E. grew fainter astern and we turned by slow degrees on to the course that would take us to more open water.

0130　　All H.E. ceased. Came to periscope depth. Sighted one of the chasers lying stopped only half a mile astern. Returned to 120 feet. Occasional H.E. heard, but nothing close.

0210　　Last H.E. passed up the starboard side and faded out on 330°. Decided to remain dived and come up for an airing shortly before dawn.

0427　　Surfaced. Very dark, moon had set. Nothing in sight. Started port engine and air conditioning.

0455　　Sighted blue flashing lamp close on port beam

0455¼　Dived hurriedly. Continued deep on course 310° until daylight.

At daylight I came to periscope depth and could see no sign of our pursuers. We had shaken them off, but at least one of them was almost certain to be still poking around near the scene of our midnight attack. All the same, we must return to our billet. The renewal of anti-submarine activity might mean that the expected merchant-ship was coming through, and we must be in our appointed place.

0630   Turned round to return to billet.
0746   Slow reciprocating H.E. reported, bearing 110°, 90 revs.
0750   Sighted masts and funnel bearing 110°. Commenced attack. Target course 310°
0752   Sighted submarine-chaser about five miles to the southward.
0756   Target zigged to port, putting me on his starboard bow. Still hull down over the horizon. Began to suspect this was the same small vessel sighted on March 2nd. He came on very slowly; as I saw more of him my impression was confirmed. Both target and chaser were proceeding zigging on a mean course of 285°. Chaser disappeared over the horizon.
0840   Heavy rain completely blotted out target, but I had already decided not to fire. From his H.E. bearing he appeared to alter course away. When the rain cleared it was seen that this was so, but he shortly after returned and passed me at a range of 4,000 yards on a course of 285° and finally disappeared. Both these vessels were presumably carrying out an A/S sweep as a result of the previous night's events.
0908   Resumed course for billet.
1130   Sighted Aroa Islands and fixed position on billet.

The rest of the day passed without incident, but we were suffering from a certain amount of discomfort. We had been dived for four and a half hours without air conditioning during the night, and our spell of twenty-five minutes on the surface had scarcely sufficed to refresh the air completely. By mid-afternoon we were noticing the lack of oxygen more than usual, breathing with difficulty and finding every movement an effort. We were also a little concerned about the battery. At the time of the attack the charge had only been half completed, and although there was no cause for immediate anxiety we knew that if we had more trouble during the coming night, and could not get in a full charge before daylight the following day, we should be in a serious position.

I wondered, too, if we had missed any vital wireless signals. In the Malacca Straits we were too far from Colombo to receive

W/T submerged (in home waters we could receive Rugby at periscope depth), so all signals had to go out during the hours of darkness, when the submarines would be on the surface. Signals were, however, always repeated two or three times in later routine broadcasts for the benefit of any submarine which had perforce been submerged while the original signal was being transmitted. It was about time we received our recall signal, and we certainly didn't want to miss that.

On surfacing after dark we were relieved to find nothing in sight. Unfortunately this peace did not last, and although we managed to complete the battery charge this time and were never actually forced to dive, we had a continually disturbed night. Half an hour after surfacing we sighted a white flashing light to the eastward, as of a vessel making the letter "T" several times over; we altered course away and retired to the westward. The alarm was sounded two or three times for dark objects that turned out to be junks. And at half-past two in the morning a black shape was sighted that did in fact turn out to be a submarine-chaser; this time we recognised him for what he was and crept discreetly away. By the time the night was over I was thoroughly exhausted.

We had missed two signals, but neither of them was addressed to us. Our recall signal came shortly before midnight, ordering us to leave patrol three nights later and return to Trincomalee by a prescribed route.

The remaining days were uneventful. We were now getting used to the conditions of tropical submarine life. While dived we wore nothing but a towel or sarong wrapped round the waist, and sandals to give ventilation to the feet. In our bunks we lay on rush mats, for they were cooler and less irritating than sheets or blankets. The air-cooling fans were a godsend. Glimpses of what a whole patrol would have been like without them were given us on the occasions when we were so close to the enemy that we had to switch them off—at the very time we most wanted to keep cool. For within five minutes the heat began creeping about us like a deliberate evil and the sweat welled up from every pore, glistening on our naked backs, trickling down our ribs and dripping over our eyebrows. If you were looking through the periscope the perspiration steamed the glass of the eyepiece so that you had to keep wiping it clear with tissue paper. When the air-conditioning fans were running, louvres in the ventilation shaft directed currents of chilled air into various corners of every compartment. Even then the humidity was such that we were never free from perspiration. Towards the end of the day the air grew heavy and foul from the sweating and breathing of fifty men. Tiny, untraceable leaks in the compressed-air pipes (under the enormous pressure of 4,000 pounds to the square inch) seeped into the atmosphere and gradually increased the pressure inside the boat. By teatime we would be feeling lethargic, suffering from headaches and breathing shorter and faster. Then, taking a tip from Lumby's practice in the Mediterranean, if no enemy was in sight through the periscope I would give the order to run the air-compressors for about ten minutes. This would take the excess pressure out of the atmosphere and put it back into the air-cylinders, not only making life pleasanter but obviating the dangerous sudden escape of pressure when the time came to open the hatch on surfacing.

Water being precious, we could not wash as often as we should have liked. I used to wash face and hands once a day, and all over every second or third day. Some of the men did not shave at all during the whole patrol, but I personally felt horribly scruffy with a three- or four-day beard and found a clean shave every other day was a good tonic for one's morale.*

Our amusements were much the same as in northern waters: the usual uckers, cribbage and liar dice. We read a good deal. My own reading was very miscellaneous: the short stories of Somerset Maugham, *The Oxford Book of English Verse*, Balzac's

---

* There were two "heads," or lavatories, in *Storm*: one just for'ard of the wardroom, reserved for Officers, Chiefs and P.O.s and E.R.A.s, and the other right aft. The contents of the pan were blown out by compressed air; but here you had to be careful, for if you worked the valves and lever in the wrong order you would suffer the unpleasantness of what was known as "getting your own back." If enemy ships or aircraft were about while we were dived, blowing of the heads would be forbidden, as the air bubbling up to the surface might have given us away.

Droll Tales, any light novel that was going the rounds, Macdonell's *England, Their England*, and of course dips into Shakespeare. We had now acquired a gramophone, though few records; Bing Crosby we ran to death, and we had a tune called *Beyond the Blue Horizon* which is still sometimes played and always has an absurdly nostalgic effect on me. In later patrols, when we were closer to land, it amused me to be looking through the periscope at an enemy harbour to the accompaniment of music from the wardroom.

At midnight on the 11th we began to withdraw from the billet in accordance with our orders.

But the patrol was by no means over.

March 12th

0312   Sighted darkened vessel. Closed to investigate. Eight minutes later decided I was getting too close and turned away.

0324   Vessel, which now looked unpleasantly like a small destroyer or large submarine-chaser, turned towards. I dived and went to 150 feet.

0353   Two depth-charges. Not very close, no damage. Enemy now began a very persistent hunt. His tactics consisted, apparently, of moving slowly in a wide circle round my diving position (why he didn't rush in and drop his two depth-charges on me straight away, I don't know), and stopping every two or three minutes to listen. Mine consisted of trying to keep his H.E. astern and gradually working round to a north-westerly course.

0423   Steadied on course 325° and maintained this course until I sighted Pulo Jarak at daylight. [Pulo means island.] Enemy's H.E. kept approaching and then fading, but gradually dropped astern.

0545   Came to periscope depth. Daylight. Sighted large chaser astern, hull down over horizon. Obtained fix off Pulo Jarak.

0550   Sighted masts of two other chasers on approximately same bearing as the other.

0700   Sighted mast bearing NW. This developed into yet another submarine-chaser, who presently passed me on an opposite course, three miles on my starboard beam, evidently on his way to join the others. Went to 80 feet while he passed.

0756   Returned to periscope depth. Chaser well past, hull down astern. The others had almost disappeared. Horrified to find we were towing a length of wood about 50 feet astern. Wonder how long I had been attached to these "buffs"?

0815   All chasers out of sight Decided to remain dived until I was beyond Pulo Jarak.

1358   Surfaced. Removed my "buffs," evidently part of some fishing gear. Several junks in sight all round.

1541   Dived for object on the horizon which looked like a possible submarine. It turned out to be a drifting tree trunk.

1615   Surfaced.

1740   Sighted mast bearing 300°   Stopped, raised periscope and examined it.

By looking through the periscope with the submarine on the surface I was able to see much further than I could have done from the bridge. We had to stop engines while I did so because the vibration they set up in the top of the periscope made it impossible to see anything.

I now saw that the vessel was a small modern coaster of about 500 tons. He was steering a south-westerly course which would take him to Belawan in Sumatra, and he was unescorted.

1742   Dived and commenced attack. It soon became evident that he was too far away for us to catch him up submerged, and the light was already failing.

1801   Surfaced, and closed on main engines, standing by gun action.

1819   Range 3,000 yards. Opened fire. Obtained first hit at 2,500 yards with the sixth round. Fall of shot difficult to observe in the gathering dusk. Target offered no resistance, but turned right round, stopped, and showed no further signs of life. Whether he launched a boat or not it was too dark to see, and knowing the submarine-chasers were not far away to the south of me I could not afford to wait for investigation. He did not catch fire, though one or two of our hits produced lurid flames for a moment.

We fired altogether fifty-five rounds. This was a lot of ammunition for a small target, but it was getting so dark that Blake, controlling the shoot as Gunnery Officer, could not tell whether our shots were hitting him on the water-line, although we had closed to a range of 900 yards. I did not want to get any closer in case the target was carrying ammunition and blew up. When he settled down in the water on an even keel and finally disappeared, I fell out the gun's crew and wasted no time in getting under way to resume our north-westerly course. It was quite on the cards that the chasers astern had heard the sound of the shooting and were on their way to investigate. It occurred to me that perhaps the last chaser I had seen going south had originally been escorting the coaster and had left him unattended in order to join the others in their search for me, a thought that helped to compensate for the sleepless hours of the previous night.

It was now quite dark. The sinking of our first victim, small though he was, acted as a tonic to our spirits, and all was cheerful in the messes as we sat down to our evening meal.

But the Malacca Straits had one more alarm in store for us. Shortly before two o'clock in the morning I was woken up by the now familiar call of "Captain on the bridge!"

0153   Ten miles south of Perak Island sighted small darkened ship ahead, looking very much like a submarine. Altered stern on. Lost target. Turned back and closed fifty degrees to right of previous bearing. Could not sight target, so stopped to listen. Asdic reported "H.E. fading on Red 45," but we could see nothing. At the same moment the officer-of-the-watch and one of the lookouts saw a red-flashing Aldis on Red 50, making a short and a long once only. Turned hard-a-starboard and retired at speed, working round to a course of 270°. Decided this must have been a patrol vessel, not a submarine.

I was wrong. I discovered later that we had run into one of our own submarines, *Trespasser* I think it was, on her way to patrol, and that the red light we had seen was part of her recognition challenge. However, we had done the right thing in retiring.

Soon after dawn we dived to keep out of the way of a flying-boat sighted by our starboard look-out, but he did not seem to have seen us, and we were able to surface and proceed a few minutes later. We were now in much more open water, turning north of Sumatra towards the Nicobar Islands. That evening I sent off a signal to Trincomalee giving a brief summary of our patrol. By dawn we were proceeding dived in the Nicobar Channel. This was where we had seen the Japanese submarine on our outward journey, but this time the day passed without incident. It was the last day's dive of the patrol. The next three nights and days gave us an uninterrupted surface run across the Indian Ocean in fine weather. On the fourth night we were navigating with extra care to make sure of arriving at the right place and at the right time for the appointed rendezvous with our escort.

But I still had time to sit down and type out the day's issue of *Good Evening*:

At the time of writing we have not been informed who our escort to-morrow will be. However, the rendezvous time is 0630, and it is then four hours' steaming into Trinco.

I should like to say, in this last issue of *Good Evening* for this patrol, how immensely encouraged I have been by the general behaviour of the Ship's Company throughout what has been a somewhat disappointing, and at times a trying and wearisome, patrol. The gun action, carried out by the crew of the gun with efficiency and enthusiasm, was a good experience and a welcome tonic. Our two skirmishes with submarine-chasers were invaluable experience for everybody, and for me in particular. We have at least caused a certain amount of annoyance to the enemy. In all, shall we say, a highly instructive Far Eastern "working-up" patrol, with a suc-cessful gun action as a kick up the enemy's backside.

Looking back through the file, I find that I had managed to produce an issue for every day of the patrol, a journalistic feat of which I feel modestly proud. My editorial labours had been frequently interrupted by the enemy, and the paper had now grown to two closely-typed sides of foolscap, with serials, quizzes, crossword puzzles, competitions and other similar features. I had also had to write up my official Log each day, no small task when things had been pretty lively.

We reached Trincomalee the following morning, all fit and cheerful. (The only sickness during the whole patrol had been two mild cases of prickly heat, or sweat rash, and these had cleared up during the three days' surface passage.) Turning the corner towards the defence boom I recognised a new arrival in the harbour—the submarine depot ship *Maidstone*, anchored within a stone's throw of *Adamant*. A signal began winking at us from *Adamant*'s bridge, ordering us to berth on *Maidstone*, and as we drew alongside I was delighted to see Bertie Pizey, still Commander Submarines, waiting to greet us at the foot of the gangway, just as he had done when *Saracen* arrived at Gib-raltar in September 1942.

When I went over to *Adamant* a little later to report to the Staff Office, I learnt that *Stonehenge* (Verschoyle-Campbell) had not returned from patrol off Sabang and was presumed to be lost.

XV

BETWEEN PATROLS : CEYLON

THE arrival of H.M.S. *Maidstone* from the Middle East was an indication that the submarine offensive against the Japanese was increasing. A single depot ship was no longer capable of supplying the needs of all the boats that were already operating here or were on their way out from England. For convenience of administration the submarines were now divided into two flotillas, the T-boats forming the Fourth Flotilla based on *Adamant* under Captain Ionides, and the S-boats forming the Eighth Flotilla based on *Maidstone* under Captain Shadwell. But since the Malacca Straits area was too small to permit of the submarines operating under two separate commands, the tactical direction of both flotillas was to remain the responsibility of Captain Ionides.

Captain L. M. Shadwell had not come out with the ship, but he arrived by air a few days after we got in from patrol. You did not have to know him for long before you became aware that behind the comfortable exterior was a man of natural dignity who commanded great respect and loyalty. He was unlucky in not getting the chance to direct his submarines operationally; even later when he took the Eighth Flotilla to Australia we worked in conjunction with an American flotilla and came under the operational command of an American admiral. However, he was free to concentrate his energies on seeing that his men went to sea in a high state of efficiency and that when they were in harbour everything possible was done for their welfare and recreation. Certainly during his reign *Maidstone* carried on and even increased her traditional reputation as a happy ship.

As the Fourth Flotilla consisted of the larger T-boats, the C.O.s in *Adamant* were inevitably senior to those in *Maidstone*.

But the two depot ships were anchored within a minute's boat-trip of each other, and there was a good deal of social inter-course between us. In *Adamant* were several old friends and acquaintances. Wingfield (my C.O. in the ill-fated *Umpire*) was now nearing the end of a successful commission in *Taurus*; he had done very well on a recent patrol when, badly damaged by depth-charges, he had surfaced and fought his assailant to a standstill in a fierce gun-action, and would have sunk him if a Jap aircraft had not appeared on the scene. Bennington, who had been my C.O. exactly three years before when he took over *H.28* as his first command, was now driving *Tally-Ho* and add-ing to his reputation for coolly calculated aggression; in a mid-night skirmish with a Japanese destroyer on his latest patrol he had come to such close quarters that the enemy's propeller had gone down one side and ripped open his main ballast tanks like a can-opener; although this did not prevent him from diving, on his return journey he had had some difficulty in keeping afloat. Also here were Favell, Collett, Rimington, Rufus Mackenzie, Robby Alexander, Bill King and others.

Operating from *Maidstone*, besides myself in *Storm*, were Tony Spender (*Sirdar*), Peter Angell (*Sea Rover*), Douglas Lambert (*Surf*), Sam Marriott (*Stoic*), Phil May (Spare C.O. but afterwards in command of *Tantivy*), and later on, Freddie Sherwood (*Spiteful*), Singey Anderson (*Sturdy*) and Pat Pelly (*Stratagem*). Pat Pelly had taken over command of *Stratagem* when Mike Willoughby, under protest, was ordered on to the sick list by the doctors just before the submarine left England for Ceylon. Later in the year, while operating in the Malacca Straits, Pat was cornered in shallow water and *Stratagem* depth-charged to destruction. A few men from the torpedo-stowage compartment escaped by opening the fore hatch and swimming to the surface, where they were taken prisoner.

During *Maidstone*'s time in Ceylon, Bertie Pizey, after his long term of office as Commander Submarines, was relieved by Commander A. C. C. Miers. Tony Miers had won the V.C. in the early part of the war when he was in command of the submarine *Torbay* in the Mediterranean. On one occasion he had entered Corfu Roads at night and, compelled to wait for daylight before attacking his prey, had charged his batteries in full moonlight on the surface in the middle of the enemy harbour. He brought the same pugnacious audacity to his job of Commander Submarines. He was a fire-eater in the best tradition, blustery, often rude almost to the point of insult, but vibrantly alive, generous-hearted and fanatically devoted to the support of his submarines at sea. We were certainly devoted to him.

Between patrols we made the most of our leisure. We swam daily in the warm water, sometimes wearing goggles to gaze down at the brightly coloured fish darting among the coral formations. We organised swimming and sailing picnics with the Wrens from the cypher office ashore, and went surf-riding on the palm-edged beaches further up the coast. Swimming in the harbour had one minor drawback: as a deterrent to midget submarines, small depth-charges were dropped at the entrance to the boom whenever the gate was opened, and if you were in the water within a mile of one of these depth-charges the sound-wave hit you in the stomach like an electric shock. We had plenty of sailing. *Maidstone* possessed four or five dinghies, and these were out on the water most days. We invented an exciting game of sailing battles, in which every resource of seamanship was needed to get up wind of your opponent and then soak him by scooping water over him with a bailer; we soon entered too vigorously into the spirit of the game, and after we had had a few collisions, grappled alongside, boarded, and hurled each other into the water to our hearts' content, we had to abandon the sport because of damage to the boats.

I was at sea when the jeep-hunts began. Phil May and two or three of the others thought it would be good fun to take a jeep into the jungle at night, carrying with them an aldis lamp which they hoped would mesmerise the game while they shot at it with their ·303 rifles. They met with indifferent success, and one night the jeep was chased by an elephant. The sound of the great beast crashing after them in the dark was too much for them, and soon afterwards the new enthusiasm died a natural death.

Sam Marriott was the only one of us who did anything original in the way of exploration. He and one of his officers, Sub-Lieut. Perowne, paddled a canoe from Kandy down the Makaweli River until they reached the sea at Trincomalee. In the course of their trip they negotiated rapids, saw herds of wild elephant, and even shot a crocodile, bringing back the skin to prove it. But the mosquitoes in the swamps by the river had found their mark too, and when the explorers reached Trinco-malee young Perowne went down with malaria. Not Sam—he had the constitution of a horse.

All submarine officers and ratings were given ten days' leave after every two patrols. I spent my first two leaves racketing around in Colombo, once with Peter Angell and the second time with Freddie Sherwood, who first met here the Wren officer who later became his wife. Colombo was amusing, hectic and very expensive. On one occasion I flew back to Trinco-malee in the mail plane; as always in air travel, the height flat-tened out all the natural beauty of the land, diminishing the vast tracts of jungle forest to nothing more than thickly-grow-ing parsley. Circling over Trinco before coming in to land, we peered down at a harbour full of toy ships of an extra-ordinary neatness; *Maidstone* and *Adamant* were easy to spot because of the submarines nestling alongside, but the flight-deck of the aircraft-carrier *Illustrious* looked like an elongated ping-pong table.

For my third and last leave in Ceylon later in the summer (to run ahead of chronology for a moment) I was invited to stay on a tea-plantation up in the mountains near Nuwara Eliya, over 7,000 feet above sea-level. I took Chief with me, and we set off from Trinco in a naval lorry. It was a morning of oppressive heat. At first the road was flanked by jungle on both sides, and monkeys swung and screamed in the branches arching high over our heads. We came out of the jungle and drove among bright green paddy-fields and through native villages swarming with wizened old men, bright-eyed women and naked children, all very attractive until they smiled and showed teeth hideously discoloured by the blood-red juice of the betel nut. We saw oxen at the plough, and from time to time a tame elephant hauling a log along the road, or chained up to a tree and waiting patiently, as a horse might be tethered to the porch of a house. Presently the road began climbing more steeply among the foothills, and the vistas grew longer and more superb, and in spite of the August sun we found the air turning chilly and had to put on extra clothes. We reached Nuwara Eliya in the late afternoon, and there Mr Astell, our host, met us in his car and took us down a dropping road to the Holyrood Tea Estate at Talawakelle, reaching his comfortable bungalow before dark. The contrast between the cool mountain air and the tropical heat we had left only that morning was delightful. For the first time for six months we really enjoyed getting into a hot bath, and after a superb meal we stretched at ease before a roaring log fire, blissfully content. That night I could hardly sleep for the incessant chatter of a million frogs and crickets.

Mr Astell provided all the ingredients of bachelor hospitality. In the evenings we drank whisky by the fire and talked until midnight, but by day he left us to our own devices. Chief and I went for long walks, explored the terraces of the tea plantations, lost our way in the rambling forests, stumbled across sudden waterfalls, native temples, and unimagined beauties of exotic landscape, and one day, like a couple of schoolboys, played "pooh-stick" races hour after hour in an irrigation duct that wandered for miles along a valley.

Those few days made one of the best holidays I can remember, certainly the most enjoyable leave I had in Ceylon, although we never saw a woman and spent not a farthing.

But that was later on, in August. It was still only the beginning of April when *Storm* sailed from Trincomalee for the second time, with orders to patrol off Port Blair in the Andaman Islands.

XVI

ANDAMAN ISLANDS

(From the log)

April 6th

0857. Slipped and proceeded, escorted by *Maid Marion*.
1853. Parted company with *Maid Marion*.

April 7th and 8th

On passage.

April 9th

Dived by day through Ten Degree Channel.

April 10th

Arrived in billet.

0434. Dived 8 miles south-east of Port Blair.

0700. Fixed position off Ross Island.

1330. Sighted fighter aircraft circling aerodrome inland. (Aircraft were sighted over the land on several occasions throughout the patrol.)

1935. Surfaced. Charged batteries, patrolling south of Sir Hugh Ross Island.

April 11th

0503. Dived. Decided to spend the day patrolling close inshore to the south of Ross Island.

1347. Four vessels appeared from the south—three small nondescript river cargo boats, and a small yacht or fishing vessel flying the Japanese naval ensign. The yacht, when about three miles away, suddenly came out of line towards me and turned a complete circle for no apparent reason, falling back

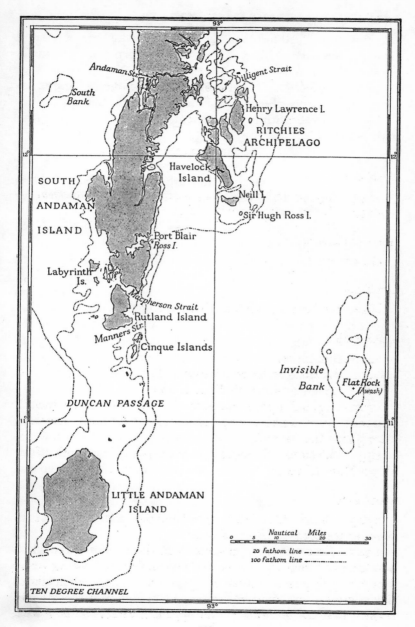

93°

Andaman Str.

South
Bank

Dilligent Strait

Henry Lawrence I.

RITCHIES
ARCHIPELAGO

12°   12°

SOUTH

ANDAMAN

ISLAND

Havelock
Island

Neill I.
°Sir Hugh Ross I.

Port Blair
Ross I.

Labyrinth
Is.

Macpherson Strait
Rutland Island
Manners Str.
Cinque Islands

DUNCAN PASSAGE

Invisible

Bank

Flat Rock
• (Awash)

11°   11°

LITTLE ANDAMAN
ISLAND

Nautical   Miles
0   5   10   20   30

20 fathom line ⎯·⎯·⎯·
100 fathom line ⎯··⎯··⎯··

TEN DEGREE CHANNEL

93°

231

into line again. All four vessels passed close inshore of me and
finally entered Port Blair. None worth a torpedo. Too many
for gun action.

1938. Surfaced. Charged batteries NE of the Cinque Islands, to cover possible approach route from the south.

2328. Passed within fifty feet of floating mine; spherical,
with horns.

April 12th

0510. Dived and patrolled three miles off Ross Island. During the forenoon asdic reported two distant small underwater
explosions.

1815. Sighted smoke close inshore, puffing like a train. No
railway or road on bearing, so assumed it must be small vessel
going south. Decided to follow him after surfacing and try to
find him when the moon rose.

1905. Sighted flashing light, possibly signalling, on Ross
Island.

1915. Surfaced. Ran to south, charging batteries at the
same time. Circumnavigated the Cinque Islands. No sign of
my prey, though one or two small lights, probably fishing boats,
sighted close inshore towards mainland.

April 13th

0328. Two vessels sighted to the southward, approaching
Port Blair. Closed to identify, then turned and ran in towards
land to hide silhouette, hoping to shadow by radar and deter-
mine target's speed. Target appeared to be a small coastal
tanker, anything from 500 to 1500 tons, escorted by one submarine chaser. Obtained three good radar ranges, the first at
4,800 yards and the last at 5,400. Obtained a plot speed of ten
knots. The moon was right overhead and giving very good
visibility, so at 0430 I went ahead, dived, and closed the track.
Soon after diving I found him in the periscope. Steadied on a
105 track, closing slowly, and watched him come on. Soon I
picked up the escort in the periscope.

The bearings were now altering far more slowly than I expected; perhaps the enemy was slowing down for the approach to Port Blair. Asdic could not hear any H.E. I decided to use a D.A. for five knots. On they came, painfully slowly. Fifteen degrees before the D.A. came on, the target's bearing suddenly stopped moving ahead and remained steady for about two minutes, although the escort passed on and across my bow. At about this time two distant underwater explosions were heard, which I presume were an accompaniment to the opening of the boom inside Port Blair. The target had now altered course, almost bows on; whether he had stopped or not I could not tell, but he began signalling by lamp, presumably towards Ross Island. Then he suddenly altered back to his original course and started going ahead again. There was no hope of re-estimating his speed at this short notice, so at 0505 I fired four torpedoes with a D.A. for five knots. All missed, probably astern. Went deep after firing and retired on a course of 145° until daylight. There was no counter-attack, but my hopes that the attack had gone unobserved were dispelled later.

0600. Came to periscope depth. No ships in sight. Returned to normal patrol line off Port Blair and re-loaded tubes.

1226. Small vessel came out of Port Blair on a course of 075°. Probably the same yacht who escorted the three small coasters on the afternoon of the 11th. He soon disappeared to seaward.

1355. Submarine-chaser came out of Port Blair, also steering 075°, and disappeared to eastward. This may have been the escort of the ship I had fired at during the night.

1445. The yacht returned from the eastward, this time two miles to the south of me, and passed towards the shore, then turned north, five minutes later turning south again along the shore. His behaviour convinced me he must be an anti-submarine vessel, and I began to wonder if he and the chaser were carrying out a sweep for me as a result of my torpedo attack early in the morning. I decided to trickle slowly southward during remainder of afternoon to make sure of being well clear of Port Blair when surfacing. The vessel hung about inshore all afternoon.

1918. Surfaced.

2045. Received signal indicating the possibility of ships approaching Port Blair at dawn, "hugging the coast."

April 14th

0303. Sighted small vessel to northward. Retired for twenty minutes. Suspected this to be our A/S friend of the afternoon.

0400. Closed to within two miles of coast, to get in as close as possible and prevent ships passing up inshore unobserved.

0452. When opposite entrance to Macpherson Strait, observed gunfire coming from close inshore. Dived. Heard slow diesel H.E. on the bearing. I had evidently been caught napping by the A/S vessel, who had managed to "hug the coast" even closer than I had. Ten depth-charges were dropped at varying intervals. No damage. I retired slowly south-westward at 150 feet, and the H.E. gradually faded astern.

0600. Came to periscope depth. Daylight. Sighted A/S vessel lying almost stopped, still in approximately my diving position. I altered round to a northerly course, while considering the possibility of coming up and gunning him.

0647. Sighted smoke to the eastward. Assuming this to be a ship making for Port Blair, I closed at speed.

0700. Target now seen as a medium-sized merchant-ship of some 3,500 tons, with three escort vessels (one of which was a destroyer), and with two aircraft circling overhead. Range estimated at about five miles. Target zig-zagging irregularly with 20° and 30° alterations, about an apparent mean course of 270°. This deceived me into thinking I was closer to enemy's track than I was. Later in the attack the mean course was found to be 300°. The result was that I failed to close in as much as I could have done.

To judge from the look of her puffing, thick, black smoke, she seemed to be a diesel ship, and this was confirmed by asdic, who eventually picked up diesel H.E. at 200 revs. Asdic detected two alterations of speed during the attack. Plot gave speeds of nine, seven and nine knots.

0840. Decided to use a D.A. for nine knots and enemy course of 300°. Steadied on to a 100 track. In view of the unusually strong escort provided for one merchant ship of her size, it seemed to me she must be worth a full salvo. Shortly before firing, three distant depth-charges were heard, but consider these were merely random preventive measures on the part of the "screen."

0852. Fired six torpedoes at a range of 5,000 yards [2½ miles]. At the moment of firing the target's course was 320°, but I was anticipating that at any moment she would alter to port on to her mean course of 300°. My last glimpse of her just after the last torpedo had been fired showed that she had in fact begun to alter to port.

I went deep after firing and ran south-eastward. Three minutes and twenty seconds after firing the first torpedo, there were two sharp explosions. The time was correct for running range. The explosions, which were quite unlike those of the depth-charges which followed, might possibly have been bombs from the aircraft, but if so why weren't there more of them? Asdic could not detect the target's H.E. after these explosions. I claim them as torpedo hits. [Later Intelligence confirmed that I was right. I had made my first sinking by torpedo.]

0901. Counter-attack began. Between now and 1050 twenty-one depth-charges were dropped. None was very close. At 0910 I ventured to periscope depth, but as the destroyer and an aircraft were approaching and only a mile away, I had no time for a careful look round. I could see two of the escorts, and a lot of thin smoke on the target's last bearing, but could not see the target itself. Went deep again.

1110. Periscope depth. No ships in sight. Continued to retire, to get well clear by dark. Re-loaded tubes.

1130. Sighted two of the escorts some way astern, evidently still hunting. Remained at periscope depth, watching them until they gradually dropped out of sight.

1839. Surfaced while it was still twilight, to make sure no patrols were in the vicinity. Charged batteries in the deep field all night.

April 15th

Decided to work up towards north-western edge of Invisible Bank and approach Port Blair from the eastward to avoid possible patrols further south.

0458. Dived eighteen miles ESE of Port Blair. Ran in at four knots.

0810. Sighted merchant ship steering eastward from Port Blair, escorted by same "screen" as for previous day's target, namely one destroyer, one submarine-chaser and one other A/S vessel rather like a river gunboat. At first I thought, pessimistically, that the target *was* the ship I had attacked yesterday, but on closer examination she was seen to be larger, about 4,000 tons, with a large derrick for'ard which the other ship did not have. Moreover, asdic counted 95 revs with *reciprocating* H.E., and the smoke was coming out of the funnel in typical coal-burning fashion.

I ran in at speed for as long as I dared. Even then the range was large on firing. I had only two torpedoes remaining in my bow tubes, and the stern torpedo. I considered firing the two bow tubes and then turning quickly to complete a salvo of three with the stern tube. However, by the time I could have turned and steadied for the stern shot, the first two torpedoes would be well on their way to the target, and before the other could be of any use the first two would either have hit or been sighted, resulting in either case in an alteration of course on the part of the target. I therefore decided to fire the two bow tubes only, and reserve the stern tube for a possible *coup de grâce* if I managed to damage her.

0837. Fired two torpedoes. Range on firing 5,000 yards. Three and a half minutes later there were two sharp explosions. The periscope was dipped at the time of the bangs, but a moment later this is what I saw:

Target turning hard-a-port just past the line of fire, half hidden by a veil of thin smoke; the destroyer, this side of the target, also just past the line of fire with a column of what looked like spray or white smoke just astern of him. I thought at first that this must have been the aftermath of a shallow depth-charge, until I looked at him again two minutes later and saw black smoke and orange flame pouring out of his stern. He was obviously hit. It looked very much as though the target had been hit too; she seemed to be making more smoke than usual, began to pursue a very erratic course, and finally almost stopped, pretty well beam on. Seeing this I began to manœuvre to attack her with my stern torpedo.

Two muffled depth-charges were heard shortly after the first two explosions, but the hit on the destroyer seemed to have demoralised the screen, as no further attempt at a counter-attack was made. I was able to watch the whole affair quite happily from a range of two miles or so, and Petty Officer E. R. Evans, the T.G.M., was able to have a look at his victim burning furiously.

The target was now at a range of three miles, zig-zagging wildly in all directions at a plotted speed of five knots. (Asdic counted 65 revs.) From her reduction in speed I felt certain she must be damaged. However, in spite of speeding up I could not get near enough to shoot with any chance of success.

In the meantime a submarine-chaser had come out from the shore and taken off the destroyer survivors, all of whom had been waiting disconsolately on the forecastle. An aircraft had also arrived and was performing inefficient aerobatics over the scene of confusion (all of which, incidentally, was well within sight of the staff office on Ross Island).

At 0952 the destroyer emitted a huge sheet of flame and a pall of thick black smoke and slowly sank. The submarine chaser returned to harbour with the survivors, and the remaining two escorts caught up with the merchant ship and made off towards the ESE. I decided to follow submerged, and surface for a chase when sufficiently far from Port Blair.

1030. Target now out of sight. I was hoping that her speed was still only five knots and that I would therefore have no difficulty in getting ahead of her and attacking again before evening.

1224. Surfaced. Smoke in sight bearing 103°. Proceeded at thirteen knots to follow and shadow. It soon became evident

that the party was making good a speed of ten knots, suggesting
that the damage, if any, must have been very small.

1430. Masts of target now in sight. Closed on the surface
until the tip of her funnel was just visible over the horizon.
Look-out on the periscope standards could just see the masts of
the escorts. Target zig-zagging about 40° either side of her
mean course.

1530. By now it was evident that the target, having crossed
the northern edge of Invisible Bank, had altered course to approximately 135° [south-east], presumably to make Penang.
Plot gave a speed of ten knots. It was now obviously impossible
to get in my attack before dark, so decided to shadow until
dusk, then close in to radar range to get accurate course and
speed, and proceed ahead to carry out submerged attack at
dawn.

1810. Passed W/T signal to Captain S/M 4, reporting the
merchant-ship [for the benefit of *Surf*, patrolling in the Penang
area] and my intentions.

1830. Fairly dark now. Began to close in for radar-
shadowing.

2134. Obtained radar echo bearing 360°, range 6,400 yards.
This was very satisfactory so far, as the target was only four
minutes adrift on the position expected from our previous estimations. I was, however, slightly ahead of her and on her starboard bow. I slowed down and turned south, aiming to get
into a position 6,000 yards on her starboard beam to obtain
accurate plot. Unfortunately the target chose this moment to
do one of her starboard zigs, and began coming almost directly
towards me. Radar showed range was closing rapidly, and
then detected a smaller echo at 4,200 yards, also closing. I increased speed and turned south-west to open the range, but it
seemed that I had somehow been detected by one of the escorts,
for his range now began shortening very fast and at 2202 he
swept a searchlight through an arc of about 60°. The beam
crossed over the submarine but he did not appear to have
spotted us. However, at this point I dived and went deep, expecting a hail of depth-charges. To our surprise, although his

H.E. was heard at intervals for some forty minutes afterwards,
no depth-charges were dropped. Either he was not sure if he
had seen anything, or else he had used all his depth-charges on
us the previous day.

I reckoned it would now be impossible to get into an attacking position until the following afternoon at the earliest. In
view of my shortage of torpedoes, I decided to abandon the
chase and go home. Moreover, lack of sleep during the last
two days was beginning to have a dangerous effect on the
efficiency of the crew.

April 16th

0113. Surfaced and proceeded towards Little Andaman
Island.

0300. Received Captain S M 4's signal acknowledging
my Enemy Report and giving my homeward route.

If I now proceeded direct for the Ten Degree Channel, I
would have to spend most of this day dived. I thought it might
be worth while using this time to return towards the vicinity
of Port Blair, with the double purpose of (a) trying to find a
small coaster among the islands to the south of the port and
taking two or three prisoners [in my patrol instructions I had
been told to take a few prisoners if a suitable opportunity
occurred], and (b) deceiving the enemy into thinking I was still
on patrol there. I therefore turned northward on sighting
Little Andaman Island and proceeded on the surface towards
Port Blair.

1056. Japanese heavy bomber flew directly over us on a
northerly course at a height of 1,000 feet but did not appear to
have seen us.

1418. Abeam of the southern tip of the Cinque Islands,
look-out sighted vessel bearing 320° about eight miles away.
At that range he looked a very possible coaster making up
coastwise towards Port Blair, but as I increased speed to close
the range he turned towards and began coming south at speed.
He was now identified as almost certainly our old A/S yacht
friend who had fired at and depth-charged us in the early hours

of the 14th. Knowing he had only a twelve-pounder gun, I reckoned there was no reason why a successful gun action should not be carried out. One hit on his frail hull ought to be fatal to him. Went to "gun action" stations.

The protagonists were now rushing towards each other at full speed on opposite and parallel courses about two miles apart.

1432. Enemy opened fire, range approximately 5,000 yards. A moment later *Storm* followed suit. The enemy's range was found with sixth round and the target straddled. None of his shots had fallen close as yet. After our tenth round there was an unaccountable delay in the supply of ammunition from below, and the next two rounds came up with an agonising slowness. During this infuriating pause the enemy also found the range, and was keeping up a remarkably rapid fire. His alternate shorts and overs were falling closer and closer with alarming accuracy. For some reason I could not understand, our ammunition supply had now practically petered out. It was clearly only a question of moments before the enemy scored a direct hit on the submarine. There was nothing for it but to break off the action.

1434. Dived, went deep, and grouped up for five minutes in an ESE direction. As the periscope went under I had a last glimpse of the enemy turning furiously towards for the kill, still firing.

1445. Six depth-charges with "closing H.E." No damage. Shortly afterwards the H.E. faded out astern and was not heard again.

[We had with us on this patrol one of the doctors from *Adamant*, Surgeon Lieut.-Commander I. F. Logan, R.N.V.R., investigating at first hand the effect of tropical conditions on the efficiency of submarine crews. Doctor Logan gained more practical experience than he bargained for. In the last three days we had fired twelve torpedoes, come under gunfire twice, and survived three different series of depth-charge attacks during which a total of forty-four depth-charges had been dropped by the enemy. During the depth-chargings Doctor Logan went calmly from compartment to compartment with his scientific instruments, measuring the humidity in the atmosphere and observing the reactions of the crew. As the last attack ceased and we knew we'd got away with it once more, I sent a message along to the doctor asking if there was anything else he would like to try. A gloomy voice from the wardroom replied, "No thanks, I've had it."]

I now investigated the mysterious and lamentable failure of the ammunition supply. It was caused by the fuse caps, which are supposed to be only hand-taut, having been screwed down so tightly that by no means could they be unscrewed, in spite of frantic efforts on the part of the supply party, assisted by the Engineer Officer. [The most annoying part of the whole business was that the shells would probably have exploded on the target even if they had been fired with the fuse caps on.]

1620. Periscope depth. No vessel in sight. Turned south and proceeded at four knots.

1843. Surfaced. Set course to pass through Ten Degree Channel and thence for Trincomalee.

April 19th

0613. In company with escort of three M.T.B.s.
1040. Secured alongside *Maidstone*.

Signal from Commander-in-Chief, Eastern Fleet

WELL DONE, STORM. THE JAPS MUST HAVE THOUGHT YOU WERE A TYPHOON.

Entry in Storm's *Visitors' Book*

"6th–19th April. Innes F. Logan, Surg/Lt. Cdr. R.N.V.R., 'M.O., H.M.S/M *Storm*.' A harrowing experience. Not (repeat *not*) to be repeated. God bless you."

XVII

CLOAK AND DAGGER

WHEN we sailed for our next patrol we had on board an R.A.F. inflatable rubber dinghy and three extra passengers: an Army major, a naval rating and a native of Sumatra. We were under secret orders for an unusual mission.

Leaving Trincomalee at dusk on May 6th we travelled all the way across the Indian Ocean on the surface as usual. During the afternoon of the 9th white cumulus clouds billowing up over the horizon on the starboard bow showed that we were approaching the northern mountains of Sumatra. Soon after dark, radar reported land echoes thirty miles ahead, and by midnight we had made our landfall and fixed our position. Slowing down so as to arrive at the right place just before dawn, we passed to the north of Pulo Bras and dived in the middle of Bengal Passage, about eight miles west of Pulo Weh, our objective.

Pulo Weh is an island off the north-west tip of Sumatra. Commanding the bay on the north side is the port of Sabang, which at that time was occupied by the Japanese as a naval base. The object of our Special Operation was to land an "agent"— the Sumatran native—to obtain information about the facilities and defences of the port. The Sumatran had volunteered for the job and had been under training in India for several months. We were to land him on the south side of the island and pick him up at the same spot four days later. The landing party consisted of the Major and the naval rating, a Leading Seaman. They were to row the Sumatran ashore in the rubber dinghy and then return to the submarine. We had rehearsed the drill at Trincomalee a day or two before sailing, and it was just as well that we had.

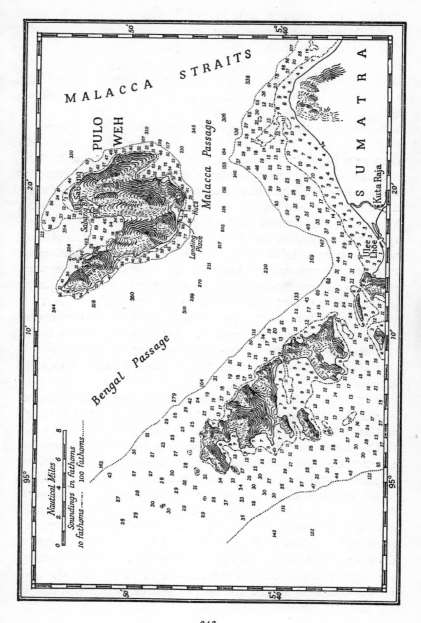

After diving we went deep to wait for daylight, closing slowly in towards the island. A little later we came up to thirty-two feet and examined it carefully through the periscope. The land rose steeply from the shore to a high ridge which ran like a spine down the whole length of the nearest arm of the island, rising gradually to a pair of humps in the south-west corner. Silhouetted in the half-light it had the semblance of a gigantic stranded whale. It was thickly wooded everywhere, and when the dawn came up behind the land and threw a pink flush all over the sea and sky, we saw that the steep slopes of the shore were covered in luxuriant foliage which came tumbling right down to the water's edge, with rust-coloured rocks showing here and there amongst the vivid green. Although no swell was apparent to seaward we could see an occasional surf exploding lazily against the rocks and drenching the overhanging creepers. No place for a landing here. Even if a landing were possible, no one could have forced a way through the jungle undergrowth which climbed abruptly to the skyline. We steered in until we were no more than a mile off-shore, and then turned south-east along the coast.

Our inspection was interrupted by three small river cargo-steamers which appeared from the northward and passed in line abreast down Bengal Passage within a mile or two of our position. They would have made a perfect gunnery target, but we were obliged to keep quiet until the Special Operation was over, and therefore had to watch them go by unmolested.

I spent most of the morning trying to train the Major in the use of the periscope. He appeared to have no sense of how long he had had the periscope up, and time after time I was obliged to tell him rather sharply to lower it. He seemed oblivious of the fact that the whole operation might be jeopardised if the periscope were spotted from the shore. Nor was he very intelligent in the matter of identifying landmarks. Spread all over the wardroom table was a large-scale aerial photographic survey of the whole island, and the Admiralty chart was open on the chart-table; the Major and I took it in turns to look through the periscope and then brood over the plans.

We had already selected a possible landing-place on the south-west coast of the island. Here the photograph showed what appeared to be a sandy beach with a wide clearing in the jungle behind it, and issuing from the clearing a path which led in the direction of Sabang, following a valley between the two humping hills. I hoped it would be possible to use these hills for fixing our position off the landing-place at night.

Accordingly we followed the coast until at noon we were opposite the place we had chosen. The soundings on the chart showed deep water up to a short distance from the shore. We closed to within four cables (800 yards) and through the high-power periscope were able to see everything in great detail. The beach was there all right, a fine stretch of white sand, with palm-trees nodding over it, and on the slope of the hill behind it a large open space clear of jungle. We could even identify the track leading up between the two hills. But at the top of the beach was a group of straw-thatched huts, and we could clearly see the dark-skinned inhabitants moving about among the trees. The place was unhealthily over-populated from our point of view. Moreover, a little to the right of this village, where the hill curved forward, I noticed a small square construction set high up on the bluff which sloped steeply down to the sea. It looked suspiciously like an observation post or gun-emplacement, perhaps both.

However, we had earlier observed a narrow strip of beach about three-quarters of a mile back, and we now returned to examine its possibilities. It seemed to suit our purpose excellently. The two hills were still well placed to give me a fix by night, and immediately behind the beach was another small but conspicuous patch of clearing in the jungle which, if we were lucky, might stand out in the dark and provide a leading-mark for the boat party. I took careful bearings of all useful landmarks, and then retired slowly to seaward, satisfied that we ought to be able to get the party ashore at the right spot.

We surfaced three miles to seaward when it was quite dark. We had agreed to wait for moonrise before sending the boat party in, for they would need a little light to identify the beach we had chosen and find the inland path without stumbling on the village. The moon would rise behind the island, so there was no danger of our being silhouetted towards the shore. We had an hour to wait. I decided to make use of the time by putting in a short battery charge. Not only should we be making our approach to the beach on the motors, but if we were unlucky enough to run into an anti-submarine patrol we might be forced to dive and spend the rest of the night being hunted. Every amp we could get back into the battery now would be valuable, and at the same time the engines would be drawing fresh air into the submarine.

I stayed up on the bridge while we cruised slowly back and forth, three or four miles out from the shore. Down below the boat party were making their final preparations. We were not at full buoyancy, but trimmed down to reduce our silhouette, to simplify the launching of the boat and to enable us to dive more quickly if we ran into trouble. Being lower in the water than usual, the engine exhausts were submerged and muffled, and threw up continuous little fountains of spray. While the officer-of-the-watch and the look-outs concentrated to seaward, I trained my binoculars along the murky shore and tried to identify the landing-place. After some minutes I thought I could just make out the patch of clearing which was to be our leading-mark. The island was black and sinister. From time to time lights flickered among the huts under the palm-trees. It was very quiet.

Presently I was aware of a gradual lightening of the sky behind the right-hand hill. I looked at my watch and saw that it was nearly eight o'clock. The moon was about to rise.

"Control-room! First Lieutenant on the voice-pipe."

"First Lieutenant speaking, sir."

"Number One, tell the boat party to stand by. Open the fore hatch and get the boat up on deck. When the boat is through, shut and secure the hatch as quickly as possible."

"Ay, ay, sir."

"Control-room, break the charge, out both engine clutches."

The noise from the exhausts died away. I was pleased to notice that a little breeze had got up and was ruffling the face of the sea to a darker grey. This would help to make the dinghy less conspicuous during its approach to the shore.

"Bridge! Both engine clutches out, main motors ready."

"Slow ahead together."

As I brought the submarine round on to a course which aimed straight at the patch of clearing, I looked for'ard and saw the lid of the fore hatch swing open. Wade and the Second Coxswain stepped out, and began hauling up the deflated dinghy. This hatch was the one normally used for loading torpedoes and conveniently led down into the submarine at a forward-sloping angle. It was the only hatch which could have been used for getting the boat out, since all the others were vertical. But being so close to the water-line, it was a dangerous hatch to have open at sea. As long as it was open we were in a vulnerable position, and I was very relieved when the loose folds of the dinghy were safely up on deck and the hatch slammed to. So many dark figures had emerged after the dinghy that it now seemed as though half the crew were down there on the fore-casing, but in fact there were only six men: the three members of the boat party, with Wade and two of our men to give them a helping hand. The Major pulled the string which released the compressed-air bottle inside the rubber skin, there was an explosive hiss and the dinghy ballooned out with an alarming suddenness, nearly slithering off the casing as it did so.

I proposed to take the submarine to within half a mile of the shore before launching the boat. Even so they would have a heavy pull before them, but it would be madness to take the submarine in any closer. We still had a mile and a half to go when the Major came softly aft to the bridge to report that all was ready. With his blackened face he looked like a desperado out of a boys' adventure story. We made a final check on our watches and ran quickly once more over the arrangements. He and his Leading Seaman would row the Sumatran ashore. I would wait in the vicinity for half an hour in case of trouble, then retire to seaward to continue the battery charge. Meanwhile, having concealed the boat, they would push inland to find the path, and when the Sumatran was safely on his way to Sabang, return to the beach. Three hours from the time of the first launching I would return to pick them up. As we might have difficulty in sighting the dinghy, the Major would flash his torch towards us, making the letter R—short, long, short.

The moon was just beginning to appear over the shoulder of the hill. We had timed it perfectly. The patch of clearing was now easily visible, but its bearing had moved a little to the right, showing that a slight current was taking us sideways towards the north-west. I pointed this out to the Major and warned him he would have to allow for this on his way in. In the darkness the island seemed appallingly close, the skyline rearing high and black before us, but I had memorised the crucial bearings and knew we were still outside the half-mile limit.

When the bearings were nearly on I stopped the motors, waited until the way was off the ship, and then gave the order to launch the boat. It slipped into the water with no trouble. The three men climbed gingerly down into it and within half a minute they were away, the Major and the Leading Seaman with an oar each, pulling steadily for the land, and the cheerful little Sumatran sitting erect in the stern steering with a paddle. I immediately ordered "Half astern together," and began to retire discreetly to a safer distance. Through my binoculars I watched the boat pursuing a somewhat erratic course until I lost it against the dark line of the shore; but they seemed in the end to be making for the right spot. I waited half an hour as agreed, a mile and a half to seaward, then turned north-west into the middle of Bengal Passage and re-started the battery charge.

We were due to pick them up at ten minutes to midnight. Half an hour beforehand I began to return towards the landing-place, but keeping three miles offshore. The moon was now very bright indeed, and I hoped we should not have to go in quite so close as we had done before. To our surprise, fifteen minutes before the appointed time we suddenly saw the letter

R flashing at us from not very far away, and there they were already half-way out from the shore and coming to meet us. We swung towards them, and ten minutes later they were both back on board and the dinghy had been deflated and taken down through the fore hatch.

The adventurers were delighted with the way everything had gone according to plan. They had had no trouble in hitting the right beach and concealing the boat in the undergrowth. In less than twenty minutes they had found the track leading up between the hills. They had gone a little way along it with the Sumatran and finally left him to make his own way in the best of spirits. Returning to the beach, they had stayed hidden for a time, but then decided they would prefer to wait for us out on the water.

I now turned away from the island and, after running out until we were well in the middle of Bengal Passage, set course eastward to pass out through Malacca Passage, the strait which divides Pulo Weh from the mainland. Part One of the Special Operation had been carried out successfully.

We now had four days to waste, during which we could make no attacks on shipping, lest we attract anti-submarine patrols to the area and endanger Part Two of the operation. So we moved round the corner, eastward along the north coast of Sumatra, examining the shore at our leisure. We investigated the little port of Sigli, but saw nothing of interest except a small vacant jetty and a number of corrugated-iron warehouses. Further east we found a place where the only railway line in northern Sumatra ran close to the sea and crossed a small bridge within easy gun range. This bridge would be a tempting gunnery target for the last day of a patrol, particularly if the action were timed to coincide with the railway time-table. West-bound trains were sighted at 1100 and 1300. It was galling not to be able to attack them.

Early in the morning of the fourth day we returned towards the scene of our operation, diving before dawn in the middle of Malacca Passage. During the day we moved round the corner

to have another look at our landing-place, and after nightfall
surfaced well out to sea. We were not due to pick up the
Sumatran until midnight, so we spent the intervening hours
charging batteries about six miles west of the island. With half
an hour to go we stopped the charge, prepared the dinghy on
deck ready for launching, with the Major and the Leading Seaman standing by, and stationed ourselves about a mile from the
shore to await the agent's signal—the letter N (a long and a
short), which he was to flash by torch at intervals of a minute,
starting exactly at midnight.

The suspense of the last five minutes was almost unendur-
able, and several times I had to put my watch to my ear to make
sure it was still going. But at last both the luminous hands were
pointing firmly to twelve, and it was midnight.

It was a terrible anticlimax when no signal came. Perhaps his
watch was slow. But the minutes passed and nothing happened.
The moon began to rise over the hill and threw our patch of
clearing into prominence. The Major came aft along the casing
and climbed up beside me on the bridge. It was certainly beginning to look as though something had gone wrong. There
was just a chance that the Sumatran had for some reason been
unable to get back to the beach on time. This possibility had
of course been foreseen, and it had been agreed that if either
party were prevented from keeping the rendezvous a second
and final attempt would be made the following night. I said,
"Well, Major, if he hasn't shown himself by half-past we'll
pack up for tonight and give him another chance tomorrow."

Precisely at the half-hour, and just as I was about to give the
orders for going astern and falling out the boat party, we saw
the signal, a long and a short winking at us from the shore, clear
and unmistakable. But there was something peculiar about the
exactness of that half-hour delay which made us pause and
consider.

Our clocks and watches were still keeping Ceylon time (six
and a half hours ahead of Greenwich). Being so much further
east, one would have expected Sabang local time to be ahead of

Ceylon. It ought to have been well past midnight. However, man can decide to keep whatever time he likes, and it was possible the Japanese here were keeping a time that was half an hour *behind* ours. Perhaps it was a Jap who was making the signal, unaware of the difference in time. Perhaps the Sumatran had been caught and tortured and forced to give the whole show away. Perhaps he had turned traitor.

On the other hand, it was still possible that there was a more innocent explanation. His watch might have stopped, and in restarting it he might have set it by a local clock. Or again he might have been delayed in his return to the beach and the exactness of the half-hour was just a coincidence.

However, there was in any case another disturbing feature of the signal. It was coming not from the landing-place but from a position well to the right. It was in fact so much to the right that it was bang in the middle of the beach in front of the village. If the game *had* been given away, it seemed that the Japs were nevertheless not sure of the right spot. But perhaps the Sumatran had only just got back to this side of the island and had not had time to find the correct beach.

Whether he was all right or not, we still did not want to land the boat right in front of that village. So we decided to postpone the pick-up until the following night, hoping that in the meantime he would be able to re-discover the original beach. Accordingly we withdrew, and continued the battery charge out in the deep field.

I thought it better to patrol well away from the island during the following day. After diving in the early hours we kept over to the southern side of Bengal Passage. Half-way through the morning a small ferry-boat came out from Ulee Lhoe, the little port at which the Sumatra railway terminated, crossed the strait and disappeared round the eastern edge of Pulo Weh. This was probably the connecting-link between the railway and Sabang. Looking at the passengers as the boat passed within a mile of us, I reflected that they had probably been aboard one of the trains we had seen further along the coast, and that if it had not been for the operation in hand we might have surfaced and taken one or two useful prisoners. Perhaps there would be another chance later in the patrol when the operation was over. I decided to spend the rest of the daylight hours investigating this port of Ulee Lhoe, which the ferry had just left. And here occurred a curious incident which puzzled me at the time but took on a new significance in the light of what happened later.

Towards evening we were patrolling about two and a half miles north of the place, in a depth of about thirty fathoms, when two apparently innocent motor fishing-vessels cast off from the jetty and began to move slowly in line abreast towards our position, stopping occasionally and then coming on again. I feel certain now that they were some form of anti-submarine patrol, but at the time I was completely at a loss to account for their behaviour. It was more than a coincidence. Yet I was confident that our periscope could not have been spotted, for there was a considerable lop on the sea and we were two and a half miles from the shore. It was possible that our propeller noise had been detected on shore hydrophones, but in that depth of water it seemed unlikely. Somewhat disturbed, I retired north-westward until I had lost sight of them in the falling dusk.

At midnight we were sitting once more opposite the landing-place. This time, in case of trouble, we had the gun's crew standing by at the gun, with a shell all ready in the breech.

When the signal again came exactly half an hour late we were faced with an extremely difficult decision. As Captain of the submarine I had an over-riding power of veto. If I considered that the situation exposed the submarine to too great a risk it was my duty to call off the operation. On the other hand, I had no power to order the Major to proceed with it if he on his side thought the odds against success were too great. The circumstances were now, to say the least, extremely suspicious. At the same time, we still had no positive proof that anything had gone seriously wrong. The flashing signal on this second night, although not quite in the right spot, was at least much nearer to it and certainly a good quarter-mile away from the village. I did not see how I could abandon the operation on the evidence available. I should have to justify such a decision to Captain Ionides on my return, and the more I thought about it the more I realised my reasons would look pretty feeble. Besides, we had a duty to the Sumatran, who had after all taken a bigger risk than any of us. We could not leave him so callously to what would undoubtedly be a ghastly fate at the hands of the Japanese. It seemed to me that we were bound to give him the benefit of any doubt we might have.

Standing together on the bridge, the Major and I argued the problem back and forth for a good five minutes. He had the wind-up properly. I could hardly blame him for that; it was he, and not I, who would have to go in to the beach; the smell of treachery was in the air, and the island loomed ominously before us in the dark like a crouching beast waiting to spring. But however much I might sympathise, I was convinced it was his duty to go forward with the operation. One thing was certain: this was no time for dithering. The longer we waited the greater the risk.

All this time the signal was flashing from the shore. Finally I lost all patience.

"Major, it's for you to decide. But I can't keep my ship waiting here all night while you make up your mind. If you don't take the boat away in five minutes I shall call off the operation and report my views to the Staff when we get back."

He turned without a word, went for'ard and told his Leading Seaman to stand by. In that moment I admired him very much. He was extremely frightened, but in cold blood he was going ahead with the job he had to do, and you can't be braver than that. I ordered "Half ahead together," and we began moving in. This time I took the submarine to within 800 yards of the shore before giving Wade the order to launch the boat.

As they pulled away I felt I was probably sending them to their death, but the die was cast, and I had too many other things to worry about now. We were still pointing towards the shore; if there were trouble and we had to dive quickly we might hit the bottom in the shoaling water. Yet I couldn't turn

my stern to the shore, for if I did we shouldn't be able to fire
the gun, which was for'ard of the bridge. So I manœuvred the
motors until we swung slowly round to port and came to rest
roughly parallel with the beach. From that position a half-turn
to port would take us immediately into deeper soundings. The
recognition signal was still flashing away, much too brightly, I
thought . . . N . . . N . . . N . . . N . . . and with increasing
frequency as the boat drew nearer to the shore. Wade and
Blake were up beside me on the bridge, Blake at his post as
Gunnery Officer, looking down at the men waiting in silence
on the gun platform. I told him to train the gun on the
flashing torch and be ready to open fire at the first sign of
trouble. The barrel swivelled round until it was pointing out
on the starboard beam. I still had my binoculars fixed on the
boat, but presently lost sight of it against the dark reflection
of the land.

When the torch stopped flashing, the darkness of the island
sprang out blacker and more intense than ever. We waited for
the climax in a silence that was as taut as a wire stretched almost
to snapping point—a wire that might have been strung between
my binoculars and that point on the shore-line where I had last
seen the boat. And then suddenly in the lenses I saw a black
dot on the water, emerging from the shadows and moving towards us. It was the boat returning. For a moment I dared to
hope that all was well. But then that torch started up again . . .
N . . . N . . . N . . . flashing much faster now, moving a little
towards the left along the shore, and at once it was certain that
something was wrong.

In the same instant the silence split asunder and the whole
basin of the hill erupted into a crackle of noise and flame. We
found ourselves the focal point of a radial cross-fire from four
machine-guns set in an arc round the lower slopes behind the
shore. Fiery streams of tracer stuttered towards us across the
water, accelerating swiftly, ricocheting off the sea like molten
pebbles, whipping over the periscope standards. And simultaneously, from the emplacement high up on the bluff astern of
us, came the sharp boom of a larger-calibre gun, probably a

four-inch. Fortunately this gun seemed to have no idea of our range, and its shells went hurtling over our heads and far into the seaward darkness. The general shindy, after the long silence, was appalling.

Blake was yelling in my ear.

"Open fire, sir?"

"Yes, open fire."

We cracked off a shell and saw it burst on the slope of the hill in a muffled shower of sparks. Over. "Down 200 . . . Fire!" The second round landed near the spot where the torch had been flashing. But we were unequally matched for a shooting contest: we could not hope to silence five guns whose exact positions were not easy to pin-point. Already machine-gun bullets were striking the casing of the submarine, and sooner or later we should have casualties among the gun's crew. There seemed no point in exposing the men if they could serve no useful purpose. So I ordered them to fall out, and sent everybody down below except Wade.

One of the machine-guns had shifted its fire to the dinghy, which at this point seemed to be about 400 yards away. Now that I could see the boat clearly with the naked eye, I realised that there was only one man in it. This was disastrous. And it seemed impossible that the one man now rowing with such desperate haste could get through to us without being hit.

I was extremely frightened. It was my first experience of being under machine-gun fire, and instead of acting up to tradition and standing boldly and calmly at the front of the bridge regardless of danger, I sheltered myself as well as I could behind the for'ard periscope standard, cocking an eye occasionally to see how the boat was getting on. I was in something of a quandary. I had to think of my duty to the ship. We had run into what was obviously a prepared ambush, and at any moment we might find our retreat cut off by a hidden fleet of submarine-chasers. All my instincts were to dive and get the hell out of it, and I daresay that if I had done so there and then my action would have received official approval. I was responsible for fifty men and a valuable ship; one unlucky hit on the pressure hull from the four-inch gun would be fatal to us. Ought I to continue risking *Storm* for the sake of one man?

The correct answer was undoubtedly No, yet somehow I could not bring myself to desert him while there was a sporting chance. The big gun was still overestimating our range, its shells roaring well over our heads with a noise like an express train. I compromised by deciding that I would wait so long as this gun showed no signs of finding our range. The machine-guns could do no serious harm to the submarine itself.

Someone was calling up the voice-pipe. It was Number One.

"Are you all right, sir?"

"Yes," I replied testily, "of course I'm all right."

But Number One was quite correct to ask. For all he knew Wade and I might both have been dead, and they would have looked silly waiting below for orders if there was no one alive up top to give them.

The boat was coming on at a maddeningly slow speed, but with every yard he put between himself and the shore the rower's chances were increasing. When he was about 100 yards away I recognised him without doubt as the Major, and then suddenly saw the Leading Seaman in the water, hanging on to the stern of the boat and swimming with his free arm. Wade and I were now wildly agitated; it was like the last lap of a neck-and-neck race, but a hundred times more exciting. We yelled crazy words of encouragement which they could not possibly hear above the din. I even urged the Major to get out and swim, though what good that would have done I cannot now imagine.

At last the incredible was coming true. They had run the gauntlet. They were within a few yards of us, and the Major was turning his head to choose the best place for coming alongside. I sent Wade down on to the fore-casing to give them a hand up, and in a few moments they were scrambling over the ballast tank and up on to the casing. "Get them up to the bridge," I shouted. "Don't worry about the boat." And then:

"Control-room! Full ahead together. Hard-a-port. Steer

210." As the submarine gathered headway I caught a glimpse of the abandoned dinghy drifting down the starboard side.

The Major and the Leading Seaman were completely done in. Retching and groaning, they struggled through the little door at the front of the bridge, staggered past me and somehow got themselves into the hatch and down the ladder.

I ordered Wade to follow them. He had been splendid.

"Control-room! DIVE, DIVE, DIVE!"

As I pulled the hatch down over my head I could still hear the four-inch shells screaming overhead and the bullets whining

and pinging all round us. In a few seconds we should be safe under water. Landing hurriedly on the control-room deck I ordered "Thirty-two feet" and told Blake to switch on the echo-sounder, for I was not sure how much water we had below us. As the machine recorded the increasing depth so we went

R

gradually deeper too, keeping about twenty feet between us and the sea's bottom, finally steadying at eighty feet.

What now? I was still expecting a flotilla of anti-submarine vessels to close in on us. We slowed down and listened, but heard nothing. Feeling it was imperative to get as far from the scene as possible before daylight, since I was sure submarine-chasers would soon be on the spot, I made a bold decision to surface almost at once and get away on the main engines.

When we came up, only two miles from the shore, the firing had ceased. At this distance we were not visible against the background of the islands to the westward, and our surfacing produced no reaction from the enemy. We started the engines without further ado and proceeded at full speed to the south-ward. Five miles from the shore we doubled back eastward and passed out through the Malacca Passage.

It was remarkable that we had got away without a single casualty, but the most surprising feature of the whole incident was that we had seen no enemy ship of any kind. Perhaps the Jap soldiery were jealous of their naval forces and hoped to win the kudos of sinking us unaided. If so, they had been very stupid: properly organised land-and-sea co-operation should have had us absolutely cold.

When we dived that dawn, we were nearly forty miles away, well off the northern coast of Sumatra in the Malacca Straits. We badly needed a restful day to soothe our nerves and recover lost sleep, so I decided to spend May 16th patrolling quietly a good four miles off shore.

When the Major and the Leading Seaman had recovered from the shock of their experience, I elicited from them the story of what had happened when they reached the beach.

As they neared the shore they got the impression that the flashing light was moving gradually left, and finally it seemed to recede into what appeared to be a little creek, thickly sur-rounded with trees and bushes, and very dark. When the boat touched bottom, the Leading Seaman got out and waded through the water up to the entrance of the creek. The torch was still flashing. And then he heard the Sumatran's voice, more high-pitched than usual and calling out in an agitated manner from the head of the creek. He said he was wounded and would have to be carried.

"It will take both of you. The Major must come too," he said.

The Leading Seaman didn't like the sound of this, and returned to the boat for consultation. While they were discussing the situation in low tones they became aware of rustling and crackling noises in the undergrowth to the side of the creek.

"The whole thing stinks to me," said the Major. "Come on, we're going to beat it. Jump in."

And he started rowing away from the shore as fast as he could. Shortly afterwards the torch began its damned flashing again, and then pandemonium broke loose. Presently, when the machine-gun fire began to get pretty close, they decided that the Leading Seaman should hop out and swim astern, both to reduce the target and to give them a second chance if one of them should be hit. They were terrified that at any moment we would dive and not realise they were on their way out to us.

We speculated miserably on what had happened to the Sumatran. It was of course possible that he had deliberately betrayed us, but from the description of the way he had spoken in the creek it looked rather as if he had somehow got caught, spilt the beans under torture, and had then been forced to act as a decoy, probably with a revolver at his back. The thought of his probable fate cast a gloom over our spirits for the remainder of the patrol.

And the remainder of the patrol was gloomy indeed. We knew that the whole neighbourhood would be alerted by now, and it was extremely unlikely that any targets would come our way for some time. On the night of the 16th I ran out to seaward and sent a signal to Trincomalee reporting the failure of the operation, and then went off to pass two days at the extreme eastern end of my area, off Diamond Point.

On the 19th we returned to Pulo Weh, and spent the next

four days patrolling off its eastern and north-eastern coast—the opposite side of the island from the scene of our abortive operation. On the 21st expectations were aroused by the sighting of a torpedo-boat which entered Sabang from the eastward, but although we thereafter kept a close watch on the harbour entrance he did not reappear with the merchant-ship we hoped he had come to escort. On all these days we wallowed in a heavy south-westerly swell caused by the onset of the monsoon period in the Indian Ocean.

One afternoon when I was doing a spell of periscope watch-keeping, as I usually did once a day if things were quiet, I found myself surrounded by a lively school of porpoises. The swell was particularly heavy that day, and the planesmen were having difficulty in keeping the submarine at a steady depth, sometimes dropping her several feet and leaving me staring up at the underside of the tumbling surface. I had often looked through the periscope under water, watched the light filtering down through the pale green water like afternoon sunshine into a forest of beech-trees, and gazed up at that quicksilver roof which refraction made so unexpectedly opaque. I had seen it from below on calm, windless days when it was as hard and definite as a sheet of mirrored glass, reflecting every speck of solid matter that drifted close to the surface, every mote of dust, every scrap of spongy seaweed, every jelly-fish, every water-logged twig. I had seen it under the lash of tropical rainstorms, when the greyed silver was spangled with a million dancing pricks of light; and I had seen it many times in rough weather when it reared up and away from the periscope and as quickly dropped back towards it with a violence that was all the more impressive because of the absolute silence. On this day off Sabang the sea was so rough that the whole surface was broken into a tossing welter of foam, one mass of water falling on another in a soundless avalanche of froth. To the majesty of a breaking sea viewed from below was added the incomparable spectacle of porpoises leaping. There were six or seven of them at a time within my field of vision, and they were jumping clean out of the water across the troughs of the waves, re-entering it smoothly with a trailing plume of white bubbles. Once by a coincidence the periscope broke surface and dipped again simultaneously with one of these porpoises, and I was able to follow its leap from beginning to end, the seemingly effortless forward and upward thrust from the powerful tail, the brief thrilling flight through the air, and the clean plunge at the finish. The whole school was moving forward in parallel curves, leaping one after the other, over and under in a graceful rhythm of *perpetuum mobile*, like the piston-ends on the crank-shaft of a slow-moving engine, until presently they had all gone past us and on into the impenetrable green underwater darkness beyond my vision. This was the only occasion on which I ever saw fish through the periscope—I suppose they are normally frightened away by the great mass of the hull—and I am glad to have been the privileged observer of that day's magnificent sub-marine display.

We were all mightily relieved when the signal came ordering us to leave patrol. The Major had in the meantime gone down with an attack of dengue fever. We reached Trincomalee on May 29th, thoroughly fed up with ourselves, and so ended *Storm*'s only "cloak-and-dagger" experience.

XVIII

DESTINATION PENANG

DESPITE our failure to obtain information about the defences of
Sabang, a heavy air raid was made on the port shortly after our
return, in the course of which much damage was done to oil-
tanks and harbour installations. Privately we had the feeling
that even if our Special Operation had been successful it would
not have made much difference, and that we had lost the Sumatran and exposed ourselves to grave danger for an object that
in the end seemed hardly worth the risks.

However, the air raid was significant. It was made by Fleet
Air Arm planes from aircraft-carriers which had sailed quite
close to the coast of Sumatra with impunity. It showed that
Admiral Somerville was beginning to feel a growing confidence
in the strength of his surface forces, and that the Eastern Fleet,
which after the loss of Singapore had been forced to fall back to
Ceylon and even at one period to Kenya, could no longer be
regarded merely as a containing force while the main attack
came from the Americans in the Pacific. Nevertheless, for the
moment the burden of harrying the Japanese sea traffic in the
Malacca Straits must continue to be borne by the submarines.

There were three distinct shipping requirements for the
enemy in the Straits. First, in order to meet the increasing
threat from the British Fleet, he must keep his advanced
bases like Sabang and Port Blair supplied with war materials.
Second, owing to the difficulties of overland transport, he must
use the sea for carrying the valuable raw materials of Malaya—
tin ore, manganese, rubber—back to Japan. Third, he must
support his army up north in Burma with military supplies
shipped to Rangoon. The Jap was undoubtedly aware of the
growing strength of our submarine force and was finding it less
and less profitable to send large or even medium-sized mer-

chant-ships through the area. Already there were signs that he was resorting to the use of smaller vessels—converted local craft of all sorts, wooden motor-ships and even junks. Commander Rimington in the submarine *Tantivy* had recently boarded a junk and taken a sample of her cargo of tin ore. Henceforth we were given permission to sink junks of twenty tons or over.

The only enemy ships, apart from submarines, that ventured the passage across to the western side of the Straits were those carrying or escorting supplies to Sabang and Port Blair. Even this traffic had to start from the eastern side, and now the majority of our submarines were concentrated along the coast of Malaya. A focal point for most of the shipping routes was Penang, and it was to the southern approach to this large port that *Storm* was assigned for her next patrol.

Before we sailed, my promotion to Lieutenant-Commander (R.N.V.R.) had come through. At last I was senior to my First Lieutenant! Previously visitors to the boat had looked at Brian's two straight stripes and then at my two wavy ones, and naturally taken Brian for skipper, a mistake which was apt to cause embarrassment all round. I may as well also mention here, because I am not sure of the exact dates, two other promotions which occurred during the next few months: Blake put up his second stripe (R.N.) in the natural course of seniority, and Chief, after strong recommendation from me, was given an unusually early advancement to Engineer Lieutenant.

It must have been about this time that we had a change of Coxswain. Chief Petty Officer Wells, who had seen much service, agreed to change places with a younger C.P.O. from the depot ship who was keen to get to sea again in an operational submarine. Chief Petty Officer Selby was a somewhat heavily built man with a pale skin and a melancholy air that at first made me regret the exchange. I soon discovered that I had gained a Coxswain of superlative worth, as will be seen later. When he came to *Storm* he had had several remarkable escapes from death, the latest of which had followed the sinking of the submarine *Olympus*, through hitting a mine off Malta, when he and only a few others managed to swim the long distance to the shore. In recent years he has had two more narrow escapes. He left *Truculent* very shortly before she was sunk in collision at the mouth of the Thames, and he would have sailed in the *Affray* on her last and fatal trip in the Channel if he had not been taken off to hospital an hour before her departure. Fortunately, while he was with us his luck was never put so severely to the test.

At Trincomalee I had an unexpected visit from an old peacetime friend, Ruari McLean. After joining up in the R.N.V.R. he had been awarded the Légion d'Honneur for his work as liaison officer in the Free French submarine *Rubis*. Now he was one of a group of crazy heroes who were preparing the way for future amphibian invasion forces by measuring the gradients of likely beaches. He had in fact come to Trincomalee to find out if I would take him with me on my next patrol, launch him in a boat off an enemy beach in Sumatra in the dead of night and recover him when he had completed his soundings. I roared with laughter and told him he could hardly have asked me at a worse moment; for the present I was extremely allergic to special operations of any sort. I said I would take him if I was ordered to do so by Captain Ionides, but not otherwise. Poor Ruari was rather taken aback at my pusillanimity, but saw my point when I outlined the events described in the last chapter. In the end he went in one of the other S-boats and carried out his operation without a hitch.

We slipped from *Maidstone* on the evening of Tuesday 13th June, escorted out by *Eritrea*, the Italian sloop which had met us when we first arrived in Ceylon. She left us at one o'clock the next morning, and with the moderate south-west monsoon now helping us along on our starboard quarter we rolled gaily and comfortably across the great stretch of Indian Ocean towards the Nicobar Channel. Passing through it on the night of the 16th, we set course to sight Pulo Perak. Inside the

Malacca Straits the sea was like molten glass, and desultory lightning flickered out of a velvet sky. Pulo Perak was as good as a lighthouse, its sugar-loaf outline rearing abruptly out of fairly deep water and providing a perfect navigational departure-point for any approach to the nearby coast of Malaya. We sighted the island on the port bow in the very early hours of the 18th. Realising that we had no hope of reaching our billet south of Penang by dawn, I decided to work round to the south of Pulo Perak and spend the day patrolling between it and Penang, in the hope of seeing a U-boat or a convoy routed away from the inshore channel. With such a prominent island as Perak in sight all day I should also have a chance to discover what the currents were doing on this coast; the navigational landmarks on my billet were reputed to be almost non-existent. By making this diversion I would be poaching on *Sea Rover*'s area, but I knew that Peter Angell was not due to reach it for a few days.

Nothing happened until at tea-time the officer-of-the-watch reported distant smoke towards the mainland. (These things always seemed to happen at meal-times.) I went to the periscope and saw a faint but distinct wisp of smoke beyond the eastward horizon. I imagined this was probably some vessel intending to pass immediately outside the offshore islands on its way northward, and that it would be well beyond our range. However, I decided to surface and have a look at it from the bridge. So up we came. But I had hardly got to the front of the bridge when one of the look-outs climbing out of the hatch behind me called out, "Aircraft, sir, straight ahead!" The plane was about five miles away at a height of about 1,500 feet and flying directly towards us. We dived hurriedly, without having had a look at the cause of the smoke, and shot down to eighty feet. I felt sure the aircraft, even if he hadn't actually spotted us, must have seen the disturbance in the calm water. There were no bombs, however, and ten minutes later I came gingerly up to periscope depth. A quick sweep round showed me that the aircraft had disappeared. The smoke was still in sight, the new bearing indicating that the unseen ship was moving north. In the rather forlorn hope that it might presently alter course westward for Sabang, I turned and ran northward at about four knots, occasionally planing up to about fifteen feet to get a better view.

Eventually, about an hour after the smoke had first been sighted, the tip of the funnel and two masts of a small merchant-vessel came into view at a range of about seven miles—much nearer than I had dared to hope. Moreover, her course was approximately north-west. Our chances were definitely improving. Soon afterwards I sighted the masts and funnel of a second merchant-ship some way astern, and at the same time two other small masts which I correctly assumed to be escort vessels, one on each side of the convoy.

I now began an attack on the first ship, which I estimated at about 1,500 tons. My hopes were still further raised when I realised she was zig-zagging between north-west and due west. This indicated that Port Blair was her probable destination. On account of her slow speed of eight knots, coupled with the large alterations of course every few minutes, the attack was long drawn out. Even so, I still thought I would be left some distance off the target's track, in spite of my occasional bursts of speed.

Suddenly the situation was radically altered when my target obligingly zigged towards me, so much so that on her port leg I found myself right ahead of her. A quick glance at the chart convinced me now that she had altered her mean course to due west, aiming straight for Sabang, and that she was carrying out a complicated zig-zag similar to that sometimes used by our own ships—several zigs to starboard of the mean course, followed by several zigs to port, then to starboard again and so on. This is a very difficult zig-zag plan for a submarine to cope with, unless it is lucky enough to be in the right position. Now it seemed that my target was playing into my hands. Sure enough, after another return to what I assumed to be her new mean course, she zigged to port for the second time, putting me only five degrees on her port bow, very nearly right ahead of her at a range of about two and a half miles.

The situation was now rather exciting. The sea was so smooth that I had to use the small periscope and show it for no more than a second or two at each glance. In that time I had to judge accurately what the target was doing and also keep a wary eye on the port escort, a large submarine-chaser which was weaving from side to side on the target's beam. Now, with the target coming almost straight at me, I was gambling on my guess that within a few minutes she would alter to starboard back on to her mean course of due west. If she did not, if she decided to keep on her present course, our own forward move-ment would take us so close to her that I could not fire, lest the torpedo explosions should damage us as well. There was even a danger that we might collide with her. All depended on her doing what I expected her to do, but in wartime the unexpected often happens.

The log records that it was at one minute to six p.m. that I observed my target beginning her swing to starboard. I could see her quite clearly now. She was an old-fashioned ship, so ugly with her stiff, straight lines that she seemed little more than three piles of boxes held loosely together with rusty iron plates. Her two derrick masts stood in the deep wells separat-ing the forecastle from the bridge and the bridge from the poop. She had at some time, though not recently, been painted a dark grey all over, except for the tall, black, upright funnel that was belching filthy smoke and leaving a stain hanging in the air for miles astern. Where her stem cut the water, the little bow wave made the only clean thing about her, a white chalk-mark which hardly trembled in that glassy sea.

I looked round for the chaser, and saw him pointing straight at me less than two miles away. Now was the time to fire. The target's next zig would probably be to starboard and leave me in a very poor position fine on her port quarter. I must fire as soon as possible, before she was due to make that next zig. I therefore altered course ten degrees towards her, and when the helmsman was steady I put the periscope up and found my tar-get was only five degrees short of the firing angle.

I said, "Down periscope," but before it had reached the deck

I ordered it to be raised again, and as soon as it was trained on the firing angle I saw the target's bow just entering the right-hand side of my circle of vision.

"Stand by."

In a sea so calm as this I could not afford to keep the periscope up long enough to aim four torpedoes individually. But we knew from our tables what the firing interval ought to be, and we should have to time them by stop-watch.

When the target's bow touched the vertical centre-line on the periscope it was as though an electrical circuit had been closed inside my brain.

"FIRE ONE . . . Down periscope . . . Carry on firing by stop-watch . . . Eighty feet . . . Shut off for depth-charging."

The E.A. stood beside the fruit machine, stop-watch in one hand, the other on the little panel of torpedo-firing indicators which sent the orders to the tube-space for'ard. Every eight seconds he turned one of the switches, the word "FIRE" appeared in small red letters on the light panel, we felt the little lurch as the torpedo shot from its tube, and McIllmurray on the asdic set reported, "Torpedo running, sir." All the time we were beginning to sink below periscope depth. I was itching to stay up and watch the results of my attack (I never saw any of my torpedoes exploding), but the torpedoes would leave a track in the smooth water which would lead the chaser straight to us if we stayed where we were. We held our course until the fourth torpedo was fired, but as soon as it was away we turned to port at full speed, planing rapidly down to eighty feet.

Nearly two minutes after I had given the order to fire the first torpedo, we heard a tremendous explosion, followed a few seconds later by a second, and then by a third. They were all sharp explosions, not followed by the long rumbling aftermath characteristic of depth-charges, and I felt sure they were torpedo hits. And a moment later McIllmurray confirmed my belief by reporting. "Target H.E. appears to have ceased, sir."

However, I had no doubt that depth-charges would follow. We reduced down to slow speed on one propeller only, steadied on a westerly course, dropped to 100 feet, and settled down grimly to await developments. Only the two planesmen and the helmsman had something to occupy their attention now; the rest of us had nothing to do but wait, listen, guess what the enemy was doing, and wonder if one of those lethal cylinders was already sinking down towards us with the sea pressure gradually squeezing in on the trigger to detonate the explosive. I moved to the after end of the control-room and stood behind McIllmurray's shoulder.

"Can you hear anything?"

"Nothing at the moment, sir."

I imagined the chaser lying stopped somewhere overhead, waiting for us to make a false move, listening, listening, listening.

"Diesel H.E. right astern, sir."

"Is the bearing changing at all?"

"Bearing seems pretty steady."

At eleven minutes past six three loud explosions in quick succession announced the opening of the enemy's attack. I did not think they were very close to us, but three minutes later came four more, a good deal nearer, thundering one after the other like a pattern of bombs. He seemed to be on our trail, but whether by good guesswork or because he had actually detected us I could not tell.

Five minutes passed, and the attack did not develop. McIllmurray could still hear him, thrashing about somewhere astern, continually starting and stopping, moving about from one quarter to another. After ten minutes I felt certain he had never gained contact with us and that provided we persevered with our quiet withdrawal we were in no danger.

Half an hour later, at a quarter to seven, having heard very little of our adversary for some time, I decided to come up to periscope depth to have a look at the situation before the daylight faded altogether. As the periscope broke surface I swept quickly round, and was at once alarmed to see the chaser, a black shape in the evening light, lying stopped only 400 yards away on our port beam. I felt as though I had been escaping down a tunnel only to find my pursuer waiting for me at the other end. He was much too close for comfort, and after sweeping rapidly all round the horizon without seeing any other ships, I immediately ordered a return to 100 feet. We were still on the way down when McIllmurray suddenly reported:

"Diesel H.E. speeding up and closing on Red 100."

I was alarmed and baffled. Had he suddenly heard us when we came up to periscope depth? Perhaps we had risen above a density layer which had blanketed our propeller noise so long as we stayed deep. Surely he hadn't spotted the periscope!

"H.E. still closing, sir, bearing steady."

And then we could all hear him with the naked ear, a steady thrashing beat growing in volume and menace—*schoo-schoo-schoo-schoo-schoo-schoo-schoo-schoo* . . . like a steam locomotive coming rapidly towards you up a long gradient. Icy fingers began closing round my vitals. This time I felt sure he knew exactly where we were. He was going to pass directly over us, and in a moment a pattern of frightful explosions would be bursting under, over and all around us with God knew what disastrous results. Ostrich-like, we could not help hunching our shoulders as the sound rose to its climax and crossed overhead. Any moment now . . .

To our amazement, nothing happened. McIllmurray followed the enemy until he faded right away on the starboard bow, and we never heard him again. His choosing that particular moment and course to leave the area was clearly a coincidence. I thanked my stars that I had not come to periscope depth a minute or two later, for we might easily have been rammed.

By eight o'clock I felt safe enough to surface, and we came up into a pitch-black, starless night with a horizon so woolly that it was difficult to separate sea from sky. Before starting the diesels we made a careful radar sweep all round, but finding nothing on the scan we set off on a south-westerly course to locate Pulo Perak once more. We sighted the island within the half-hour, no more than a murky thickening of the darkness, but enough to provide the navigational check we wanted, and immediately set course westward to pass round the island and make our way to our appointed billet south of Penang. We had not gone far, however, when we received a signal ordering us to proceed immediately to a position eighty miles NE of Pulo Weh, to attack an outward-bound Japanese submarine which was believed to be passing through that position on the surface about 0900 on the day after the morrow. This new billet being about 125 miles west-nor'-west of our present position, we turned immediately on to the course that would take us there.

At 0447 on the morning of the 20th we dived in what we imagined to be the correct position. I was a little anxious, however, because we had not been able to get a star sight the previous evening, and had therefore run on dead reckoning from the morning sight nearly twenty-four hours ago. When daylight revealed the distant blue mountains of Sumatra to the south of us, I set about trying to get a fix off the more prominent peaks, not a very accurate way of fixing, but a useful check if nothing else is available. I could not achieve a precise result from these bearings, but all the indications showed that we were something like ten miles to the south of the position ordered. This was serious, for we had exactly an hour to retrieve the error. We should have to surface if we were to get there on time, and that would mean running the risk of the enemy's sighting us first.

0758　Surfaced and proceeded northwards to gain correct position.

0905　Sighted smoke bearing 100°. [It was Leading Seaman Taylor, the gunlayer, perched up as lookout on the periscope standards, who made the sighting.] Dived. Shortly afterwards sighted the mast and then the conning-tower of a submarine, which continued to produce a surprising amount of black smoke Commenced attack. Could not detect any zig-zags, but there was a moderate swell which gave me only occasional glimpses of his casing. From later analysis of the plot, however, I consider he must have been zigging.

0940　Fired six torpedoes on a 110 track at a range of approximately 2,500 yards (though I thought it was closer at the time). During the firing the boat became very light, though the firing interval was 6½ seconds and we had a bow-down angle on firing, and it was necessary to flood to prevent our breaking surface.　By the time

trim was recovered three minutes later, the enemy was seen to
have turned away and had not even crossed the line of fire.
Whether he had sighted either (a) the torpedo tracks, or (b) the
swirl made by our efforts not to break surface, I could not tell.
Eight minutes after firing, four torpedoes were heard to explode
on the sea bottom. This caused the target to alter hard-a-port
and perform a series of violent zigs, pouring out yet more smoke,
until he disappeared to the southward. The H.E. bearings later
indicated that he had resumed his westerly course.

I bitterly regretted my failure to sink that submarine. He
was believed to be the same that had a few months earlier sunk
an unescorted British merchant-ship not far from the Gulf of
Aden, taken the survivors on to the casing and hacked them to
pieces with swords. We had been after this particular chap ever
since. Besides, I had had plenty of time and my whole attack
had proceeded quite calmly, without any of the frenzy often
associated with attacks on submarines. I had been told beforehand not only what time he would be passing through that
position but at what speed and on what course, and he had
come along absolutely on schedule, like a crack express train.
It was miserable to have failed.

Except for a two-minute surfacing to take the noon altitude
of the sun, we remained dived until the middle of the afternoon,
then came up to proceed once more towards the Penang billet
which we had not yet reached. I felt I ought to let Trincomalee
know that I had only three torpedoes left, so I sent a signal reporting the results of my two attacks and the total number of
torpedoes fired. I expected to be told to stay on patrol until
another submarine could get out to relieve me, but before dark
the reply came back ordering me to leave patrol forthwith and
return to Trincomalee. Once again we altered course back to
the westward.

We always enjoyed those homeward runs across the Indian
Ocean. There was an easing of the strain, and more laughter
and singing in the messes; we were on the surface all the way,
with fresh air ventilating the boat by day as well as by night;
the crew had a chance to get up on the bridge and feel the
breeze and the sun on their faces. I myself would often spend

hour after hour leaning over the front of the bridge to watch the bow lifting and dipping to the endless monsoon rollers, the waves breaking continually on the port bow and sending a fine spray arching across the deck, so that in the afternoons, when the sun was ahead of us, we carried along with us our own intermittent rainbow; flying fish skeetered away before our approach, gliding between the watery valleys until the momentum of their flight was exhausted; and the hot blue of the sea burned with an inward fire. Life was good then.

But though we could relax in some ways, I felt it necessary to sound a warning note in one of my evening bulletins:

> The greatest danger which faces a submarine leaving patrol is the "we're on the way home" complex. It is a fact that the majority of German submarines which have been sunk by our own submarines have been homeward bound. Everybody naturally feels the need to relax a bit, the constant anxiety and dangers of the nights on the billet itself having been successfully survived, and unless you guard against it the temptation to ease off in concentration is almost irresistible. But fatal. This applies of course principally to the officer-of-the-watch and the lookouts. In the Indian Ocean, where both we and the enemy have a constant stream of submarines going backwards and forwards across this no-man's-land of empty sea, the danger of such relaxation is obvious. It would be stupid to get sunk by torpedo just as we were getting home, merely for want of keeping up the same standard of vigilance for a few extra days.

On the last evening before we got into Trincomalee my daily news-magazine proudly reached its hundredth issue. I had put out an urgent request for special contributions, and the crew responded so well that I was able to produce a really bumper number of *Good Evening*, consisting of no fewer than twelve pages. A good half of the contributions were in verse. My most faithful contributor was Stoker Rooke, especially after a depth-charging or a gun action; generally the more noise there was the more his inspiration blossomed. He could reel the stuff off by the yard.

And so the time passed, pleasantly enough, until at five o'clock on the morning of June 25th we were met by the trawler *Maid Marion* and escorted into Trincomalee harbour.

XIX

MERGUI ARCHIPELAGO

OUR next billet was a submarine captain's dream—almost virgin territory (no submarine had visited it for nearly a year), and a roving commission to look for trouble along a 300-mile coastline studded with hundreds of islands. The area assigned to us was the Mergui Archipelago and the western seaboard of the narrow isthmus which joins the Malay Peninsula to Burma and Siam. It was suspected that, in pursuance of their policy of using small, shallow-draught coastal craft in place of larger deep-water ships, the Japs were working some of the many channels hidden behind the islands, and that the port of Mergui itself might be the departure point for seaborne traffic taking military supplies to Rangoon.

As we expected to use the gun far more than the torpedo tubes, it was decided to increase our outfit of ammunition. By converting a little-used trimming tank and various stowage spaces we finally managed to pack in twice as many rounds of three-inch shells as usual. We also organised a Boarding Party with a view to inspecting, and if necessary blowing up, junks and other small cargo-carrying craft. An edict had recently gone forth that all submarines in the Far East were to carry an additional officer for watch-keeping duties, and we were lucky in having appointed to us a young sub-lieutenant R.N. called Dicky Fisher, who was not only an extremely likeable fellow and a great asset to the wardroom, but also burning to distinguish himself in some personal fracas with the enemy. I immediately appointed him Boarding Officer and told him to decide for himself how many men and what equipment he needed. He entered into his commission with enthusiasm and intelligence, selected five men, fitted the party up with grappling-hooks, revolvers, demolition charges, and collected from God knows

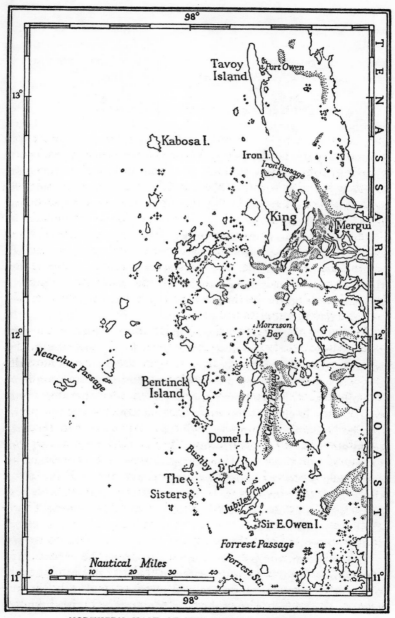

Tavoy
Island

Port Owen

13°

Kabosa I.

Iron I.

Iron Passage

King
I.

Mergui

12°

*Morrison
Bay*

Nearchus Passage

Bentinck
Island

Celerity Passage

Domel I.

Bushby I.

The
Sisters

Jubilee Chan.

Sir E. Owen I.

Forrest Passage

Forrest Str.

Nautical Miles

0   10   20   30   40

11°

13°

12°

11°

NORTHERN HALF OF THE MERGUI ARCHIPELAGO

where a most fearsome assortment of knives and daggers for self-defence in case of treachery. When fully kitted up for the first dress rehearsal they looked as bloodthirsty a crowd of pirates as ever slit throats on the Spanish Main.

We left Trincomalee on the evening of July 15th, and after an uneventful passage entered the patrol area in the early hours of the morning of the 20th. I had chosen to make a landfall in the vicinity of Tavoy, since all the islands here are so steep-to that the navigational approach would be easy. We set course to arrive just to the north of Kabosa Island, and a good radar fix was obtained off this and the neighbouring islands before any land was sighted.

Patrol conditions during the first few days were trying and depressing. A monotonous swell from the south-west made depth-keeping difficult, and we had heavy and almost continuous rain—as was to be expected in the wettest month of the monsoon period on one of the wettest coasts of the Bay of Bengal. By day the heavily wooded islands were half hidden by the curtain of falling water, and at night on the bridge we were miserable under the tropical downpour which penetrated everywhere and rendered binoculars useless. When it was not raining, the heat turned the universal damp into a shrouding mist. Visibility was always poor; there was no moon; and at night we had to rely entirely on radar for fixing our position.

The bad visibility foiled my first attempt to inspect the sheltered anchorage on the inside of Tavoy Island known as Port Owen, but on the 23rd I determined to try again. Diving before dawn a few miles out, we crept round the northern tip of the island and turned south towards our objective. The visibility was still down to about three miles, but I hoped it might clear later in the day.

At a quarter past nine the officer-of-the-watch suddenly saw a dim shape on the port bow emerging from the mist of rain. Examining it through the periscope, I could not at first make out what it was, but soon realised it was a small north-bound coaster of about 200 tons, heavily camouflaged with branches

of trees and other foliage. I had never before met this form of
disguise, an ingenious attempt to make the vessel hard to see
when close in against the land.

I turned hard-a-port to bring the submarine on to a parallel
course with the enemy, and gave the order,

"Stand by gun action."

This was the signal for a tremendous bustle and clatter as
the gun's crew opened the lower hatches of the conning-tower
and the gun-tower (situated over the wardroom) and clambered up the ladders to wait for the order to open up. Next to
the wardroom, in the passage-way by the galley, the ammunition supply party were lifting the hatch-cover off the magazine
under the deck and passing out the three-inch shells to be
stacked on the wardroom table. Within a minute Blake was
able to report, "Gun's crew ready."

I waited to let the coaster pass me, intending to surface on
his port quarter.

"Target is a small coaster," I said. "Bearing Green 40.
Range 800 yards. Open fire on surfacing. Point of aim the
wheelhouse."

And then the coaster had drawn past our beam and the
moment had come.

"Surface. *Gun action!*"

Number One at once gave the order to blow all main ballast.
In accordance with the gun-action drill, the planesmen at first
tried to hold the submarine down, but when the blowing tanks
began forcing her up they reversed the planes and let her shoot
to the surface like a cork. At fifteen feet, when the top of the
gun-tower was still under water, Number One blew a whistle,
the hatches slammed open, a little shower of water fell down the
gun-tower, and then the men were climbing the ladders at the
double. I had to wait until Blake and the gun's crew were clear
of the conning-tower, so I kept my eyes at the periscope.
watched the target still chugging along in the rain, quite unconcerned, and saw our bow rising out of the sea in a surge of
whitened water. A moment later I was climbing the tower.

I got to the bridge just as the gun cracked away the first

round. It was a direct hit, and made a shambles of the wheel-house. There was no sign of opposition from the enemy, but although we pumped round after round into him, most of them along his water-line, he maintained his course and speed for some minutes with apparently no one at the helm. One shell produced a burst of flame from the deck-cargo of oil-drums. At last, after we had fired twenty-eight rounds, he came to a dead stop, so we ceased fire and closed slowly in towards him. There was still no sign of life, and I began to wonder if we had killed the entire crew, but as we approached figures began to emerge hesitantly from the after cabin and jump into the water. Some were Japanese, some Malays. Although the coaster had settled slightly by the stern he looked like taking some time to sink, but as I was manœuvring *Storm* alongside to board him and blow him up with a demolition charge, the shattered vessel sank slowly aft and dived vertically stern first. As he did so, numerous oil-drums and odd bits of wood floated off the deck.

I decided to take only two prisoners. It was too early in the patrol to encumber ourselves with many passengers; the other survivors had plenty of debris to cling to, and land was less than half a mile away. We cruised slowly among the bobbing heads trying to select our prisoners. I was anxious to have one Jap if possible, but the first three we tried to pick up—all unusually large men for their race—swam away at our approach and could not be reached. However, one small Jap consented to be rescued, so he was hauled out of the water and taken below.* We also picked up a Malay, whom we found to be wounded in the thigh; he was assisted down the conning-tower and handed over to the Coxswain.

I now decided on the spur of the moment to put into action a plan I had been toying with the previous day—to enter Port Owen brazenly on the surface. There was no large-scale Admiralty chart of the place, but at the last minute before I sailed George Perrin, the Staff Officer in *Maidstone*, had given me a plan prepared by the India Survey and Topography Division which charted the anchorage in great detail. Although this

* See photograph facing page 288.

showed that the water inside was too shallow to allow us to dive in the event of serious opposition, I felt there was an excellent chance of getting away with it if we could achieve a tactical surprise.

It seemed to me that everything was now favourable for such an attempt. The rain, which was still falling heavily and which had thwarted my periscope inspection of the anchorage, would conceal our approach long enough to give us the advantage of surprise. Moreover, we had just tasted blood; the gun's crew were in buoyant spirits at their quick success; we were already on the surface and in a mood to stay there. It seemed unlikely that the noise of the action could have been heard as far away as the anchorage. I decided to go ahead.

It was ten o'clock when we left the scene of our sinking. Proceeding southward, we found ourselves half an hour later at the northern entrance and able to see right across the harbour.

Three vessels were lying at anchor, close inshore. One of them was clearly the empty hulk of a large junk, but the other two were much more difficult to identify, being painted light grey and closer to the land. Blake and I began to have a nasty suspicion that they were submarine-chasers, and for a moment I lost my nerve, so much so that I ordered "Hard-a-starboard" to bring our nose pointing back towards the deeper water. However, on second thoughts we decided they were some kind of river gunboat or patrol vessel, and that having come so far and revealed our presence we must go ahead with the desperate enterprise. I therefore ordered gun action stations and kept the starboard helm on until we had come full circle back to our original course. The gun's crew had been fallen out after the previous action, but now came tumbling out of the hatches to take up their stations once more.

As we approached we observed great activity aboard the enemy ships and realised they were desperately trying to lift their anchors. One of them did in fact succeed in getting under way and turned towards us just before we opened fire at a range of 1,200 yards. This vessel was engaged first, hit and stopped with the third round, and after that every round was a hit. The enemy replied with machine-guns firing the alarming Japanese "clap-clap-clap" explosive bullets, which had at first so confused our troops in the retreat to Singapore, and with these bangs going off all round like Chinese crackers it was impossible to tell whether the firing was coming from the ships or the shore. Our shots were making a pretty good mess of the first patrol vessel, and presently the crew—all Japanese—began to leap overboard. As soon as we saw this we shifted aim to the second vessel, and after a bit of punishment her crew also took to the water. Further rounds were then fired at the first target and several water-line hits observed. Finally, as we swept past at a range of 400 yards, the second vessel was also punctured along the water-line.

At this point the breech-worker, Telegraphist Greenway, suddenly spun round as though kicked by a horse, and there was a cry of "Greenway's hit, sir!" from the gun's crew. I immediately sent him below, the second casualty for the Coxswain to look after within the hour. Fortunately, the action was in any case nearly over.

All this time I had been contending with the navigation of this constricted piece of water. I had no time to take bearings and put fixes on the chart, so there was nothing for it but to navigate by eye. As an extra precaution I ordered the echo-sounder to be started, with instructions that I was to be informed of the soundings every minute, or immediately they shortened to less than five fathoms. And what with the enemy machine-gun fire and watching the results of our own shots, manœuvring the ship so as to bring the gun to bear with the best advantage, listening to the soundings coming up the voice-pipe, looking at the chart in the drenching rain to make sure we did not go aground, and passing my helm orders to the helmsman below, I was pretty busy.

Owing to the narrowness of the anchorage I considered it would be unwise to attempt to turn round and go back by the way we had come. When the gun could no longer be brought to bear, I broke off the action and set course to pass out through the south-eastern exit. Before we could turn to port to make our get-away we had to go fairly close in to the shore on our starboard hand, and there under the trees by a large wooden hut we saw a group of Malays, women and children included, who waved gaily to us as we swept past them. Passing through the narrows towards more open water, we looked back at the anchorage in time to see the sinking of the second target; the other, which had received at least as much damage, was settling low in the water and would obviously be sinking very shortly. These two successes had been achieved at a combined cost of only twenty-nine rounds of ammunition, not bad going in view of the opposition. It had all been very exhilarating, in spite of the torrential rain and the navigational worries, but I was troubled about Greenway; it turned out, however, that the bullet had passed straight through the fleshy part of his right shoulder and left a clean wound with no complications; he was shortly able to resume his telegraphist duties, and when we reached harbour at the end of the patrol, the wound, thanks to the Coxswain's attention, was almost healed.

Not content with our two gun actions in the day, we went off to look for more trouble, and found it:

1118   Set course southward on the surface towards King Island Sound. This involved crossing a six-mile patch of water too shallow for diving, but the risk was considered worth while since it was intended to investigate the anchorage in King Island Sound, at the entrance to the Mergui River, before dark.

1334   Dived 9½ miles due north of King Island Sound and proceeded to close.

1615   Obtained a good view of the Sound and sighted it clear of shipping. A small fishing vessel was seen crossing the entrance.

1636   Sighted two landing craft proceeding down river from Mergui. One was observed to be armed with two light machine-guns, the other with one. Manœuvred for attack.

1700   Surfaced when both targets were in line and engaged the nearest one with gunfire at a range of approximately 1800 yards. This vessel turned stern on and showed no fight after we had obtained two near-misses, but the other, the one armed with two machine-guns, turned towards and began firing. We had fired ten rounds at our first target, and were about to shift aim to meet this new menace, when the three-inch gun ceased fire, with the extractor apparently jammed open. The two Vickers guns opened fire successfully, but to my dismay the Oerlikon gunner could not get his weapon to fire. The three-inch failure was later discovered to be due to the new breech-worker (put in at the last moment to replace Greenway) holding down the breech-mechanism lever instead of releasing it, thus preventing the new shell from going home. The failure of the Oerlikon remains a mystery, as it was tried on the following day with the same magazine, and in subsequent gun actions never gave the slightest trouble.

1704   Not wishing to see my gun's crew mown down by the enemy fire, which was getting pretty hot by this time, I dived. Proceeded northwards at high speed for thirty seconds as deep as was safe (sixty feet). Half a minute after diving, much to my surprise, a depth-charge was dropped, followed by a second one five minutes later, the closest *Storm* has had yet. A few lights were put out, and one cockroach fell stunned on to the chart-table, but otherwise there was no damage. Our Japanese prisoner was very alarmed, and asked permission to visit the heads.

1711   In view of the navigational dangers, came to periscope depth shortly after the second depth-charge, to find one of the landing-craft ahead of me and the other astern. Decided, therefore, to escape through Iron Passage, the tide being on the ebb, and altered course westward accordingly. Neither of the enemy vessels seemed to be in asdic contact with me, and both eventually moved close in to the eastern shore of Iron Island, presumably hoping to be hidden against the land and tempt me into surfacing early.

1730   Iron Passage was successfully negotiated. The chart is correct in reporting "strong eddies"! The tide swept us through at a tremendous rate, and at one point the submarine was sucked down from periscope depth to sixty feet in a few seconds.

1830   Surfaced when clear of Ant Island and set course to pass round the north of Kabosa Island

I now had a strong feeling that we had caused enough disturbance in the vicinity for the time being. In any case, the enemy would probably suspend the sailings of small craft for a few days and send out chasers to look for us. It would be advisable to spend a little time in the southern half of our huge area. That night, therefore, we shaped a course southward to pass outside the Mergui Archipelago until daylight, after which I intended to turn in among the islands and explore the inner channels as far as the Pakchan River, if possible on the surface.

There followed what were perhaps the most extraordinary two days of my submarine experience. From the time we turned in through Nearchus Passage to our emergence at the southern end of Forrest Strait, we moved everywhere on the surface, travelling freely among the innumerable islands, often in narrow waterways and always in full view of supposedly enemy-occupied territory. The absence of shipping in the inner channels of the archipelago, and the way we were able to proceed on the surface at will, even through Forrest Strait, were astonishing. We saw not a single aircraft. "It would even seem possible," I wrote in my patrol report, "for a large force of warships to approach the islands between Mergui and Pakchan unobserved, and to remain within their shelter unmolested perhaps for days on end. The islands appear to be largely uninhabited and contain numerous anchorages surrounded by steep-to hills."

Between some of the outer islands of the archipelago the sea-bed is in places only sparsely charted, so that on some courses we took a risk, like the old circumnavigators, of running on to uncharted rocks. In daylight, therefore, we always had a man posted on the periscope standards to keep a look-out for breakers, and by night we played for safety. Wherever possible, courses were set along lines of known soundings.

Moving still further south, we spent two days patrolling dived off the Pakchan River in the hope of sighting small vessels carrying tin from the local mines, but without result. On July 28th we carried out a periscope reconnaissance of Hastings Harbour, an extensive anchorage formed by three islands which provided, by the looks of the chart, excellent shelter from both the south-west and the north-east monsoons, but although we had a good view into the anchorage through both eastern and northern entrances, no ships were seen, and we had to content ourselves with making panoramic sketches of both entrances through the periscope. That evening, having drawn blank for five days, I made up my mind to return to the Mergui area, and sent a signal to Trincomalee telling them of my intention to do so unless they had anything better to offer.

We had been steaming north for about four hours when we received their reply offering me the Puket area, further south and outside my original patrol area, as an alternative if I wished. I immediately turned south, and informed them that I was doing so. Fourteen hours later yet another signal ordered us back to the northward again. It seemed they had new intelligence of some unspecified target arriving at the entrance to the Heinze Basin, to the north of Tavoy and again outside my area. All that night and the next day we travelled north, keeping just outside the islands, and at dawn on July 31st we were in position off the Heinze Basin. Here I soon came to the conclusion that it was not a good spot to wait for a target; in the prevailing bad visibility we could see the coastline only in patches, the shoaling water at the river-mouth making it impossible for us to patrol close in, and it would have been easy for a target to enter or leave the harbour unobserved by us. I accordingly began moving south, soon after midday, to patrol off the end of the Tavoy peninsula, where we could take up a better strategic position. The afternoon produced nothing, but we patrolled in the same spot during the night, no more than two miles off shore, and on the following morning, August 1st, reaped our reward.

The alarm sounded at 0442. I shot out of my bunk and up to the bridge to find Number One and the for'ard look-out, Petty Officer Blight, peering to seaward through their binoculars. It was still dark, but the rain had stopped. Blight had seen a small light flicker for an instant in the darkness, and now Number One said he thought he could make out a black shape on the same bearing. A few moments later I could see it myself, a south-bound modern coaster with funnel aft.

I spoke into the voice-pipe. "Control-room . . . *Gun action!* Tell the men to move as silently as possible. Anything from radar yet? Tell the operator we have a target bearing Green 40, range about 1,500 yards."

The gun-hatch opened quietly just below the front of the bridge, and the men climbed out on to the gun-platform in their

sandalled feet, moving about the deck on tiptoe like a gang of
conspirators; some came up the conning-tower and swung
themselves quietly over the side of the bridge. Blake stood on
the little raised step and in a low voice passed his orders down
to the men round the gun.

There was still no report from radar. How I cursed the
temperamental nature of this wonderful new invention! The
set had so far given good results during the patrol and been a
great assistance to the navigation, but now, on the first occasion
when we badly needed an accurate range for a night gun
action, it could not find the target which we knew was there. I
had in fact under-estimated the size, and so the range, of the
coaster, and consequently many rounds were wasted before we
got our first hit.

The first crack of our gun seemed a desecration of the
silence. In the darkness Blake could not see where the shot
fell; it was not on the target, so he could only assume it had
dropped short and raise the range by 200 yards. Another difficulty was that the gunlayer could not yet see the target and was
obliged to lay his open sight on the muzzy line where he
imagined the horizon to be. Our second round also whined
away into the night and fell without visible trace, and it was not
until the sixth or seventh round that we saw the little orange
flash and heard the muffled *crumph* which indicated our first hit.
After that we continued to hit the enemy with nearly every
round. He came slowly to a dead stop, and then just sat there
taking our pounding in silence. It was like murder, but our
job was to sink enemy supply ships. By this time the dawn
was coming up, and in the early light we saw that he was a
steel ship, fairly new, and larger than I had originally thought.
I put him at about 350 tons. We continued to pump shells into
him until, after the expenditure of fifty rounds, he sank at last,
going down slowly by the stern.

We had no time to stop to see if there were any survivors, for
the vessel had hardly disappeared under the water when we
sighted another ship on the horizon to the northward coming
towards us in the gradually increasing light. We at once dived

and ran towards him at full speed. I wanted to reach him before he was put on his guard by sighting the debris of the first sinking.

He turned out to be a small wooden two-masted motor schooner of about 100 tons. When he was passing our position we surfaced and fired a round ahead of him, hoping he would stop and abandon ship. Instead, he increased speed and turned towards the shore with the obvious intention of trying to beach himself. I also speeded up, altered course to head him off, and resumed the attack. The crew soon jumped overboard, but the vessel kept on and did not slow down for some minutes. Closing to short range we poured into him a burst of Oerlikon fire which set the wooden hull ablaze from stem to stern, but although we riddled him with holes along the water-line with the three-inch gun we could not sink him. Finally I gave up the attempt and went alongside with the intention of placing a demolition charge for'ard. However, we could then see that he was thoroughly on fire below decks, and decided to leave him to burn himself out. He sank all right in the end, for when we came back to the same spot later in the day we could find no trace of him.

There were several heads dotting the water. I had previously decided that we would take one other prisoner, but no more; passenger space below was very limited. Again we found the Japanese were not anxious to be picked up, but we rescued an Indian who (unfortunately for the Coxswain) turned out to be suffering from two nasty wounds. As we began to withdraw from the scene our attention was attracted by a young Malay, swimming a little apart from the others and waving and shouting in great excitement. I did not want to take on any more passengers, but I was impressed with the look of this lad and his obvious desire to be picked up, so in spite of Number One's ill-concealed disapproval I manœuvred close to him and took him on board. The Coxswain was even more disapproving when this man too was found to be wounded in the thigh: he now had four patients to look after.

However, I was very glad we had picked up this boy, whose

name was Endi. He was extremely friendly and co-operative, and claimed to have been at the Malay R.N.V.R. Training School in Singapore before the Japanese arrived. In spite of his wound he was full of spirit, and delighted to be a prisoner of the British, even declaring that he would now be able to join the British Navy. He had been one of the quartermasters in the little ship we had just attacked, the *Kikaku Maru*, bound from Rangoon to Mergui with a cargo of rice. The crew consisted of the Captain, the First Mate, the Chief Engineer—all Japanese—and five Malays, two Chinese and one or two Indians. When we surfaced and opened fire, he said, all the Malays in the crew went to the wheelhouse and tried to persuade the Japanese officer to stop and abandon ship. The officer shot four of the Malays out of hand, and compelled Endi to remain at the wheel and obey his orders. A moment later one of our shells hit the wheelhouse and blew him and the Jap overboard in opposite directions. Endi spoke excellent English, and later volunteered much useful information.

Meanwhile I decided to shift patrol northwards, a few miles along the coast. This last action had taken place within a short distance of the shore, and it was possible that the Japs had a look-out post at this focal point on the coastal traffic route. We ran for an hour or so on the surface and then dived fairly close inshore, just to the south of Oyster Island.

Nearly three hours later another coaster, of about 250 tons, was seen approaching from the north. I let him pass as usual, and surfaced for gun action astern of him. When I reached the bridge, machine-gun bullets were flying all round us and the enemy had turned in an attempt to ram. However, he soon changed his mind when our first shell demolished his bridge and a devastating fire from our Oerlikon and Vickers guns poured into him and set him ablaze. The crew, mostly Japanese, panicked and jumped overboard, and the vessel stopped, stricken and deserted. Soon the stern had slumped until the deck was awash, but then refused to sink any further despite all our efforts. Suddenly, while all this was going on, one of the look-outs called my attention to another vessel, coming towards us from the south. I immediately called off the action, dived, and proceeded towards this fresh target at high speed. This time I did not see how, if he was keeping a proper look-out, the new arrival could fail to sum up the situation ahead of him.

However, to my great relief, on looking astern five minutes later I found that our late target had finally sunk, leaving the usual mess of wreckage floating on the spot. The new target, a fine, new-looking coaster of about 300 tons, was still coming on, apparently unaware that anything was wrong. Once more I let him pass and then surfaced astern of him. Our first round went over him, the second splintered his bridge into a mass of wreckage. Figures were running for'ard to man the machine-gun mounted on the forecastle, but they never had a chance. Our third shell hit the deck in front of the bridge and set the ship on fire with an oily, billowing flame and high clouds of black smoke. This was the signal for the crew to abandon ship. We fired nine more rounds, until the whole ship was a writhing inferno. It was a most satisfactory result for the expenditure of only twelve shells, and as we were now running short of ammunition (only twelve more shells remaining in our magazine), I decided to cease fire and let the flames do their work.

At this point Number One asked to speak to me on the voice-pipe. It seemed that Endi believed our target to be an ammunition ship and urged me not to approach too close to it. I took his advice and retired to a safer distance. The information was correct. Shortly afterwards the vessel began to produce a succession of muffled explosions, bursts of enormous flame, shooting debris and great columns of black smoke. This was such a wonderful firework display that I gave permission for the whole of *Storm*'s crew to come up on the bridge, two at a time, to enjoy the spectacle, which continued for the best part of an hour while we cruised backwards and forwards on the surface in full view of the shore. When the target sank at last we turned away southwards once more, and sat down to a long-delayed lunch.

When I turned in that night and tried to sleep, visions of blazing ships came floating towards me in endless succession.

But the patrol was nearly over. We had received our recall signal the evening before, and the following afternoon, August 2nd, we left the billet for the homeward voyage.

We now had altogether four prisoners on board, all of whom presented certain problems. Three of them were wounded and needed constant attention, a duty which fell to the Coxswain and proved to be such a full-time job that we had to relieve him of his watch-keeping. Besides these prisoners he had Greenway to look after. Poor Selby loathed this work, the tending of the torn flesh inducing in him a physical revulsion, yet so well did he perform it that two of his patients were soon able to get up and move about, and by the time we reached Trincomalee all the wounds were healing nicely. The M.O. in *Maidstone* said he had done a professional job.

The fourth prisoner was the Jap. Altogether, we had him on board for a fortnight. He was not wounded, but we could not allow him to wander about the submarine of his own free will. He lived and ate in the fore-ends, with an armed sentry guarding him day and night, which meant that the watches were always short of one man. However, he gave no trouble. From a photograph of himself found in his wallet, we discovered that he was a soldier, not a sailor as we had imagined; presumably he had been taking passage to Rangoon when captured. Other articles found in his wallet were Japanese occupation currency notes, and two Chinese postage stamps. Besides the wallet, we removed from his person a Swiss-made watch, a key, a string bag containing wooden strips with inscriptions, and a folded paper chart bearing mysterious circles and probably representing a charm or prayer diagram. Every morning he was made to scrub the decks throughout the boat, and he did this job without complaining and more thoroughly than my own sailors. He was a little inclined to curiosity, and in the control-room would cast his eyes around at what was going on; once I caught him glancing at the chart-table as he passed it, and angrily sent him packing with an unwonted torrent of abusive language. At first I was taken aback by his hissing at me every time he came near

T

me, but eventually tumbled to the fact that this was the Japanese indrawn-breath mark of respect. He spoke, apparently, almost no English, but the seamen for'ard discovered that his home town was Kobe and that he seemed to think we operated from Calcutta. In view of the language difficulty I decided not to interrogate this prisoner, as my questions might prejudice the official interrogation later.

The Malay whom we had picked up from the same ship became very friendly after recovering from his wound and his initial shock, and frequently volunteered for work in the engine-room. He lived aft in the stokers' mess and proved himself an expert draughts player. But he did not really like submarine life; it was a terrible shock to him when he discovered we were still off Mergui a whole week after his capture, for we had travelled so many miles in the meantime that he thought we must be nearing base.

The Indian survivor from the second coaster of August 1st spoke practically no English, had two nasty wounds and seemed to be rather unhappy. He appeared to think he was going to be shot. It was obviously useless to attempt an interrogation.

On the other hand, the Malay lad Endi was only too eager to answer questions. He told us that the coasters travelling from Mergui to Rangoon usually carried ammunition and filled up with rice for the return trip; there was a large ammunition dump just north of Pakchan, the ammunition being transported thence to Mergui by rail; it seemed there was a good deal of traffic on this railway. He said that in place of balloon barrages the Japanese had stretched wires between the peaks of hills in the vicinity of Mergui and Penang, that two American bombers had recently been brought down by this means and that the crews were now prisoners in the hands of the Japs. He also said the Japanese were laying traps in some of their junks in the Malacca Straits, the practice being to leave one man on board who would try to lob a hand-grenade down the conning-tower as the submarine went alongside, while the remainder of the crew would pretend to abandon ship and leap overboard on the opposite side after fusing an explosive charge to scuttle the vessel and damage the submarine as well. When he was last in Singapore, about five months earlier, he had observed several Japanese warships; a battleship, three destroyers, three submarines and some two-man submarines. He believed there were two torpedo-boats in Mergui. (We met one of these in our next patrol.) I was not sure how much of all this to believe. He was so anxious to please that he might have been inventing, or exaggerating, perhaps unconsciously, in order to produce information he thought we wanted to hear. I felt inclined to take some of it with a pinch of salt; on the other hand, none of it seemed to be the sort of thing anyone would make up.

We reached Trincomalee on August 7th. Going alongside *Maidstone*, with our black Jolly Roger flying from the periscope standards and spangled with seven new stars to represent our gun actions, we received a great welcome. We had the distinction of being the first submarine to bring back a Japanese prisoner, and tremendous curiosity was aroused by the sight of our passengers being marched up the gangway ladder.

At the conclusion of my patrol report I was glad to be able to add the following general remarks:

1. The plentiful opportunities for gun action were seized on with avidity by the gun's crew and were popular with the entire ship's company. I wish to commend my Gunnery Control Officer, Lieutenant R. L. Blake, R.N., for his coolness and skill in conducting the shoots; also my Gunlayer, Acting Leading Seaman W. Taylor, for his accuracy, determination and spirit during the actions; and indeed the whole gun's crew for their coolness under enemy fire, even when one of their number was wounded.

2. I also wish to commend my Coxswain, Acting Chief Petty Officer F. Selby, for his skilful and patient attention to the wounded, one of whom was an unpleasant sight when brought on board.

3. During the patrol a total of over 4,000 miles was registered. The fact that during this long mileage the Main Engines were kept running without any serious defect arising, reflects, in my opinion, great credit on the Engine Room staff as a whole, and in particular on my Engineer Officer, Mr W. H. Ray, Warrant Engineer, and the Chief E.R.A., R. Brown.

The only dissatisfied man was Dicky Fisher, who had had no opportunity of bringing his boarding party into action.

XX

GUN ATTACK ON CONVOY

GREAT changes affecting our future were about to take place. H.M.S. *Maidstone* and the Eighth Submarine Flotilla were to move to Fremantle, Western Australia, to combine with the United States Submarine Fleet operating in the South-West Pacific. The change-over involved some tricky staff work and precise timing. It was arranged that the submarines would sail for patrol in the Malacca Straits area as usual, all within a few days of each other, and then carry on to Fremantle instead of returning to Trincomalee; in the meantime *Maidstone* would sail direct and be ready to look after the submarines on their arrival. H.M.S. *Adamant* would remain in Trincomalee, and the Fourth Flotilla continue operating in the Malacca Straits.

When, on August 25th, we sailed for our next patrol, we therefore knew it would have to be a comparatively short one, so that we could make the long journey to Australia without refuelling. We were assigned to the same billet as on the previous patrol, but I had no illusions that we were likely to find such easy victims. That sort of patrol happens only once in the same area. Since then two of our submarines had patrolled in the archipelago, *Sturdy* near Pakchan and *Sea Rover* further north near Mergui; *Sturdy* had sunk two armed coasters by gunfire, but *Sea Rover* had reported a blank patrol. We must now expect the enemy to have learnt his lesson and stopped sailing his coasters independently. Instead we should probably find them, if we found them at all, travelling in convoy under escort.

During our surface exploration of the Mergui Archipelago we had seen no ships whatever, but the Staff had received information that the enemy was from time to time sending coasters from the Pakchan River northward through the islands to Mergui, and they were anxious to find out what route the coasters were using. As *Sea Rover* had recently drawn blank just north of Mergui, the scene of our former depredations, I decided to spend my patrol in Forrest Passage, a comparatively open stretch of water in the centre of my area which it seemed all the inner routes must somehow cross.* I was hoping that the calmer weather and the bright moonlight nights would tempt small craft to make the passage of the archipelago in greater numbers.

We reached the area some hours before dawn on August 30th, dived in Forrest Passage and settled down to keep an eye on the head of Forrest Strait. We had passed through this spot on the surface during our voyage of exploration on the previous patrol; this time the situation seemed to demand a waiting game, and we remained submerged during daylight, patrolling the same spot on the surface at night. Nothing happened for the first two days, but at half-past ten on the third morning several distant columns of smoke were sighted to the southward. They were so far away that I felt sure it would be safe to surface and get a better view. We came up, and from the bridge I could see nine small vessels—seven coasters and two escorts of the landing-craft type—proceeding in convoy up Forrest Strait. A minute later we dived and began to manœuvre for a good attacking position.

While it was interesting to have confirmation of the Staff's intelligence that coasters were plying between Pakchan and Mergui, I was still at a loss to know how to attack such a convoy. Our experience on the last patrol had shown that these coasters were now armed with machine-guns. We could fire torpedoes, but the targets were so small and of such shallow draught that they were hardly worth the expense of torpedoes and also extremely difficult to hit. As for gun action, it seemed too much of a risk to take on seven armed adversaries at once— not to mention the two escorts, probably equipped with machine-guns and depth-charges. It was a problem which had been worrying us in the flotilla for some time, and neither my

* See previous map on page 275.

senior officers nor my fellow C.O.s had been able to find a satisfactory answer to it. Here I was faced with the situation, and
I had to do something about it.

The convoy was approaching so slowly—we plotted the
speed as six knots—that I had nearly an hour in which to make
up my mind. I finally decided to get in to as close a range as
possible, fire torpedoes set to run at a depth of four feet, and
aim each torpedo at a different ship. I hoped that I would hit
at least one of them and that such confusion would ensue that
we could surface and pick off one or two individual ships with
the gun.

Once more the sea was mirror-smooth, so that in the final
stages of the attack I had to make do with the briefest of
glimpses through the low-power periscope. To aim the torpedoes at individual ships I should have to keep the periscope
up all the time I was firing, so I decided to fire with the submarine's head swinging across the convoy, and thus shorten
the interval between each torpedo. I managed to get to within
600 yards of the nearest ship without being sighted, and, with
starboard helm on, fired at five separate ships, aiming at the
middle of each.

To my dismay, there were no bangs, no eruptions of flame,
no skyward leapings of disintegrated metal. The whole convoy,
alarmed by the tracks of the torpedoes, began zig-zagging
wildly, though not in time to account for my lamentable failure
to obtain one single hit.* The two escorts seemed to think I had
fired from a greater range, for they passed either side of me and
fussed around some way astern while I watched them from periscope depth. Meanwhile the convoy regrouped and proceeded
in good order northwards towards Celerity Passage. One of the
escorts presently disappeared round the western corner of Sir
Edward Owen Island, presumably rejoining the convoy later
through Jubilee Channel.

---

* Commenting later on my description of the attack, Captain Shadwell wrote
that he considered my failure was "probably due to an over-estimation of speed,
combined with the fact that the torpedoes were fired on the swing. Against such
small targets the aim has to be very accurate indeed if a hit is to be obtained, and
this is unlikely to be achieved with helm on."

Looking back afterwards, I realised that this would have been the moment to come up and gun the convoy, with one escort out of sight and the other nearly two miles away from me. Moreover, this would have been a better spot than the one forced on me the following day, for the water was deeper here and there were fewer navigational worries.

Half an hour after I had made the attack, the remaining escort, still two miles away, for no apparent reason suddenly dropped two depth-charges. These were probably intended as no more than a face-saving farewell gesture, for immediately afterwards he went off and joined up with the rear ship of the convoy, the head of which was now disappearing amongst the islands to the north.

I was furious with myself for failing so completely to inflict damage on the coasters, and determined to try to intercept them again. They were obviously bound for Mergui, and looking at the chart I reckoned they had the choice of two separate routes through the inner channels. They could turn sharp left and pass round the outside of Domel Island, thence proceeding north by the normal passage east of Bentinck Island—in which case I could attack them very soon by Domel Island. Or they could make the narrow journey through Celerity Passage on the inside of Domel Island, reaching Morrison Bay (the next point at which I could get in close enough to make an attack) at some time during the night. Unfortunately at this vital moment we were handicapped by having one engine temporarily out of action, owing to a defective lubricating oil pump, and it was doubtful if I could get there in time by the roundabout route. However, on a closer examination of the large-scale chart we realised that part of this inside channel was only navigable at high tide, and the next high tide was not until nine o'clock that night. It was possible that the convoy would not attempt this tricky passage in darkness, but would wait for the morning tide. If so, we could reach the entrance to Morrison Bay in plenty of time.

In any case, the sooner we got moving the better. Before the last of the convoy had vanished among the islands, a heavy rain-squall gave us the opportunity to surface. On our one engine we proceeded nor'-nor'-west through the gap between The Sisters and Bushby Island. There was no sign here of the enemy coming outside Domel Island, so we pressed on northward, passed outside Bentinck Island, and by midnight had reached a position from which we could keep an eye on the entrance to Morrison Bay. We spent the rest of the night there, charging batteries in the moonlight, and before dawn dived and moved closer in.

All this time I had been racking my brains to find a plan of action for my next attack—if the convoy should appear as expected. I could hardly waste any more torpedoes on these small ships, and the only alternative was to come up and use the gun. But suppose they all turned towards us when we surfaced, and tried to ram us? With our one three-inch, our one Oerlikon and our two Vickers light machine-guns, we could not hope to stop them all at once. If they were all armed, as was only too likely, we might easily have the gun's crews and the bridge party wiped out when the fighting came to close quarters. Clearly, in such an engagement we should need room to manœuvre, and enough water to dive in if the opposition got too hot.

Unfortunately it was obvious from the chart that there was very little room to manœuvre. The water everywhere was fairly shallow, and we were surrounded by shoals that were deep enough in most places for surface navigation but not for diving; even on the surface we should always be in imminent danger of going aground. I did not like the position at all, and cursed myself for not having attacked with the gun after my torpedo attack the day before, when I had plenty of deep water all round me. However, here we were, and it was the last chance of having a go at this convoy before it reached Mergui. Beyond this point its route would follow channels too shallow for submarine approach.

It was not until half-past nine that morning that we saw the head of the convoy emerging from the inner channel exactly where I had expected. As on the previous day, it was a long time—about an hour and a half—before the slow-moving ships reached our position. In the intervals of watching them through the periscope I studied the chart and memorised the general shape of the sea's bottom so that I had a fairly accurate mental picture of the shoal dangers. I knew that once the action started there would be no opportunity of precise fixing, and that this would be another case of navigating by eye.

Beyond deciding to let all the ships pass me before surfacing, hoping thus to minimise the chances of a massed ramming attack, I still could not make up my mind what tactics to adopt. Submarines had never been designed for this sort of work, and I had a strong foreboding that the odds were weighted too heavily against us. But we could not sit tamely there and watch them pass unharmed. We must *do* something.

Once again I had to contend with a sea that was as unruffled as a sheet of polished glass. It was desperate work trying to keep track of the movements of so many ships with only split-second observations through the periscope. The two escorts seemed very much aware that they were approaching a danger point, for they were moving in a rapid and continuous zig-zag on the seaward beam of the convoy. However, although they passed within about 200 yards of us, they did not spot the periscope, and when the second of them was well past us we were abeam of the last coaster of the column. Now, if ever, was the moment for gun action.

When I gave the order to surface it was the first time I had ever done so without knowing exactly what I meant to do when I got to the top. Climbing the ladder to the bridge on the heels of the gun's crew, I was in a blue funk and full of a premonition of disaster.

Yet as soon as I reached the bridge and stood in the sunshine under the blue sky all my apprehensions were miraculously swept away. Every one of our guns opened fire at once without a hitch and continued firing for the next thirty-six minutes without any of the stoppages which had sometimes let us down in the past. Action, once joined, produced its own stimulus to the brain; our tactics were adapted every moment to meet the changing situation, and we were never at a loss.

1117   Opened fire at the rear ship at a range of 2,000 yards, obtaining seven or eight fairly destructive hits. She turned away and limped towards the shore. We then attacked and stopped the ship ahead of her, but both the escorts were now racing towards us, firing their machine-guns. Turned to port to bring them both on to the starboard bow, and directed the fire of all our guns on to them. In turn they were each hit and stopped by several direct hits from the three-inch. This part of the action was most exciting, the range eventually closing to four hundred yards. The enemy were very brave, and we were lucky not to suffer any casualties. Both these escorts were carrying a score or so of Japanese, presumably troops. One of them released a depth-charge (or it may have been shot over the side) when it was 500 yards away, and it went off on the bottom causing the submarine to heel slightly to starboard for a moment. One of the escorts got out of control, and eventually drove itself under, still with way on. The other remained afloat and was sunk later when things calmed down.

In the meantime, a small vessel had been sighted approaching from the northward at great speed. This looked too much like a motor torpedo-boat to be healthy, so it was the next target to be engaged. At the same time a constant-helm zig-zag was maintained. Several near-misses were seen before the torpedo-boat, at a range of about 3,000 yards, turned and fired two stern torpedoes. The tracks passed about 100 yards astern of us. One definite direct hit was scored on this M.T.B. as she was retiring, at a range of about 4,000 yards, and she took little further interest in the proceedings. I think our shooting had put her off quite effectively.

Before this, some vessel had opened up with a pom-pom. We traced the firing to a small ship not previously sighted which lay stopped about 4,000 yards away and began to get uncomfortably accurate. Fortunately this fellow, probably a motor gun-boat, obtained only one direct hit, which struck *Storm*'s bridge casing below the Oerlikon and caused no casualties. Neither the motor torpedo-boat nor the gun-boat had been previously seen through the periscope, and it is considered that they came out from Mergui to meet the convoy.

All this time, also, there was a perpetual whine of machine-gun bullets, but it was difficult to see exactly which ships were firing. They caused no casualties. It was now decided to finish off the coaster which had been stopped earlier (the second target engaged) and also the other escort. These both sank after a few short-range water-line shots. Meanwhile, the first coaster we had attacked and severely damaged appeared to have beached herself; later, however, she seemed to be still under way and may have succeeded in proceeding with the remainder. Fire was now directed at a coaster which had stopped about 4,000 yards away. Two direct hits were obtained, and his bridge demolished.

But by this time we had fired over 150 rounds of three-inch and the barrel was so heated that the next round jammed. Moreover, the remainder of the convoy was getting out of range, we had exhausted all our pans of Oerlikon and Vickers ammunition, and I was getting anxious about the navigation. I decided to call it a day, as the situation did not justify the risk of running the submarine aground.

1153 Broke off the action and retired westward on the surface, passing through the gap north of Bentinck Island. There seemed no point in remaining in the vicinity.

The net result of the action was: Two escorts and one coaster sunk, two coasters damaged, one torpedo-boat hit. Also, the last clue to the inshore convoy route had been uncovered. An interesting point was that all the survivors seen in the water were apparently Japanese. Not a single Malay or Burman was among them, though these had been plentiful in the coasters sunk on the previous patrol.

I was staggered, and profoundly thankful, that we had survived those thirty-six minutes without a single casualty. There was great elation throughout the boat at our success. The gun's crew were no doubt regaling their messmates below with vivid descriptions of the action; they had enjoyed themselves, and were only too disappointed when the engagement was broken off. Inspired by the grim determination of Taylor, the gunlayer, they had done very well, quite unperturbed by the machine-gun fire coming at us from all directions; even Greenway, now back in the gun's crew as breech-worker, was unshaken by any memories of his previous wounding in somewhat similar circumstances. My highest admiration went to Richard Blake, who as gunnery control officer had been faced with unusually rapid decisions—for my constant shifts of target, and the wild zigzag forced on us by the threat of torpedoes from the M.T.B. had demanded frequent and immediate corrections to range and deflection. In spite of these difficulties he had remained cool, patient and accurate. At the end both he and I were hoarse from shouting our orders above the inferno of noise. For several hours afterwards we were partially deaf, and I think it must have been on this occasion that Blake suffered the damage to his eardrums which led, five years after the end of the war, to his being invalided out of the service.

Needless to say, all this noise inspired Stoker Rooke to one of his longest and most glorious epics, which ran as a serial in many subsequent issues of *Good Evening*. Neater, perhaps, was the crop of clerihews produced by another contributor:

> He takes the cake
> Does Lieutenant "Whaley" Blake.
> He's just as accurate, though himself no boaster,
> At shooting stars or an enemy coaster.

> "Captain Kettle" Taylor *
> Is a most belligerent sailor.
> At the sight of his gun every Nippo and Hun
> Turns considerably paler.

> A Jap, not so quick as
> His pals, didn't know that a Vickers
> Was death in the hands of a Hewetson—
> But he knew it soon!

> Now Brown (A.A.3),
> A quiet enough fellow is he,
> But in the midst of a good hurly-burly can
> Make a big noise with his Oerlikon.

Out of the original nine ships we had sunk three and damaged two. It was better than I had hoped for when we surfaced, but I could not help remembering that if I had been quicker in the uptake on the previous day we should probably have taken a heavier toll and might even have sunk the entire convoy.

There were five more days to go before we were due to leave for Australia. I decided to spend these in the south of my area, and that night we travelled down outside the islands to reach the northern entrance to Hastings Harbour by dawn. Here, as

* Taylor was so nick-named on account of the red beard he wore at this time.

on the previous patrol, we drew blank. One morning we sank a northbound junk at the southern entrance to Forrest Strait, afterwards transferring the survivors to a fishing-boat, but saw no other targets. On the afternoon of the 7th we surfaced and proceeded to leave the billet. We had not yet cleared the islands when we were caught napping by an enemy plane, the first aircraft we had seen in the whole area in two patrols. He saw us and came for us as we dived, circled the position for a while, but dropped no bombs. Presently he went away, and at dusk we came up again and set course for Australia.

It was a long voyage, but we were on the surface nearly all the way. On the 10th we crossed the Equator in longitude 95° 50′ E, tying an imaginary loop round the line by diving back under it and re-crossing it on the surface. On diving we left open the upper hatch of the gun-tower to allow it to fill up and provide a ducking-pond for King Neptune's traditional ceremonies. During the fun the weather deteriorated rapidly, and the last few latherings and duckings were carried out in the midst of a chilly squall that was distinctly un-equatorial. On the 14th, our route taking us close to Christmas Island, then under Japanese occupation, we spent the day making a periscope examination of the island, and of Flying Fish Cove in particular. But there were no ships alongside any of the piers, and at nightfall we surfaced and went on our way.

Four days later, at six o'clock in the morning, a low-lying strip of land was sighted on the port bow. It was hard to believe that this unimpressive line on the horizon was the north-western outpost of a great continent, but the fact was that we had, as the log laconically records, "sighted Australia." Soon we were entering Exmouth Gulf, a shallow bay surrounded by a waste of sand dunes. Here we took in some much-needed fuel, continued down the west coast and reached Fremantle on September 22nd. *Maidstone* had been there for nearly a week.

XXI

THROUGH THE LOMBOK STRAIT

THE Eighth Submarine Flotilla was the first unit of the Royal
Navy to operate from Western Australia. The people of Perth,
Fremantle and the surrounding districts opened their hearts
and their doors to us with a generosity beyond our previous experience. The ground had been admirably prepared by Commander Miers on an earlier ambassadorial visit, in the course
of which he was able to make a variety of attractive arrangements for the recreation of the submarine crews in harbour.
Leave could be spent at private homes in Perth or Fremantle,
at country hotels further down the coast, or in outlying farms.
The place most favoured by some of the C.O.s was the sheep-
farm at Boraning, about a hundred miles inland, the home of
Harold and Joan Klug. These two remarkable people treated
us as their own sons. I spent two leaves under their hospitable
roof, one with Freddie Sherwood and Tony Spender, one with
Sam Marriott, and of those sun-scorched days I have a hundred
crystal memories: getting up at five in the morning to shoot
rabbits at dawn, riding horses among the blue-gum trees,
watching the sheep-shearing, sitting out on the veranda in the
noonday sun with a glass of beer and drawing pictures of submarines for young George Klug, hearing the whine of the circular saw in the paddock below the house, playing the pianola,
helping with the washing-up and being upbraided by Joan for
surreptitiously adding cold to the scalding water, listening to
the two Italian P.O.W.s singing grand opera as they worked
about the fields . . . and the day we tried to find the fire.

The threat of bush fires was a constant anxiety to the farmers
in the dry season; after many rainless weeks the undergrowth
would be as dry as matchwood, and an odd spark could result
in the loss of much valuable timber. One afternoon when I was

staying with the Klugs, their nearest neighbour some five or six miles away telephoned to say that he could see smoke coming from one of their outlying timber paddocks. I followed Harold Klug as he ran out of doors. On the horizon behind the house a wisp of smoke was rising against the blue sky beyond the brow of the hill. We ran down to collect the lorry and the Italian P.O.W.s, and drove off along the rough tracks in the direction of the fire. But by now the smoke had faded away, and for nearly an hour we searched the woods without getting so much as a whiff of a fire. Finally we came out into the open at the limit of the Klug territory where it joined that of the neighbour who had telephoned the news. We got out of the lorry. Glancing at Harold's lined and sunburnt face I saw that his eyes were alert and searching the ground, and suddenly he moved forward and pounced on the branch of a sapling which had obviously just been cut and then laid in a deliberate manner on the ground. Following its direction we found other unmistakable signs in the bushes; Harold's neighbour had been there earlier and left us these pointers to the bearing on which he had seen the smoke. We drove back towards the trees and renewed our efforts, but again without result. By this time it was beginning to grow dark, and Harold had just decided to call off the search until morning when one of the Italians sang out from the back of the lorry, "Stop! I smell burning." Harold sniffed the air and said, "By God, he's right." I personally couldn't smell anything, but he confidently drove off the track into the undergrowth to our left, and a few minutes later, in the hollow of a small clearing, we came on a red glow muttering in the darkness. Coming up to it we found the stump of a tree that was being slowly eaten away from the inside by a smouldering fire, and lying near it the disembowelled shell of the trunk where it had fallen and cracked and spilled ash along the ground. Harold said the core of the tree must have been burning for months; from time to time, at the wetter season of the year, when fires could be kept under control, it was the practice deliberately to fire certain sections of the timber paddocks in order to burn off the foliage before it grew

dense enough to be dangerous in the dry season; sometimes it
happened on these occasions that the head of a tree would catch
fire internally and quietly smoulder downwards without visible
sign for many months until the roots were attacked and could
no longer support the weight of the trunk. This particular section had been fired about six months previously. We cleared
the ground for some yards around the burning stump to remove
any immediate danger of the fire's spreading, and went home.
In the morning we came back with the lorry loaded up with
water-barrels, and pumped a fine spray into the ashes until
there was no doubt that the fire was out.

But while life ashore was so pleasant, our sea operations in
the new patrol areas were far from satisfactory. When we left
the Malacca Straits we had great hopes that by operating beyond the outer ring of Dutch East Indian islands—on the
Pacific side of Java, Bali, Lombok, Soembawa, Flores and
Timor—we should once more find larger targets.* Unfortunately we were a few months too late. The U.S. submarines
working from Fremantle had scooped the field and gone on to
scour the South China Sea and the waters round the Philippines, leaving the newly-arrived British to pick up whatever
crumbs might still be found in the Java and Flores Seas. For
the first time we realised that the Royal Navy was now the poor
relation of the American Navy, and it was an unpalatable shock.
Their submarines, built from the start with a view to operations
in the vast distances of the Pacific, were larger and better
equipped than ours, which had been designed for work in the
North Sea or the Mediterranean. Theirs had a fuel capacity
which enabled them to patrol in areas far beyond our range.
Our T-class submarines, some of which had joined the flotilla
when it moved to Australia, could reach the Singapore area and
the north coast of Borneo, but even they could not compete
with the Americans; for the smaller S-boats the limits were the
north of the Straits of Macassar and the western extremity of
the Java Sea. The crew accommodation in the American sub-

* See inset map on page 311.

marines was so superior to ours that after being shown over one of them I felt downright ashamed of the conditions in which my own able seamen and stokers had to live at sea. With their greater size the Americans were naturally able to carry more torpedoes. Most galling of all was the fact that they were equipped with the latest type of radar; our set was the by now somewhat outdated "aircraft-warning" set with the X-shaped aerial, which was only fairly efficient in the detection of surface echoes, and it was infuriating to find that this British invention should be available in its latest form to the Americans and not to us. The reason was that in the American Navy submarines had top priority, while in the Royal Navy the best quite rightly went first to the anti-submarine forces fighting the Battle of the Atlantic.

Once at sea, we came under the operational direction of the American Admiral Fife, a man of great charm and impressive personality who went out of his way to treat us always as though we were the equals of his own submarines. Although his headquarters were in Perth, he made a point of coming in to Fremantle personally to say good-bye to us whenever we sailed for patrol. Even after *Storm* went back to England he took the trouble to send a signal congratulating us on the decorations awarded us at the end of the commission. He was typical of the best kind of American, and when you find one of those you have found one of the world's most delightful citizens.

In harbour we mixed surprisingly little with our American opposite numbers. But we learnt to respect them for their efficiency and bravery in operations against the enemy. As we now came under the same command we were using the U.S. Navy code, and from the signals we read while we were at sea we knew something of what they were accomplishing in the more distant and rewarding areas of which we were so envious. With their up-to-date radar and their short-range ship-to-ship radio telephony, they had brought the art of wolf-pack tactics to a pitch finer than anything achieved by the German U-boats in the Atlantic. When the Americans re-invaded the Philip-

U

pines and the Japs responded by sending large naval forces to the area, one of the U.S. submarine wolf-packs in one night sank a Kongo-class battleship and a heavy cruiser, hit another cruiser with four torpedoes, and made sighting reports of two other battleships and cruisers. A few nights later another pack caused heavy destruction to an enemy supply convoy approaching the Philippines.

By contrast with the mighty deeds of the far-ranging Americans our own efforts in Pacific waters were small beer.

Storm's first patrol from Fremantle was in the Gulf of Boni off the south of Celebes. Some idea of the vast distances we had to contend with in this part of the world may be gathered from the fact that we had to cross over 2,400 miles of ocean to reach the billet. That took us ten days of surface running. During our fortnight in the patrol area itself we covered 1,600 miles in our efforts to find targets, and by the time we returned to Fremantle we had logged altogether 6,200 miles.

We left Fremantle on October 10th and, after fuelling at Exmouth Gulf on the 13th, proceeded north across the Timor Sea and passed through the island barrier by way of the Ombai Strait along the north-west coast of Timor, turning west into the Flores Sea at dawn on the 19th. At noon the following day, on sighting Salayar Island ahead of us in hazy visibility, we submerged and continued closing in towards the land.

Shortly afterwards an enemy aircraft, unseen by the officer-of-the-watch against the sun, saw us below him in the clear water, came down low and dropped a bomb on us. The first I knew of it was the sudden explosion coming unheralded out of the peaceful afternoon. I leapt from the wardroom into the control-room, ordered "Full ahead together, 100 feet, hard-a-starboard," and thrust the startled officer-of-the-watch away from the periscope. In the moment before the top of it was dipped below the surface I saw a wide circle of tumbling foam just astern of us where the bomb had dropped. We were passing sixty feet on our way down when a second bomb exploded over the top of us—rather closer this time; it made the lights flicker, cracked the gauge glass of one of the trimming tanks and the welding of the starboard tail-clutch casing, and (as we discovered later) smashed the green shade in the starboard bow light on the side of the bridge. Fifteen minutes later I came back to periscope depth only to find the aircraft still circling. I hurriedly returned to the depths and stayed there for an hour, and when I had my next look round he was gone.

We spent more than a week off the south coast of Celebes, vainly searching for enemy traffic. We saw nothing through the periscope but white-sailed praus filled to the gunwales with natives whose skins gleamed in the sun like new chestnuts; beyond them the beaches of burning sand lying empty under drowsy palm-trees, and emerald islets scattered on a sea that was as blue and hard and transparent as zircon. On the tenth day, being due to leave patrol at dusk on the following evening, and despairing of finding anything better to attack, we moved further into the Gulf of Boni to investigate the native schooners which, as Singey Anderson had discovered while patrolling this billet in *Sturdy* just before us, had been pressed into service by the Japanese to carry nickel ore westward from the little port of Pomalaa. We had been authorised to sink these schooners if they were engaged in this traffic, but as they were known to be entirely manned by natives I had made up my mind that I would sink them only if I could do so without causing any loss of life to their crews. Dicky Fisher was delighted at the prospect of this game, for at last he and his boarding party could come into their own.

We found the first of our nickel-traders at dawn the next day. She was a handsome miniature two-masted gaff-rigged schooner, with a large boomed mainsail, a loose-footed foresail and an outer and inner jib set proudly on a long, lifting jibboom; the hull was entirely of wood, with a built-up poop cut off square and overhanging the rudder, a wide deck planked in from stem to stern, and three or four small hatches giving access to the roomy hold. She was manned by about ten Malays, who downed sail as we approached; even before we were alongside,

Fisher jumped the gap and boarded her, followed by Petty Officer Blight (the Second Coxswain) and the rest of the small party. The Malays seemed to take it all as a matter of course, and climbed obediently over our bow on to the fore casing. Their schooner had been inward bound to Pomalaa without a cargo, but Fisher, rummaging around in the empty hold, found a residue of nickel ore, and her papers showed that she had orders to carry nickel on her return trip to Macassar. It seemed a terrible shame to have to sink her, but she was useful to the enemy and we had no alternative. Having taken off all the crew and recovered the boarding party, we withdrew a little distance and sank her with a few rounds of three-inch. But we gained no satisfaction from destroying this graceful little ship.

Only one more schooner was found that day, but learning from the Malays that further nickel traffic was expected to leave Pomalaa shortly I moved south during the night and signalled to Fremantle for permission to extend my patrol by four days. A reply granting my request came back a couple of hours later, so after spending two days in the south of the area in a last attempt to find some enemy target to attack, I returned north to make further raids on the nickel trade inside the Gulf.

On November 1st we sank only two westbound schooners, both crammed to the hatches with nickel ore, later dumping our Malay prisoners on an outrigger fishing craft in exchange for one very large fish. But November 2nd was a field-day for Fisher and his boarding party; we had so many natives on board—all down below in case we had to dive for aircraft—that we afterwards called it Visitors' Day.

0540   Sighted three westbound schooners on the SE horizon.
0555   Radar aircraft echo, closing to thirteen miles. Dived. Aircraft not sighted. Surfaced and continued chase of schooners.
0635   Radar aircraft echo, closing to eight miles. Dived, but again no sign of aircraft. Surfaced and resumed chase.
0700   Came up with schooners, who continued to sail on. Fired one warning shot, and all three downed sail. Boarded each in turn and found them all full of nickel ore. Took crews off and sent them down below. This meant we had eighteen Malays in the submarine. Four more schooners had in the meantime been sighted on

the horizon to the SW. The wind being very light, however, and a convenient fishing-boat appearing to the northward, I decided to get rid of my Malays first.

0745   Left the three schooners abandoned and proceeded five miles towards fishing vessel.

0828   Disembarked Malays, and returned to the three schooners.

0900   Sank them in turn by gunfire. As the third one sank, two lads were seen in the water; they had evidently hidden during the boarding party's search earlier. Picked them up. Proceeded towards three of the four schooners which had been sighted earlier. The fourth was some distance to windward of the others, and it was decided to sink the three and then disembark the crews in the fourth, there being no other smaller vessels now in sight.

1005   Approached the schooners—all larger than the previous three. Boarded them in turn and took off crews. All three were fully laden with nickel ore. Sank them by gunfire. Again two small boys jumped overboard from one of them as she was sinking. Picked these up unharmed. The submarine was now getting somewhat crowded; thirty-eight Malays were below.* Proceeded towards remaining schooner.

1202   Came up with schooner, who downed sail. Boarded. Found cargo was again nickel ore. It seemed a pity to let this one go, but the thirty-eight Malays had to be disembarked somewhere. Hit on the plan of making them jettison their cargo. Fisher managed to get the idea across, and the work of jettisoning began. Disembarked my Malays as an extra working-party.

1219   Began circling schooner slowly. As she drifted to leeward the nickel ore dust continued to pour over the side in bucketfuls, staining the sea a rich reddish brown.

1300   Gave schooner permission to sail on, and proceeded northwards.

One more nickel-laden schooner, sighted at dusk, completed a busy day. This one had a woman and her baby on board, and for a time it looked as though we should have to have them and the crew with us for the night. But we fortunately sighted another small sail in the moonlight and were able to transfer them less than two hours later. In the early hours of the morning we boarded yet another schooner, which also contained a woman and child, and it was a relief to find no cargo in the hold so that we could allow the vessel to proceed.

It was now time to be leaving the billet for our homeward

---

* Our passengers increased the number of bodies on board by seventy-five per cent. Number One would have had quite a trimming problem on his hands if we had been forced to dive during this time.

passage. Our bag was pitifully small—only eleven unarmed
schooners whose sinking had given us no satisfaction but that
of knowing we had not killed or even wounded a single one of
their crews. During the day of November 3rd we moved southward on the surface, passed through Salayar Strait shortly after
dark, and set course across the Flores Sea. By the following
evening we were making our approach to the most dangerous
spot in the whole of our expedition.

The Lombok Strait, which separates Bali from Lombok, is
the least narrow, and was for us the only feasible, gap in the long
chain of islands that stretches 1,500 miles from Sunda Strait in
the west to Ombai Strait in the east. It is one of the sluice
gates through which any movement of water between the Java
and Flores Seas and the Indian Ocean must force itself. The
currents that flow through it are irregular, unpredictable and
often swift. At that season of the year they were usually
southerly, but until we were in the strait itself we could never
be sure. We could not hope to make the whole passage
submerged if the current was against us. It can run at anything up to five or six knots at the southern end where the gap
narrows to a width of only eleven miles. The Allied submarines therefore always tried to negotiate the Lombok Strait
on the surface at night. But the Japanese, who were in occupation of all these islands, knew that we were using this gap and
maintained a regular anti-submarine night patrol here. Most
submarines had encountered destroyers or submarine-chasers
on their way through; a few nights before we were due to make
the passage an American submarine signalled that she had been
attacked by gunfire from a shore battery which appeared to be
radar-controlled, and a little while earlier the Dutch submarine
Zwaardfisch had reported being fired on by an enemy submarine at the northern entrance to the strait.

As we made our approach on the surface that evening there
was no mistaking where the Lombok Strait was. From fifty
miles away we could see to the south of us the massive outline
of Lombok's great mountain, Rinjani, 12,000 feet high, stand-

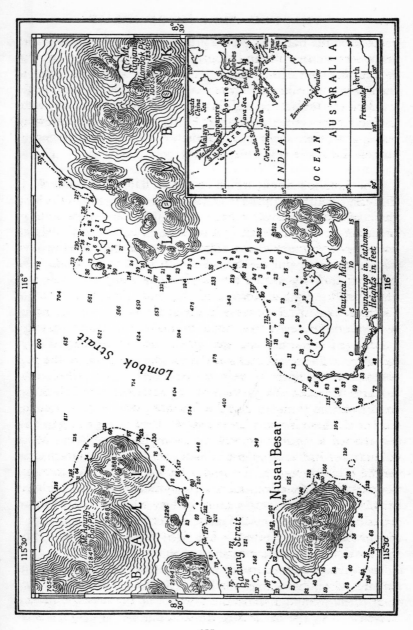

ing out on the port bow, and a little to starboard the staggering beauty of Bali's volcanic Mt. Agung, rearing 10,000 feet up in the shape of a perfect cone and flushed with the rose-petal hues of sunset. Our way home lay between the two mountains.

Darkness fell across the sea with its usual swiftness. We pressed on towards the strait, knowing that the moon would be rising about midnight and that the nearer we could get to the narrows before it did so the better it would be for us. I doubled the usual number of look-outs.

We met the first enemy patrol shortly before eleven o'clock. Since nightfall a slight haze had spread over the sea, obscuring the land. All we could see of this vessel was a dark smudge broad on our port bow. He was some miles off, and by altering course to starboard we were able to work round to the westward of him without being sighted. Soon after midnight, being now closer to the land, and the moon just rising, we could once more distinguish the shape of the islands; and by one o'clock we had obtained a good land fix and begun our passage of the strait. It was indeed a frightening prospect. The black land masses looming up on either side of us made the strait appear even narrower than it is; and ahead of us rose a seemingly impenetrable wall of darkness. At the same time we felt that the climbing moon was deliberately singling us out for illumination.

At 0140 we saw another patrol vessel, but he was already on our beam when first detected, so far off that I did not consider it necessary even to alter course; and we soon dropped him out of sight on our port quarter. The next hour passed without alarm, but just before three o'clock we began to run into trouble. The man who made the next three vital sightings was Selby, the Coxswain, who was on this occasion acting as an extra look-out on my special instructions. I used to reckon my eyesight was better than most, but Selby had a quite remarkable night vision and frequently spotted things before I did. And indeed when, at 0255, he reported, "Dark object bearing Red 10, sir," it was some seconds before I could distinguish anything through my binoculars.

When I saw the dark shape I realised it was larger than the

two ships we had seen before, and at once altered course away. Keeping him just in sight we worked gradually round to westward and south-westward of him. He had unmistakable war ship lines and was almost certainly a destroyer; he seemed to be lying stopped, and gave no sign of being aware of our presence. At last, after describing a wide semi-circle, we were able to resume our southerly course, with the destroyer fading from view on the port quarter. But we had only just lost sight of him when Selby reported another vessel, on the starboard bow this time. I turned away eastward, but in doing so caught sight of the destroyer once more and realised that this course would be taking us closer to him. I shaped a new course south-eastward which put both the enemy vessels slightly abaft our beam. We were gradually drawing nicely away from them when Selby sighted yet another black smudge—and this time it was dead ahead of us and looked like a small vessel fairly close. At this point I began to feel somewhat hemmed in; I could not turn either way without getting dangerously near one of the other two ships. I decided to dive. If the current was against us it was too bad.

I did not want to go deep unless I was forced to, so on diving I stayed at periscope depth and hoped the ship ahead had not seen us. The moonlight was so bright that I found I could see more than I expected through the periscope. The shape resolved itself into a motor launch. He was even closer than I had thought, for only a few minutes after we had dived he passed slowly down our port side, so close that at one time I could only get half his length into my field of view. He could not have been more than fifty yards away, and my heart was pounding like a steam hammer. But he went on past us, unsuspecting, and presently disappeared astern. I could no longer see the other two vessels. We pressed on southward, still keeping periscope watch, and as the dawn came up behind Lombok and enabled us to take a land fix we found to our relief and joy that the current was with us at the rate of five knots. At six o'clock we were passing out through the narrows in great style, and by noon the islands were so far astern that we were able to surface for the homeward run to Fremantle, which we reached eight days later, having been thirty-four days away. It was our longest patrol so far.

On arrival I learnt from Captain Shadwell the surprising news that we were returning to England after the next patrol. I had fully expected to have to carry out two or even three more before going home, but as I was due to get married as soon as I reached England I raised no objections to this advancement of the date.

On the evening of January 2nd we were approaching the Lombok Strait from the north for the second and last time. We had spent a blank and depressing patrol off Cape Mangkalihat, the most easterly tip of Borneo, almost dead on the equator in the Strait of Macassar.

It had been my intention this time to attempt a submerged daylight passage of the Lombok Strait, but on New Year's Eve we read the following signal made to Fremantle by Tony Spender in *Sirdar*: "Unable to make Lombok passage. Current northerly. Strong surface and air patrols, including two destroyers. No damage. Am returning via Ombai Strait."

Current northerly, he had said. This was disturbing news, and as a result of it I changed my mind and decided after all to try to get through on the surface at night as before. This is how I described the night's adventures in my log. It was *Storm*'s last brush with the enemy:

1330. Set course southward for Lombok Strait.

2200. Just after moonrise, in the northern approach to the Strait, sighted darkened vessel bearing ESE. Altered course westward towards the land.

2206. Lost sight of the enemy. Resumed course 180°.

2220. Sighted vessel again on the port beam up moon, pointing towards. Altered away to SW. Enemy, now seen to be a destroyer about three miles away, began belching black smoke, but seemed uncertain of our position, as his bearing started drawing aft. However, he soon altered towards us.

2227. Enemy evidently overhauling rapidly on the port quarter. Turned to due west.

2228. Dived, turned hard-a-starboard to a course of due north and went to 200 feet. Proceeded at full speed for four minutes, then dead slow.

2232. Turbine H.E. on the starboard quarter.

2235. Nine depth-charges in rapid succession, in two patterns of four and five. Much reverberation owing to the proximity of the shore. No damage.

2240. H.E. faded out on Red 150.

2245. H.E. bearing Red 140, moved slowly up the port side and then faded out again on Red 85. It looked as though we were down for the rest of the night. *Sirdar* had reported the current as northerly three days previously; if it were still northerly it would be difficult, if not impossible, to get through the Strait submerged. But since the currents were variable at this time of the year, it would be worth trying. If by daylight it was obvious that the current was against us, there would still be time to turn back and get clear to the north before the following night.

2250. No more H.E. was heard from the destroyer, last detected on a bearing of due west, which would put him close in to the beach. His tactics appeared very unenterprising. I decided he must be lying stopped inshore, listening, hoping perhaps I would be lulled into a false sense of security and surface up moon of him. Being uncertain of the current I decided to get out into the middle of the Strait before turning south. I altered course to starboard and steered ESE for three miles.

3rd January

0005. Altered course due south.

0140. Between now and 0210 heard several distant small explosions, sometimes singly, sometimes in groups of three, and once five together. Clearly heard on asdic, they were just audible to the naked ear, sounding as though the pressure hull had been lightly caressed by a thin wire brush.

0250. Came to periscope depth. No vessels in sight. Bright

moonlight, showing enough landmarks for a good fix. Position just over half-way through the Strait. This indicated an over-all current of one knot to the south since diving. Very cheerful news.

0445. Asdic reported diesel H.E. passing down the starboard side.

0450. Sighted vessel on starboard beam, smaller than a destroyer, possibly a submarine-chaser, range about one and a half miles. Watched him pass northward. He then crossed the stern and was last seen on the port quarter.

0530. Now in the narrow southern exit to the Strait. First signs of daylight. The current appeared variable in strength, though always southerly in direction. At one time it reached four knots.

0900. Well clear of the Strait. No ships in sight.

1835. Surfaced and proceeded for passage to Fremantle.

For two days after our return we held the all-time record for the length of time spent by an S-boat away from base—thirty-seven days. But when *Sirdar* finally got home after going all the way round by Ombai Strait she had beaten our short-lived record by one day. We passed our previous patrol's distance record by nearly a thousand miles, for the distance registered on the log this time amounted to no less than 7,151 miles. To have spent all that time and travelled all that distance without sinking a single enemy ship—and to have been depth-charged into the bargain—was a bit of an anticlimax for the last patrol of the commission.

Never mind, we had had our share of excitement, we were a happy ship, and now we were going home to England.

EPILOGUE

WE reached Portsmouth after a ten-weeks' voyage which included a hurricane off Australia, a submerged but fruitless cruise up the west coast of Sumatra, and short stops at Trincomalee, Aden, Port Said, Alexandria, Malta and Gibraltar. At Gibraltar we were ordered to join a slow convoy of merchant-ships leaving three hours after our arrival. Two days before sighting England the convoy ran into a fog so thick that we could hardly see the ship ahead of us. This fog persisted, and gave me the most sustained period of anxiety of the whole commission; for forty hours I was almost continuously on the bridge. Long-buried memories of the *Umpire* collision rose up to make these hours a nightmare. Once we came within yards of being rammed by one of the merchant-ships, and it was only our radar which saved us. But we emerged from the fog at last, and having detached from the convoy *Storm* passed the Needles and entered the Solent on Sunday morning, April 8th, 1945.

We had to lie off the mouth of Portsmouth harbour to wait until the tide was right for entering Haslar Creek. It was a lovely Spring morning. A slight haze blurred the outline of Portsdown Hill, but Fort Blockhouse, its windows flashing with reflected sunlight, stood out sharply on the left of the harbour entrance. In the interval of waiting I remembered the day when I made my first trip in a submarine, from this very place; it seemed a long time ago, but in fact it was a month short of five years. Now, after many adventures, I had brought my own ship safely home. It was a most satisfactory feeling.

Since leaving Cammell Laird's *Storm* had travelled seventy-one thousand miles and spent over fourteen hundred hours under water—the equivalent of sixty days and nights.

THE END

THE SHIP'S COMPANY

of H.M. Submarine *Storm* at the conclusion of her wartime commission, April 1945

OFFICERS

E. P. Young	Lt.-Cdr. R.N.V.R.	Captain	D.S.O., D.S.C. and Bar
C. B. Mills	Lieut. R.N.	First Lieutenant	D.S.C.
R. L. Blake	Lieut. R.N.	Navigator and Gunnery Officer	Mentioned in Despatches
R. G. Wade	Lieut. R.N.V.R.	Torpedo Officer	Mentioned in Despatches
W. H. Ray	Lieut.(E) R.N.	Engineer Officer	D.S.C., D.S.M.
R. C. Fisher	Sub-Lieut. R.N.	Boarding Officer	

SEAMAN BRANCH

F. G. Selby	Chief Petty Officer	Coxswain	D.S.M. and Bar
W. R. Cottrell	Electrical Artificer	Maintenance of electrics and torpedo tubes	D.S.M.
E. R. Evans	Petty Officer, T.G.M.	In charge of torpedoes	D.S.M.
E. Robinson	Yeoman of Signals	Visual signals	
C. E. Brown	Petty Officer, Telegraphist	In charge of wireless office	Mentioned in Despatches
A. D. Blight	Petty Officer	Second Coxswain	Mentioned in Despatches
W. Bullough	Leading Telegraphist	Wireless operator	
W. H. Burson	Leading Telegraphist	Wireless operator	

W. T. Taylor	Leading Seaman	Gunlayer	D.S.M.
E. G. May	Leading Seaman	In charge of motor room	Mentioned in Despatches
E. McIllmurray	Leading Seaman	Chief Asdic operator	
J. W. Harris	Leading Seaman	Torpedoman	
R. E. Couchman	Leading Cook	Galley	
N. A. C. Greenway	Telegraphist	Wireless operator	D.S.M
S. T. Stain	Telegraphist	Wireless operator	
G. F. Richards	Able Seaman	Chief Radar operator	Mentioned in Despatches
M. T. A. Gascoigne	Able Seaman	Radar operator	
H. Bradbrook	Able Seaman	Second gunlayer	
V. Raynes	Able Seaman	Motor room	
W. Brown	Able Seaman	Oerlikon gunner	
J. Fell	Able Seaman	Asdic operator	
R. Mitchell	Able Seaman	Asdic operator	
A. Dodd	Able Seaman	Torpedoman, and wardroom steward	
H. A. Machin	Able Seaman	Torpedoman	
A. Buchanan	Able Seaman	Torpedoman	
G. W. Grieve	Able Seaman	Torpedoman	
A. Morris	Able Seaman		
J. J. Coton	Able Seaman		

(Continued overleaf)

THE SHIP'S COMPANY (continued)

ENGINEER BRANCH

R. Brown	Chief Engine Room Artificer	D.S.M.
A. C. Jamieson	Stoker Petty Officer	D.S.M.
R. M. Hodgson	Engine Room Artificer	D.S.M. and Bar
H. Harding	Engine Room Artificer	
J. J. Ferneyhough	Engine Room Artificer	
R. A. Hewetson	Leading Stoker	D.S.M.
W. B. Taylor	Leading Stoker	
T. O'Donnell	Leading Stoker	Mentioned in Despatches
H. F. Rooke	Stoker	
L. Day	Stoker	
E. David	Stoker	
R. McClelland	Stoker	
H. Driscoll	Stoker	
D. R. Harris	Stoker	
J. E. Carling	Stoker	

It is impossible in a list like this to show all the duties that fell to each man. Every officer except myself and the Engineer Officer took his turn as officer-of-the-watch, either on the bridge or at the periscope. Any officer off watch would give a hand with the decoding of wireless signals. Every man had a special duty at "Diving Stations," and in some cases a different one during a torpedo attack or a gun action. The majority of the Seaman Branch would take their turns as planesmen or helmsmen at "Watch Diving" or as look-outs while on the surface.